WHATEVER HAPPENED TO HELL?

Other Titles by John Blanchard

WHATEVER HAPPENED TO HELL?

John Blanchard

Foreword by
J. I. Packer

CROSSWAY BOOKS • WHEATON, ILLINOIS
A DIVISION OF GOOD NEWS PUBLISHERS

Whatever Happened to Hell?

Copyright © Crossway Books 1995

Published by Crossway Books
   a division of Good News Publishers
   1300 Crescent Street
   Wheaton, Illinois 60187

This edition is published by special arrangement with
EVANGELICAL PRESS, Darlington, Co. Durham, DL1 1RQ, England.

First U.S. edition published 1995 by Crossway Books

First British edition 1993 EVANGELICAL PRESS

Cover photo: © W. Warren / Westlight

Computer Imaging: Raymond Elliott

Art Direction/Design: Mark Schramm

First printing, 1995

Printed in the United States of America

Library of Congress Cataloging-in-Publication Data
Blanchard, John, 1932–
    Whatever happened to hell? / John Blanchard ; J. I. Packer
      p.   cm.
    Originally published: Durham, England : Evangelical Press, 1993.
      1. Hell—Christianity.   2. Hell—Biblical teaching.   I. Title.
    BT836.2.B54 1995   236'.25—dc20   94-39192
    ISBN 0-89107-837-1

03	02	01	00	99	98	97	96	95
15	14	13	12	11	10	9	8	7	6	5	4	3	2	1

*This book is earnestly
dedicated to the
next generation of faithful
gospel preachers, who may
have to fight even harder than
the present one for the
maintenance of biblical truth.*

TABLE OF

CONTENTS

FOREWORD

Christian evangelists ought to give teaching on hell: it is part of their job. Granted, they are not always loved when they do it. Robert Service, bitter rhymester of the frozen north, mocked such action by the narrative of it that he put into the mouth of the religious maniac Pious Pete:

> I started to tell of the horrors of hell,
> When sudden his eyes lit like coals;
> And—"Chuck it!" said he: "Don't you persecute me
> With your cant and your saving of souls!"

Many today show the same knee-jerk reaction if ever hell is mentioned to them; contempt for hell-talk has, it seems, become part of our culture. But evangelists are on a rescue mission to their unbelieving neighbors, and it is right and necessary that, as honest men, they should undertake frankly to explain what jeopardy people are in apart from Christ. Academics sometimes look down on evangelists for affirming that hell is real and eternal, but they would be wiser to look up to them, for while academics in their ivory towers can weigh notions against each other and finally avoid embracing any of them, evangelists stand in the church's front line, and therefore find it necessary to come clean on every issue they raise. Now, John Blanchard is not an academic but an evangelist, and it is very clear why he felt he had to write this book.

According to Jesus and His apostles, personal life goes on after physical death, and the prospect for those without Christ in the world to come is as bad and terrifying as it could possibly be, and everyone needs to be told so. That is a drumbeat emphasis that the most casual Bible reader can hardly miss; and certainly, anyone who works through John Blanchard's detailed argumentation will not be able to doubt that it is what the New Testament really says. What then should we do with this teaching? May we water it down because we find it uncomplimentary, and embarrassing, and contrary to the spirit of our age? Surely not: it is as divine, and as authoritative, as anything else in the New Testament, and the fact that it jars with today's humanistic unbelief makes the declaring and defending of it all the more important. Should we then line up with the great pastor-evangelist Charles Spurgeon, who a century ago told fellow-preachers: "Shun all views of future punishment that would make it appear less terrible"? Blanchard believes we should, and I think he is right.

One particular present-day unhappiness is that the same "less terrible" view that Spurgeon opposed in the era of late-Victorian sentimentalism, namely conditional immortality or annihilationism, is getting renewed exposure through the advocacy of some well-respected evangelical veterans. Uncertainty, bewilderment, and some alienation have resulted, and John Blanchard has had to pick his way through complex cross-currents of argument. Others beside myself will admire spirit, as well as the substance, with which he voyages through these choppy waters.

To announce the reality of hell is a testing and grueling task. The compassion and fellow-feeling that should mark all Christian communicators required us to do it, not with gloating and contempt, but with tears, if not in our eyes, then in our hearts. Any appearance of off-handedness in our manner will surely discredit our matter, just because it discredits us as human beings. It is hard to take seriously a message from a messenger who does not appear to take it seriously himself, or at any rate not to feel about it as a good man should. R.W. Dale once said that D.L. Moody had a right to preach about hell because he so clearly did so from a weeping heart. I detect something of the weeping heart behind the resolutely low-key reasoning of this book, and am glad that I do.

Theologically and pastorally, John Blanchard's work is a valuable contribution on a difficult theme. It is a double-barreled book, targeting confused Christians as well as complacent unbelievers, but it is none the worse for that. I gratefully commend it, and hope it will be widely read.

J.I. PACKER
Sangwoo Youtong Chee Professor of Theology
Regent College, Vancouver,
March 1993

PREFACE

In the early 1960s I read a book written almost exactly 100 years earlier and which had recently been republished.[1] Its title was *The Rich Man and Lazarus,* and the author, Brownlow North, powerfully applied the meaning of a parable Jesus told about the lives, deaths, and afterlives of two men, one rich and godless and the other poor and godly. The book was based on messages Brownlow North had preached to thousands of people at huge open-air services held in Northern Ireland in the summer of 1859, and this may account for the passion that comes through its pages. As a young evangelist, I found it riveting.

Nearly thirty years later I had lost none of my admiration for the book but sensed that it was in danger of being sidelined because the style and language were becoming increasingly out of date. What was needed was a modern replacement, something basic, simple and brief—about 100 pages would be fine—and directly aimed at unbelievers. I decided to make the attempt, but the plan quickly came unstuck, because I soon realized that there was an even greater need for a book that covered much more territory. Brownlow North wrote at a time when the man in the street had at least a nodding acquaintance with the general flow of the Bible's teaching and many of his readers a fairly good grasp of its central doctrines. Times have changed. Ignorance of biblical truth is of epidemic proportions. Polls taken in the United Kingdom in recent years have indicated that fewer than four per cent of the population read the Bible on a regular basis. There is "a famine through the land—not a famine of food or a thirst for water, but famine of hearing the words of the Lord" (Amos 8:11), as a result of which the average person has virtually no idea of what the Bible says about hell.

What is in some ways even more serious, many of those who profess and call themselves Christians have retreated from "the faith that was once for all entrusted to the saints" (Jude 3), and the pulpit has been as badly affected as the pew. We have seen a widespread defection from biblical truth, with many preachers blurring some of the crucial issues almost beyond recognition and others abandoning the whole idea of hell. This disastrous development needed to be faced and "Brownlow North revisited" would not be the way to do it.

This explains how the present book came into being. Although it remains little more than a broad outline of the subject, it does cover more ground than I originally intended, and I hope that in the goodness of God it may serve a wider purpose. My prayer is that it will not only help unbelievers to grasp the serious and urgent implications of what the Bible has to say about hell and to accept God's wonderful offer of salvation, but that it will also encourage believers to respond as they should to the love of God, "who has saved us and called us to a holy life—not because of anything we have done but because of his own purpose and grace" (2 Timothy 1:9).

As this book goes into circulation, my special thanks are due to an unofficial "team" of highly respected friends—Andrew Anderson, Peter Anderson, Steve Brady, Brian Edwards, Paul Hill, Graham Hind, and Geoff Thomas—who kindly read through the manuscript and made numerous suggestions, almost all of which have been incorporated into the finished work. I shudder to think of the flaws that might have slipped through without their kind and careful work. I am also grateful to Dr. J. I. Packer for his very gracious foreword. With countless other Christians all around the world, I already owe him an incalculable debt for his wise and winsome teaching of biblical truth; in my case, that debt is now much greater.

My secretary, Joy Leary, has once again done a superb job and richly deserves the thanks I am delighted to give. Last, but by no means least, I would like to thank my wife, Joyce, who has patiently endured the long sessions, sometimes lasting weeks on end, when I have been virtually incommunicado in order to concentrate on this particular project.

May God graciously overrule its many weaknesses and imperfections and use this book "to the praise of his glorious grace" (Ephesians 1:6).

JOHN BLANCHARD
Banstead
Surrey

WHATEVER HAPPENED TO HELL?

Fact or Fantasy?

Hell seems to have fallen on hard times.
A poll taken in the United States in 1978 revealed that over seventy per cent of those interviewed said they believed in hell.[1] Eleven years later a *Newsweek* survey, again taken in the United States, produced a figure of just fifty-eight per cent.[2] A poll conducted in Australia in 1988 indicated that only thirty-nine percent believed in hell,[3] while in 1989 a Gallup Poll taken in Britain for the *Sunday Telegraph* revealed that no more than twenty-four per cent of those questioned did so.[4]

These are pretty poor ratings, but according to some people they are still grossly exaggerated. In novelist David Lodge's opinion the real situation is this: "At some point in the 1960s hell disappeared. No one could say for certain when this happened. First it was there, then it wasn't. Different people became aware of the disappearance of hell at different times. Some realized that they had been living for years as though hell did not exist, without having consciously registered its disappearance. Others realized that they had been behaving, out of habit, as though hell were still there, though in fact they had ceased to believe in its existence long ago."[5]

That may be putting it a bit strongly (a novelist is not the same as a historian or a theologian) but there are both historians and theologians who would be inclined to agree with Lodge, even if they disagree about when hell began to evaporate. When the American church historian Martin Marty, a professor at the University of Chicago Divinity School, was preparing a Harvard lecture on the subject, he consulted the indexes of several scholarly journals dating back over a period of a hundred years to 1889 and failed to find a single entry. His conclusion was that "Hell disappeared and no one noticed."[6] Gordon Kaufman, a professor at Harvard Divinity School, says that hell has been in decline for 400 years and is now so diminished that the process is irreversible: "I don't think there can be any future for hell."[7] Another theologian says, "Talk of hell started to fall off in western countries about the same time science began to make an impact, about the late nineteenth century."[8] Speaking on BBC television, Richard Cavendish, author of *Visions of Heaven and Hell*, commented, "In our century there has been a kind of double development. We have created hells on earth on a bigger scale and perhaps of a more horrible kind that any previous century has done. Yet there has been a very general retreat from the idea of hell."[9]

This retreat is reflected in theological literature. One volume of Christian doctrine, with nearly 800 pages, and edited by three highly respected Christian leaders, has only eight lines on hell;[10] yet even this is eight lines more than in another major work entitled *Handbook of Contemporary Theology*.[11] In 1957, an American religious writer researching the subject had difficulty getting hold of a particularly important book published toward the end of the nineteenth century. When he eventually found one in a seminary library, he discovered that it had been loaned out only twice in fifty years![12] In the course of preparing this present book, I asked the manager of a large Christian bookshop in Australia how many titles he stocked on the subject of hell. He replied, "None. We had only one, but nobody wanted to buy it, so we had to give it away." On another occasion I asked a minister with several thousand books in his library how many he had on hell and was told, "I did have one, but I seem to have mislaid it."

THE LIVELY CORPSE

Yet if hell no longer exists, or is on its deathbed, the word "hell" may never have been more active or popular; it is certainly in no danger of becoming unemployed. It is often used to covey images of violence or aggression. In the Second World War, the United States 2nd Armour Division, led by General George Patten, was nicknamed "hell on wheels" because of the havoc it caused on its way to becoming the first American unit to enter Berlin. During the popular revolution against Communism in Romania in December 1989, there was a last-ditch battle on the streets of Bucharest between the Securitate Secret Police and units of the Romanian army. One observer said, "All hell has broken loose."[13] When fifteen people were killed and 186 injured in a collision involving seventy-five vehicles near Chattanooga, Tennessee, in December 1990, a fireman described the scene as "three miles of hell."[14] On the first night of the war in the Persian Gulf in 1991, Cable News Network reporter Bernard Shaw described the American bombing of Baghdad by telling viewers, "This feels like we're in the center of hell."[15] Later in that extraordinary year, when there was a coup d'etat in the USSR, the British politician Paddy Ashdown said, "The gates of hell are going to open on the Soviet Union."[16]

People also use the world "hell" to speak of a particularly painful experience. The British comic actor Terry Thomas was once a millionaire, yet died in sad and lonely poverty after contracting Parkinson's Disease, something he described as "hell to live with".[17] Another millionaire, the Marquess of Bristol, was jailed for a year in 1988 for smuggling cocaine into Jersey about his private helicopter. Asked what it was like for a man of his social standing to live in a prison cell smaller than any room in his own palatial home, he said, "It was sheer hell."[18] Talking of the effects of taking cocaine, disgraced American football star Dexter Manley confessed, "I went through hell."[19]

Sometimes, the word is used in situations not nearly so serious, yet in a way that expresses very strong emotions. When the England team reached the semifinals of soccer's World Cup competition in Italy in July 1990, millions in Britain watched the match on television. There was chaos around London as hordes of people left work early to be home in time for the kick-off. In the words of one reporter, "Heaven was anywhere there was a screen. Hell was a faulty fuse."[20] Earlier in the same competition, England's captain had to return home because of an injured Achilles tendon, and the team manager commented, "We miss him like hell."[21]

Then there are times when the word is used to mean a great deal of power or effort. When England's cricketers were being humiliated during the 1990-1991 tour of Australia, the Chairman of Selectors defended them by saying, "They are all trying like hell."[22] In his book *How to play your best golf all the time*, Tommy Armour, the famous Scottish golfer and teacher, advised his readers to "whack the hell out of the ball with the right hand."[23]

The word is also used to mean something difficult or dangerous. When my stepmother faced critical surgery in July 1990 the surgeon warned me, "It's a hell of an operation." About the same time, the Church of England asked advertising company Cogent Elliot to come up with slogans for a campaign to recruit new clergy. One of the proposed posters read, "The money's diabolical. The hours are ungodly. It's a miracle anybody does it. C of E clergy. It's a hell of a job."[24] At other times, those who use the word seem to be coming at it from two different angles at once. In 1990, an Australian newspaper carried an article on the holiday resort of Pattaya, in Thailand, where "foreign tourists can stagger from go-go bar to brothel in a drugged stupor for as little as ten dollars a day." The story was carried under the heading "A Holiday in Hell."[25]

OBVIOUS OR OTHERWISE?

The word "hell" can also mean something good, enjoyable, or exciting. In December 1990, Iraq's President Saddam Hussein suddenly announced the release of all foreigners held against their will since Iraq's invasion of Kuwait four months earlier. When hostage David Dorrington telephoned his wife in Britain to ask whether she had heard the good news, her reply was, "Yes, all hell's breaking loose over here."[26] On another page, the same newspaper reported that Durham County Cricket Club had been granted County Championship status by the Test and County Cricket Board. The club's treasurer told a reporter that it was strange to feel so calm because "I thought I'd be as excited as hell."[27] At a funeral service for the extravagant American millionaire Malcolm Forbes, held in March 1990 and attended by 2,000 mourners, his son Robert addressed his dead father with the words, "It's been a hell of a party—thanks for the trip."

In December 1991, England's soccer captain Gary Lineker learned that his two-month-old son, George, was seriously ill with leukemia. After the baby's first course of chemotherapy at London's Great Ormond Street Hospital, Lineker spoke of the thousands of letters he and his wife had received from well-wishers, and added, "If prayers count for anything then George has a hell of a chance of pulling through."[28] During the British General Election campaign in 1992, one businessman told a newspaper reporter, "I'm voting Labour and praying like hell the Tories get back."[29]

All of these phrases are pretty clear in their meaning, even if "hell" is a rather crude expression of emphasis, but the word is also used in ways that seem to make no sense at all. Early in 1990, the legendary American golfer Jack Nicklaus was interviewed for an article to mark his approaching fiftieth birthday. In the course of the interview he said, "My dad was fifty-six when he died. I certainly hope to hell that I will be around beyond fifty-six."[30] What does "hell" mean in that statement? Why not "I hope to Outer Mongolia," or "I hope to lumbago"? When England's cricketers finally won a game on that demoralizing tour of Australia, captain Graham Gooch said, "Winning beats the hell out of losing."[31] Again, what does "hell" mean? Why not "Winning beats the wheelbarrow out of losing"?

Yet even with all these illustrations, we have hardly dented the mass of idioms that make use of the word "hell." To move "like a bat out of hell" is to move very quickly; to go "hell for leather" means much the same thing; to have "a snowball's chance in hell" is to have no chance at all; to "raise hell" is to cause trouble; to say, "There will be hell to pay," means that there will be serious trouble later on; to be "as angry as hell" is to be furious; to give a person "merry hell" is to make things unpleasant for him.

This all goes to show that we have reached the stage where the word "hell" has as many meanings as people want to give it. It is spread so thinly over the English language that for most people it has lost most or all of its original significance, although there are times when glimpses of this come through. When a jilted wife had taken revenge on her husband by setting fire to his new home in London, she telephoned him and called it "a wee bit of roasting just to give you a taste of what hell is like."[32] Other phrases also show traces of an earlier meaning—"as sure as hell," "as hot as hell," "it hurts like hell," and "until hell freezes over" for example—but by and large the word has been watered down so much that it has almost totally lost its impact upon mind and conscience and hardly affects how most people live.

But does all of this matter? The answer to that question depends on the answers to others. Is hell a fact or fantasy? Is it something concrete or nothing more than a metaphor or a myth? In the early 1970s, John Lennon had a smash hit with a song which included the words:

Imagine there's no heaven;
It's easy if you try.

No hell below us—
Above us only sky.[33]

Was Lennon right? Can we dismiss hell as what one religious leader called "only a figment of the theological imagination"?[34] Surely it is massively important that we find out? What if the traditional pictures of hell as a place of endless punishment and suffering are true? What if millions of people are on their way there? What if we are? And if we are, is there any way of getting off the road, or lessening the punishment we shall have to endure in hell, or shortening the length of time we shall spend there? Is there any way in which we can avoid hell, or evade it?

No sensible person would deliberately ignore those questions. This book sets out to find the answers to them.

T W O

Database

I have always been fascinated by words, and especially by their origin, history, and development—something technically known as etymology. If I had to be stranded on a desert island with just three books of my choice, one of them would be the largest etymological dictionary I could lay my hands on. Exploring how words began and tracing their development is not only fascinating but an education. After all, a word is a "meaningful element of speech,"[1] and if we can discover how a particular word came about, we shall have a better understanding of its meaning.

Here are three examples, deliberately chosen because they will come in very useful toward the end of this chapter. The first word is "speculation." This comes from the Latin word *"specere,"* which means "to look" (a *specula* was a Roman watch-tower and *"speculari"* means "to spy out"). This gives us the background to one of the present meanings of "speculation," which is the formation of a theory about something. The second word is "revelation." In Latin, a *velum* is a veil, a *"re"* has to do with taking something away—so a "revelation" involves a veil being taken away, enabling us to see what lies behind it. The third word is "confidence," which again has Latin roots, this time the word *"confidere,"* made up of *"con,"* meaning completeness and *"fidere,"* meaning "to trust;" so to have confidence is to have complete trust.

ROOTS

As far as the subject of this book is concerned, this brings us to some obvious questions. Where does the word "hell" come from? What do its origins tell us about its meaning? What is the history of this one tiny word which may be the most terrifying in the whole of our English language? The word can be found in Middle English (fourteenth-fifteenth centuries) and in Old English (eighth-twelfth centuries)—in both cases it was sometimes spelled "hel"—but it stems from an even older fourth-century Anglo-Saxon word meaning "to conceal" or "to cover." This gives us our first clue as to one of its main ideas, but our search is not nearly finished when we reach the fourth century.

Anglo-Saxon was derived from an earlier Germanic language with roots in the Middle East and Asia, but the trail eventually leads us back to two of the oldest languages in the world still in common use, Hebrew and Greek, and to three words (one Hebrew and two Greek) which provide the earliest building blocks we can find for constructing the real meaning of the word "hell." The Hebrew word is *Sheol* and the two Greek words are *Hades* (virtually a translation of Sheol) and *Gehenna*, and to understand what "hell" means we need to find a reliable source where these words are widely used. There is only one—the Bible.

The link between our three basic "hell" words and the Bible is impressively strong. Although there is hardly a trace of it anywhere else in ancient Hebrew literature, the word Sheol appears sixty-five times in the Old Testament; the Bible is far and away the best document we have for understanding the word Hades (it occurs seventy-one times); and the Bible is easily the clearest authority on Gehenna. If we are serious about finding out the meaning of "hell" we have no alternative but to go to the source where it is mentioned more than anywhere else and without which we know virtually nothing about it. Since that source is the Bible, it is crucially important that we establish its credibility before we go any further.

Let me interrupt myself at this point. If you have no problem accepting the Bible's reliability and trustworthiness, you might want to ignore the rest of this chapter and go straight to chapter 3. On the other hand, you may find this chapter useful in reinforcing your convictions as to the meaning and message of Scripture.

One way to establish the Bible's credibility is to examine five claims that can be made on its behalf.

CHECK IT OUT

The first claim is that *the Bible is a reliable and trustworthy document.*

Here is one simple yet remarkable example. The ancient Egyptians believed that the earth stood on five great pillars, one at each corner and one in the middle; the Greeks were taught that Atlas carried it on his shoulders; and some Eastern scientists and theologians had a theory that it rested on the back of an elephant standing on a massive sea turtle. Yet while all these theories were swirling around, the Bible spoke about "the circle of the earth" (Isaiah 40:22) and about the earth being suspended "over nothing" (Job 26:7), things now universally accepted without question—other than by members of the Flat Earth Society.

The Bible's teaching is not sealed in a vacuum but closely woven into events which took place over a period of 1,500 years. As someone has said, "Christianity is nothing without its history"[2]—which means that it is open to investigation. The results have sometimes produced banner headlines—at least temporarily. It used to be said that science had disproved the Bible, but that kind of statement has a less confident ring about it these days, not least because scientific discoveries have a habit of amending or even discarding previous "known facts," while an unchanging Bible increasingly proves to be completely reliable.

One of the most brilliant language scholars of this century was Robert Dick Wilson, one-time Professor of Semitic Philology at Princeton Theological Seminary in the United States. In his student days, he set himself a forty-five-year schedule: fifteen years of language study, fifteen years of studying the text of the Old Testament, and fifteen years in publishing his findings. In the course of this tremendous program, which he fulfilled to the letter, he learned twenty-eight languages and dialects, studying under some of the leading professors of his day. In his second slot of fifteen years, he collected over 100,000 quotations from these languages and compared them with related statements in the Old Testament itself.

His conclusion was that the Bible was consistently accurate, while all other contemporary records contained inconsistencies or contradictions. For example, he showed that the Bible's details of about forty kings living from 2,000 B.C. to 400 B.C. were so accurate that "No stronger evidence for the substantial accuracy of the Old Testament records could possibly be imagined. Mathematically, it is one chance in 750,000,000,000,000,000,000,000 that this accuracy is mere circumstance,"[3] He eventually summed up his findings like this: "I have now come to the conviction that no man knows enough to assail the truthfulness of the Old Testament."[4]

Archaeology is another field in which the Bible lies open to investigation, but the fact is that new discoveries are underlining the Bible's truth, not undermining it. The evidence is so powerful that Nelson Glueck, a renowned Jewish archaeologist, speaks of "the almost incredibly accurate historical memory of the Bible" and adds, "It may be stated categorically that no archaeological discovery has ever controverted a biblical reference."[5]

Sir William Ramsay, founder member of the British Museum and holder of nine honorary doctorates from universities in Britain, Europe, and the United States was one of the most brilliant archaeologists the world has ever known. At one point, his studies concentrated on the narrative recorded in the Acts of the Apostles, written by Luke. When Ramsay began his work, he was convinced that Luke's details were seriously flawed, but the further he went, the more the Bible was vindicated. Eventually the sheer weight of the evidence forced him to change his mind and come to this assessment: "Luke is a historian of the first rank; not merely are his statements of fact trustworthy, he is possessed of the true historic sense . . . in short, this author should be placed along with the very greatest of historians."[6]

THE MAIN MESSAGE

The second claim is this: *the Bible clearly teaches that Jesus Christ is the Son of God.*

Although the Bible is a book that deals with historical facts, it is not a history book (in the sense of merely recording matters such as political events, economic trends, and international relationships). Nor is it a textbook on human behavior (though it teaches the highest morals the world has ever known). Instead, the Bible is about God and man, and their relationship to each other. Specifically, it is about God creating man in His own image, man deliberately turning his back on his Creator, and God restoring their broken relationship. Every page in the Bible is related to that overall theme—and central to it all is that Jesus Christ is the Son of God who, as one of its writers says, "came into the world to save sinners" (1 Timothy 1:15) or, as another writer puts it, "The Father has sent his Son to be the Savior of the world" (1 John 4:14). In other words, the Bible's fundamental message hinges on who Jesus is and what Jesus did.

It is generally agreed by Bible scholars that the earliest New Testament book to be written was the Gospel of Mark, whose opening words are: "The beginning of the gospel about Jesus Christ, the Son of God" (Mark 1:1). From then on, one New Testament writer after another endorses this statement; Matthew, Luke, Paul, and John (who together wrote about ninety per cent of the New Testament) give Jesus this title nearly fifty times. The apostle Peter, one of the other writers, certainly agreed with them, because when Jesus asked him who He was, Peter answered, "You are the Christ, the Son of the living God" (Matthew 16:16). Even more remarkably, both God and Satan confirmed this declaration. When Jesus was being baptized (He was about thirty years old at the time) God spoke from heaven and said, "This is my Son, whom I love; with him I am well pleased" (Matthew 3:17). Soon afterwards, when Satan mounted a sustained attack on Jesus, he launched two assaults with the words: "If you are the Son of God . . ." (Matthew 4:3, 6). The word "if" can sometimes mean "since" and it is clear from the context that this is the meaning here. The implication is that Satan had heard God's statement about Jesus and knew it to be true. Evil spirits had the same supernatural knowledge: we are told at one point that whenever they saw Jesus they fell down before Him and cried out, "You are the Son of God" (Mark 3:11).

No other person in human history has been given this name in this way. Jesus is not merely a son of God, but the Son of God, "the one and only Son, who came from the Father" (John 1:14). This is virtually the same as saying that Jesus is God—which is exactly what the Bible teaches. In the words of one New Testament writer, "The Son is the radiance of God's glory and exact representation of his being" (Hebrews 1:3), and that same stupendous truth can be seen on page after page. As the eminent writer C.S. Lewis put it, "The doctrine of Christ's divinity seems to me not something stuck on which you can unstick, but something that peeps out at every point, so that you would have to unravel the whole web to get rid of it."[7]

The evidence that Jesus is divine is powerful and convincing. After all, a book which proves meticulously accurate in every statement capable of being independently checked, and which lays down the highest moral teaching the world has ever know, is unlikely to be guilty of blasphemous heresy on every page, especially when speaking about the one subject which holds all of its message together.

THE MAN WHO TOLD THE TRUTH

This brings us to the third claim: *as Jesus is the Son of God, He is an infallible authority on every subject.*

It is sometimes said that "God can do anything," but that is not strictly true. The Bible says that "It is impossible for God to lie" (Hebrews 6:18) and that "He cannot deny himself" (2 Timothy 2:13, NASB). When God speaks He does so with absolute authority—and that same authority marked everything that Jesus said. At the end of the Sermon on the Mount, "The crowds were amazed at his teaching, because he taught as one who had authority, and not as their teachers of the law" (Matthew 7:23-29). Religious teachers were a dime a dozen in those days, but the people who heard Jesus instinctively knew that He was different. At Capernaum, "They were amazed at his teaching, because his message had authority" (Luke 4:32).

Coupled with His authority, and in a way inseparable from it, Jesus also displayed absolute integrity; He always spoke the truth. many times in the course of Matthew's Gospel we are told that He began a particularly significant sentence with the words: "I tell you the truth . . ." (Matthew 5:18). These statements included teaching about prayer, faith, the kingdom of heaven, and the final judgment. Even in "ordinary" conversation, Jesus made such an impression on Peter that after three years as one of His closest friends he said of Him, "No deceit was found in his mouth"(1 Peter 2:22). When Jesus spoke, on any subject, everything He said was stamped with the authority and integrity which resulted from His being the Son of God.

SEAL OF APPROVAL

Now to the fourth claim: *Jesus taught that the Bible was the Word of God.*

The only "Bible" which Jesus had was what we now call the Old Testament, which was usually referred to as "the Scriptures," "the Law,"or "the Law and the Prophets." What was His assessment of the Old Testament? It is not difficult to answer that question. In the Sermon on the Mount He said, "Do not think that I have come to abolish the Law or the Prophets; I have not come to abolish them but to fulfill them. I tell you the truth, until heaven and earth disappear, not the smallest letter, not the least stroke of a pen, will by any means disappear from the Law until everything is accomplished" (Matthew 5:17-18). He underlined this elsewhere by saying, "It is easier for heaven and earth to disappear than for the least stroke of a pen to drop out of the Law" (Luke 16:17). These are powerful statements, because in making them the Son of God put His seal of approval on the Old Testament and said that all of it, even the slightest detail, had divine and eternal authority.

On another occasion He said, "The Scripture cannot be broken" (John 10:35), and what He meant comes across with tremendous power because the whole point of His argument hinged on the divine authority of a single word. By saying, "The Scripture cannot be broken," Jesus meant that not a single word could be loosened from the Old Testament and discarded as having less authority than the rest.

What about the New Testament? Can we be equally sure that Jesus gave this part of the Bible His approval? Yes, we can—though obviously not in the same way, because these twenty-seven books were written after His death, resurrection, and ascension. Yet as far as the New Testament is concerned, Jesus endorsed it before it was written. He not only appointed certain men to be His apostles (the word "apostle" means "one sent forth"), He promised them that God the Holy Spirit would enable them to remember His words, so that they could accurately commit them to writing and teach them to others.[8] A few days before His death He told them, "The Counselor, the Holy Spirit, whom the Father will send in my name, will teach you all things and will remind you of everything I have said to you" (John 14:26), and promised them that "When he, the Spirit of truth, comes, he will guide you into all truth" (John 16:13).

This explains why the apostles regarded their teaching as having the same authority as the Old Testament, which Jesus had already called the Word of God. They were not on some gigantic ego trip (they were often overwhelmed with a sense of their own weakness and unworthiness) but realized, to their own amazement, that the Son of God had chosen them to convey the Word of God to others. Paul challenged his critics, "If anybody thinks he is a prophet or spiritually gifted, let him acknowledge that what I am writing to you is the Lord's command" (1 Corinthians 14:37). His fellow apostle John said that what he was writing was nothing less than "the word of God" (Revelation 1:2). Peter claimed that the message he and his fellow apostles preached was "the command given by our Lord and Savior" (2 Peter 3:2) and in the same chapter classed Paul's writings with "the other Scriptures" (2 Peter 3:16). These men dared to speak like this because they had the authority of the Son of God to do so.

It is not difficult to see how all of this locks in together, and how impossible it is to pry the pieces apart. To accept that Jesus is the Son of God and not to accept that the Bible is the Word of God is to be guilty of dangerous double-thing; it is neither consistent nor honest. The two statements stand or fall together.

AUTHORITY AND INTEGRITY

That brings us to the final claim: *because the Bible is the Word of God, it is totally true and utterly trustworthy.*

You would think it would be taken for granted that the Word of God carries with it all the authority and integrity of God Himself. That was certainly how the Bible was originally received by the church, and for a thousand years after its completion hardly a voice was raised against its divine authority. Significantly, the authority of Scripture was never defended by any of the early Christian creeds. "The reason," as Canadian theologian Clark Pinnock argues, "is not hard to find. Creeds are called into existence by burning questions and serious challenges confronting the church. The divine authority of Scripture was never a disputed question. Controversies raged over what it taught, but not over what it was."[9]

It was 1,800 years before people began to produce statements like this one by the Swiss theologian Karl Barth: "The prophets and apostles as such, even in their office, even in their function as witnesses, even in the act of writing down their witness, were real, historical men as we are, and therefore sinful in their action, and capable and actually guilty of error in their spoken and written word."[10] This argument is so absurd that a contemporary American scholar wonders "how any one can take it seriously".[11] Nobody is suggesting that Moses, David, Isaiah, and the other Old Testament writers or John, Paul, Peter, and other writers of the New Testament were perfect, but to admit their imperfections does not mean that as a result they were guilty of error in everything they did. The argument, however, goes beyond the simple piece of logic. To say that the Old Testament writers wrote error is to accuse Jesus of ignorance at best and blasphemy at worst, and as Dr. D. Martyn Lloyd-Jones, the one-time minister of Westminster Chapel, London, pointed out, "The moment you begin to question the authority of the Old Testament you are of necessity questioning the authority of the Son of God himself, and you will find yourself in endless trouble and difficulty."[12] To say that the New

Testament writers wrote error is to run headlong into the same problem, because Jesus specifically told them that they would be guarded against any such thing, and they themselves confidently base their right to be heard on the promise He gave them.

The only consistent position to take in all of this is that just as the Son of God cannot lie, neither can the Word of God. A nineteenth-century theologian put it like this: "We do not believe in Christ because we believe in the Bible, but we believe in the Bible because we believe in Christ."[13]

One of the most influential statements of faith drawn up in the last four centuries is the *Westminster Confession of Faith*, which was completed in 1648. The first rule adopted by those who drew it up was this: "What any man undertakes to prove as necessary, he shall make good out of Scripture." That was their pre-computer age way of saying that in whatever they discussed, the Bible was to be their database; this was to be the standard source of every statement they were to lay down in the confession they eventually produced. That is going to be our approach for the remainder of this book, and we can begin by making us of the three words whose history we outlined at the beginning of this chapter.

FROM FICTION TO THE FACTS

Firstly, *the Bible rules out the need to rely on speculation.* The subject of hell is not only massively important, it has an almost magnetic fascination. For thousands of years man's thinking has run riot on the subject, with the result that scores of theories and ideas have been put forward about hell's existence or non-existence: where it is, what it means and what it is like. Yet anybody who begins to make his case by saying, "What I think . . ." is building on a hopelessly frail foundation. As we have already seen, some people think that hell is just a figment of religious imagination, some that it is just a relic from the Dark Ages, and others that its horror has been grossly exaggerated. But ideas and guesses are mere speculation which only leads to chaos and uncertainty. Who decides whether one guess is better than another? On what basis can anyone claim that he is right and another speculator wrong? And if there is even a possibility that hell is something of eternal significance, who would be prepared to risk his whole future on something as flimsy as his own theory on the subject? It is hardly the height of wisdom to throw dice with one's own destiny. Our biblical database rules out the need to take the risk.

Secondly, *the Bible is divine revelation.* Some people say that we have no way of knowing whether hell even exists, let along anything about its nature or meaning. This is a popular approach with those who limit "knowledge" to that which can be scientifically proved. As there is no way of testing "hell" scientifically, they say that the only honest approach is to join the "Don't knows." But for many people "We don't know" means "We can't know"—and at that point their case begins to crumble. The most that a person with a "scientific" approach to this subject can say it that he has not yet found any answers that convince him and doubts whether he can even do so; what he cannot say is that there are no answers. This leaves him in no better a position than that of the person who relies on his own ideas, because the Bible tells us that there are things we can know about hell—and the Bible is the Word of God.

The Bible is a revelation from God of truths we could never otherwise have known. Left to ourselves, we would have no way of answering life's greatest questions or discovering its most important truths. One theologian has said that if God did not both speak and act, trying to make sense of life would be like watching television without the soundtrack: "It throws man helplessly back upon his own human guesses as to the meaning of what God is doing."[14] The illustration is a good one. I had to break into the writing of this chapter to speak at a large conference in East Anglia. The meetings were relayed by closed-circuit television into chalets all over the holiday camp in which the conference was being held. After the first of my sessions, a friend of mine suffering from a serious disease told me that he had been resting in his chalet while I was preaching. He had had his television set on, but for a large part of the service he had not understood a word I was saying because a fault in the system meant that, while the picture was clear, the sound was not coming through. My friend was fascinated by all my body language, but it was impossible for him to grasp what was being said until about halfway through the service when the fault was corrected, and the sound came through loud and clear.

When we come to the subject of theology, we are not thrown back on our guesses because God has spoken clearly through the pages of Scripture. In the Bible's own words, "All Scripture is God-breathed" (2 Timothy 3:16). This means so much more than that the human authors were "inspired" when they wrote (in the way we sometimes think of musicians or artists being "inspired"). It means that the words they wrote down were the very words the Bible's divine Author breathed out. This is what gives them their authority and integrity. It also destroys the argument of the person who tries to escape the impact of thinking about hell by claiming to be an honest agnostic, because in the Bible God tells us certain very specific things about it.

Thirdly, *we can use the Bible with confidence*. Because the Bible is the Word of God we can trust it utterly and unreservedly. The American scholar John Warwick Montgomery describes Christ's attitude to Scripture as "one of total trust; nowhere, in no particular, and on no subject did he place Scripture under criticism".[15] This comes across again and again. When face to face with Satan, Jesus began his reply to every attack with the words: "It is written . . ." (Matthew 4:4, 7, 10). For him, the Bible's teaching was decisive and final. When a group of religious teachers asked Him a complicated question about life beyond the grave, Jesus told them, "You are in error because you do not know the Scriptures . . ." (Matthew 22:29)—inferring that they would not be in error if they did. For Jesus, the Bible "was something absolutely unique and apart; it had authority which nothing else has ever possessed nor can possess."[16]

If the Son of God had such confidence in the Bible, surely so should we? The alternative, as with relying on guesswork, is chaos, because as John Wesley, one of the founders of what we now call the Methodist Church, wrote, "If there be any mistakes in the Bible, there may as well be a thousand. If there be one falsehood in that book, it did not come from the God of truth."[17] In investigating the subject of hell, we can be absolutely sure that the Bible is a totally reliable source of information, and that we can accept it "not as the word of men, but as it actually is, the word of God." (1 Thessalonians 2:13).

NOTHING BUT THE TRUTH

In a court of law, a witness may be called upon to swear that he will speak "the truth, the whole truth, and nothing but the truth." This is sometimes shortened to "the whole truth and nothing but the truth" (presumably because the first part of the oath is included in the second). However, while the Bible is the truth and nothing but the truth, it is not the whole truth. As a boy, I remember coming across a small encyclopedia with the rather presumptuous title *Enquire Within*

Upon Everything. The Bible makes no such claim, not least because it is not an encyclopedia. It tells us nothing about the depth of the Mediterranean Sea, the specific density of mercury, or the mating habits of turtles. As we saw earlier, the Bible is about God and man and their relationship to each other, and everything else it says fits into that central message.

Not only does the Bible not contain the whole truth about everything, it does not even contain all the truth about anything, not even about any of the subjects within its central theme. Studying the Bible produced a strange paradox: The more you study the more you learn, yet the more you learn the more you learn how little you know. Thomas Edison, the brilliant American scientist who held 1,300 patents for his inventions, used to say that we did not know "a millionth part of one per cent about anything." If this is true of science and philosophy in general, it would be surprising if it were not true in the case of theology. Can we really expect frail, fallible human beings to be able to fathom out the measure and meaning of the entire body of divine truth? There would be a greater chance of a cockatoo unraveling calculus. In the Old Testament, the Bible's writers freely acknowledge man's inherent ignorance in this area: "Can you fathom the mysteries of God? Can you probe the limits of the Almighty?" (Job 11:7); "[God] has . . . set eternity in the hearts of men; yet they cannot fathom what God has done from beginning to end" (Ecclesiastes 3:11); "No one can comprehend what goes on under the sun. Despite all his efforts to search it out, man cannot discover its meaning. Even if a wise man claims he knows, he cannot really comprehend it" (Ecclesiastes 8:17).

Even in the clearer light of the New Testament, we find writers acknowledging the same basic weakness, so that Paul, who wrote more of the New Testament than anyone else, cried, "Oh, the depth of the riches of the wisdom and knowledge of God! How unsearchable his judgments, and his paths beyond tracing out!" (Romans 11:33). That may sound rather depressing, especially when we want to discover the truth about something as serious as hell, but there is another side to the coin. Although God has not told us everything, He has told us enough. The Bible might not give us all the information we want to know, but it does tell us all we *need* to know. While there is nothing outside of God's knowledge—the Bible specifically tells us that "His understanding has no limit" (Psalm 147:5) and that He "knows everything" (1 John 3:20)—it is obviously not necessary that we too should know everything. We can therefore be sure that if we grasp what the Bible says about hell we will have all the knowledge we need to some to the right conclusions and make the right decisions.

THE MEANING OF THE MESSAGE

There is one other thing we need to bear in mind as we study the Bible, and that is the form in which it is written. The Bible is not a kind of theological *Yellow Pages* or doctrinal directory. It was originally written in three different languages by about forty authors over a period of some 1,500 years. It includes laws, history, poetry, prophecy, parables, and personal correspondence, as well as theological teaching, and these are not all meant to be read or understood in exactly the same way. Sometimes the Bible uses "street language," in which the words have their obvious and natural meaning. At other times that is not the case: For example, when the Bible speaks of "the four corners of the earth" (Revelation 7:1) it is not suggesting that the earth is a cube. Sometimes the language used is metaphorical: When Jesus says, "I am the gate" (John 10:7), this no more means He has hinges than being called "the Lamb of God" (John 1:29) means He has four legs. Along the same lines, when the Bible speaks of "the finger of God" (Exodus 8:19) the language is metaphorical, not biological.

Nowhere, however, does the Bible descend to fairy stories or folklore. None of it was written for our amusement or entertainment. Instead, it "never had its origin in the will of man, but men spoke from God as they were carried along by the Holy Spirit" (2 Peter 1:21). And because the entire Bible was written in this way, we must never interpret any part of it (especially any obscure part) in a way which contradicts the general flow of what the Bible is teaching. All of this needs to be appreciated if we are to have a right understanding of what our biblical database teaches. On a subject like hell we dare not settle for anything else.

THREE

Windows on the Words

The previous chapter established the Bible as our database and uncovered impressive evidence that it is absolute in its authority and infallible in its integrity. We also discovered that the Bible's focal points are God and man and their relationship to each other. We can now begin to look at what it says about the subject of hell, but before we do so, it is worth noting some principles that follow from the fact that the Bible is the Word of God.

The first is that everything the Bible says on any subject is true. Some of its language may be figurative, it may not tell us as much as we would like to know, and it may not always be easy to understand—but it is never in error. This is vitally important because when people say that a statement in the Bible is wrong, their problem is not one of interpretation but authority. They are pitting their opinion against the Word of God.

The second is that any teaching which contradicts what the Bible says must be rejected, regardless of who is doing the teaching or how many people believe it to be true. Everything must be tested by Scripture. When Paul visited Berea in northern Greece, the people there received his message "with great eagerness"—but they also "examined the Scriptures every day to see if what Paul said was true" (Acts 17:11). They already believed the Old Testament, and if Paul claimed to be teaching the Word of God then what he said should correspond with what was already written in Scripture. They were not prepared to take anything for granted, nor to get swept along with anybody's enthusiastic opinions. Everything Paul said had to be set alongside the Old Testament. If Paul's teaching agreed with Scripture, they would accept it; if it disagreed, they would reject it. Nor was this something they did in a casual, offhand way. The word "examined" is a word we would use of a judge meticulously sifting the evidence— and they did this "every day." The Bereans are a perfect model for us in our present study, and for everyone who is seriously searching for the truth.

The third principle is that when the Bible is silent we gain nothing by guesswork. As we have already seen, the Bible does not claim to tell us everything about anything. God has set limits as to the contents of Scripture, but He has still told us everything we need to know in order to come to a living and eternal relationship with Him. In keeping back part of the truth, God is not teasing us but testing us. Even Paul, who may have received more in the way of direct revelation from God than anyone who has ever lived, confessed that here on earth "We live by faith, not be sight" (2 Corinthians 5:7). This means that we must submit to God's wisdom, not only when He speaks but when He is silent. When the Bible speaks we should have our ears open; when it is silent we should keep our mouths closed!

THE "HELL" WORDS

In the previous chapter we identified the three main words which have been translated "hell" in our English versions of the Bible.[1] We must now examine them closely, because unless we grasp what they mean we will be thrashing around in the dark.

The first is the Hebrew word *Sheol* in the Old Testament. The experts are not sure of the origin of this particular word. It may come from a verb meaning "to demand," which could be linked to the ancient practice of people trying to contact the dead and ask them questions. One the other hand, it may be connected with the idea that death is always demanding more and more people to come into its presence; the Bible itself says that death is "never satisfied" (Proverbs 27:20). The second possibility is that "Sheol" comes from a verb meaning "to be hollow," giving the idea of Sheol being a large area of "space" to which human souls go after death.

It is difficult to decide which of the suggested origins is the right one, but one thing is clear: from the earliest times there was a firm belief that after death human beings continue to exist, though in a totally different environment. As one modern writer puts it, "There is always the assumption that the dead are still there, somewhere.

Man doesn't simply disappear at death."[2] This conviction was not limited to the people of Israel, around whose history the Old Testament is woven. The Egyptians, for instance, spoke of the soul going to Amenti; the Babylonians believed it went to Arullu; and the Ethiopians referred to the soul's destination as Si'ol (notice the similarity to Sheol). The details were no doubt very different from the Bible's teaching, which had God's authority, but it seems that there was never a time when man did not believe in a conscious afterlife of some kind or another. We shall see the special importance of this in a later chapter. As theologian George Eldon Ladd says, "Sheol is the Old Testament manner of asserting that death does not terminate human existence."[3]

What did the Old Testament writers mean by Sheol? The answer seems to be that the word was used to mean different but related things at different times. It is interesting to see how some of our best-known English translations of the Bible handle this. In the Authorized Version, first published in 1611, Sheol is translated "hell" thirty-one times, "grave" thirty-one times and "the pit" three times. The New International Version, first published in 1979, has "grave" fifty-five times, "death" six times, and three other phrases for the remainder. The New American Standard Bible, first published in 1971, plays it safe by leaving Sheol untranslated, allowing the reader to determine from the context what the writer meant—though in thirty-four places it puts the note "i.e., the nether world" in the margin.

In trying to pull all of this together, it is important to realize that God revealed truth progressively, with the light becoming brighter as the centuries went by, and especially as the Old Testament gave way to the New (with a gap of 400 years in between). This does not mean that the New Testament contradicts the Old; there is not a single case where this happens. Instead, the Bible has a remarkable unity, with each part taking its proper place in the whole scheme of things. There are many statements that underline the fact that although the Bible is a unity, God revealed truth gradually, adding greater intensity to the light as He went along. This is apparent when we understand that the Bible's central message is about Jesus Christ, God's Son, coming into the world to save sinners. One New Testament writer makes the point perfectly: "In the past God spoke to our forefathers through the prophets at many times and in various ways, but in these last days he has spoken to us by his Son, whom he appointed heir of all things, and through whom he made the universe" (Hebrews 1:1-2). This is

one of the Bible's ways of telling us that the Old Testament is no less
the Word of God than the New, but that in the New Testament the
light is brighter. With that in mind, we are in a position to assess what
the Old Testament writers had in mind when they used the word
Sheol. To help us do this, I will leave the word Sheol untranslated; this
will make it clear where it is being used.

Firstly, there are a few cases where it seems to refer to *death* or *the
grave*. When he was suffering from a serious illness, King Hezekiah
of Judah was terrified at the prospect of a premature death and cried
out, "In the prime of my life must I go through the gates of Sheol and
be robbed of the rest of my years?" (Isaiah 38:10). When King David
was dying, he reminded his son Solomon of the treachery of a double
murderer by the name of Joab and said that Solomon should "not let
his gray head go down to Sheol in peace" (1 Kings 2:6)—which seems
to be no more than authorizing an urgent "search and destroy" operation which would end in Joab's death.

Secondly, it was used in referring to *the place or state to which all
men go at death*. One of the clearest examples of this is when the
psalmist asks, "What man can live and not see death, or save himself
from the power of Sheol?" (Psalm 89:48). The answer to the question
is obviously, "No one"; everyone will "see death" and be subject to
"the power of Sheol." Elsewhere, we are told that "The Lord brings
death and makes alive; he brings down to Sheol and raises up" (1
Samuel 2:6)—and again this clearly applies to everyone.

In these statements, and many others like them, there is no indication that Sheol has anything to do with reward or punishment.
Everyone goes there, from the best of men to the worst. There is no
mention of pleasure for the righteous or punishment for the unrighteous. The picture we have is of a place of shadows, "the land of gloom
and deep shadow" (Job 10:21); of darkness, "The enemy . . . makes
me dwell in darkness like those long dead" (Psalm 143:3); and of
silence, "The dead . . . go down to silence" (Psalm 115:17). The
images are those of a place in which "the color is gone from everything; a washed-out copy is all that remains"[4] and the individual person is "but a shadow of his former self."[5] In his book *The Great
Divorce* C.S. Lewis describes his travelers going to "the grey
town"[6]—his way of expressing the general feeling of Sheol that comes
across in these quotations from the Old Testament.

Thirdly, there are some places in which Sheol is seen as *a place of
punishment for the wicked*. Job says of the wicked that "Suddenly

they go down to Sheol" (Job 21:13, NASB) and that "Sheol snatches away those who have sinned" (Job 24:19); David says that "The wicked return to Sheol, all the nations that forget God" (Psalm 9:17); another writer says that the steps of the adulteress "lead here straight to Sheol" (Proverbs 5:5). It is difficult to see how the meaning of Sheol in these places can be limited to the grave or the state of being dead. If that were the case, why are warnings such as these given only to the wicked and never to the righteous? The Old Testament might not be as clear as the New Testament in its teaching on the afterlife, but there is no doubt that it does speak of a place where "God will bring every deed into judgment, including every hidden thing, whether it is good or evil" (Ecclesiastes 12:14) and where there will be "a fire . . . kindled by [God's] wrath, one that burns to the realm of Sheol below" (Deuteronomy 32:22). We would be less than honest if we ignored statements as serious as these.

Fourthly, the Old Testament teaches that *for God's people there was to be deliverance from Sheol*. One of the clearest statements about this is where the psalmist says of those who "trust in themselves" (one of the Bible's classic definitions of the unbeliever) that "Their forms will decay in Sheol" and then adds, "But God will redeem my soul from Sheol; he will surely take me to himself" (Psalm 49:15). Another psalmist writes with equal assurance of life after death: "You guide me with your counsel, and afterwards you will take me into glory" (Psalm 73:23). The British preacher Alec Motyer is hardly exaggerating when he calls this "eloquent testimony to a sure hope beyond the grave".[7] The general picture of death in the Old Testament is shadowy and gloomy, but as one writer puts it, "There are passages here and there that reveal glimpses of a more wonderful life after death for the believer."[8] When they caught these glimpses, Old Testament believers were able to break through the natural fear of death and rejoice in the assurance that they would "dwell in the house of the Lord for ever" (Psalm 23:6).

FROM THE OLD TO THE NEW

We can now turn to the New Testament and examine the use of the Greek word *Hades*, the second of our "hell" words. The first translation of the Old Testament into Greek (the New Testament language) was called the Septuagint and dates from around 250 B.C.[9] In sixty-one cases out of sixty-five, the Old Testament word Sheol is translated by the Greek word Hades, regardless of the context in which it was originally used. The word may be formed from the verb *idein* (to see) and the negative prefix *a*, so that the main idea is of something hidden or unseen. Alternatively, it may be connected with the word *aianes* (something gloomy or gruesome)[10] or *hado*, which means "all-receiving".[11] Whichever of these is the true root of Hades, one can see why the Septuagint almost always chose it as the translation of Sheol.

However, the word Hades occurs only ten times in the New Testament, and in just four books—Matthew, Luke, Acts, and Revelation. The Authorized Version always translates it as "hell," the New International Version retains Hades in five places and renders it as "grave" twice, "depths" twice and "hell" once; while, as in the case of Sheol, the New American Standard Bible always leaves the word untranslated.

What did the New Testament writers mean when they used the word Hades? We could say that they took over where the Old Testament writers left off. Yet this is only partly true, because during the 400 years that elapsed between the end of the Old Testament and the beginning of the New there were some very significant developments. In particular, the Jews came to believe that Sheol was divided into two sections, one in which the wicked were punished for their sins and the other, often called "paradise" or "Abraham's bosom" (Abraham was universally recognized as the father of the faithful) in which the righteous experienced great joy.

This is the background to the story Jesus told about a poor but good man who died and went to "Abraham's side" and a rich but wicked man who also died and went to Hades. (As in the case of Sheol, I will leave the word Hades untranslated.) The rich man in Hades asked Abraham to help him, and when Abraham refused he pleaded with him to warn his five brothers who were still living on earth, so that they could avoid Hades. But Abraham also refused this request and told him that if his brothers rejected the teaching of the Old Testament, "They will not be convinced even if someone rises from the dead" (Luke 16:31).

What was the point of the story? Jesus was familiar with current teaching about Sheol, and with the way in which religious teachers of that time used parables to get their message across, so it was natural for Him to weave Sheol into a parable in order to make two major points: The eternal destinies of the righteous and the unrighteous are vastly different, and their destinies are settled while they are here on earth.

What else can we learn from the way Jesus used the word Hades? On one occasion He warned the people of Capernaum who refused to turn from their sin, in spite of all the miracles He had performed there, that they would not be "lifted up to the skies" (a biblical phrase for heaven) but "go down to Hades" and added, "I tell you that it will be more bearable for Sodom on the day of judgment than for you" (Matthew 11:23-24). Here, and in the parallel passage in Luke's Gospel, it is obvious that Hades is in direct contrast to heaven; in other words, it means hell, a place of punishment for the ungodly. There is also more than a hint that in hell there are degrees of punishment.

The only other time when Jesus used the word was when He told Peter that "On this rock [the truth of Peter's confession that Jesus was 'the Christ, the Son of the living God'] I will build my church, and the gates of Hades will not overcome it" (Matthew 16:18). This looks at our subject from a different angle, but again the meaning is clear. Hades is the headquarters of evil, none of whose attacks would ever be able to destroy the Christian church. That promise has already held good for 2,000 years!

PETER AND JOHN

The next two uses of Hades come from Peter's remarkable sermon preached to several thousand people on the Day of Pentecost. He reminded them of the life, works, miracles, and execution of Jesus and emphasized that "God raised him from the dead, freeing him from the agony of death, because it was impossible for death to keep its hold on him" (Acts 2:24). He then proved that Jesus' resurrection was in fulfillment of an Old Testament prophecy recorded by David in which Jesus says to His heavenly Father, "You will not abandon me to Hades, nor will you let your Holy One see decay" (Acts 2:27). A few moments later, Peter explained what this prophecy meant: "He spoke of the resurrection of Christ, that he was not abandoned to Hades" (Acts 2:31). Here, either "the state of being among the dead" or "the place of punishment for the wicked" would fit into the prophecy and its fulfillment.

The other four references to Hades are in Revelation, the last book in the Bible. Some of the teaching in Revelation underlines things we have already seen, but there are two additional and important pieces of information. The first comes when Jesus tells John (the writer of Revelation), "Do not be afraid. I am the First and the Last. I am the Living One; I was dead, and behold I am alive for ever and ever! And I hold the keys of death and Hades" (Revelation 1:18). What this tells us is that Jesus Christ, the eternal Son of God, who conquered death, has absolute authority over both death and the entire unseen world beyond it. Now, as the living and eternal God, He holds "the keys of death and Hades." The fact that He holds the keys of death means that He and He alone determines when people die. As the nineteenth-century American theologian James Ramsey put it, "Not a soul can pass from this world to the next except at the time and in the circumstances which [Christ] ordains."[12] We think of death in terms of "natural causes" or "unnatural causes" (accident, suicide or execution), but whichever of these may apply it is Christ who unlocks the gate of death to let man in.

But He also unlocks the gate of Hades to let men out. This is emphasized in a statement toward the end of Revelation: "The sea gave up the dead that were in it, and death and Hades gave up the death that were in them, and each person was judged according to what he had done. Then death and Hades were thrown into the lake of fire" (Revelation 20:13-14). We shall look at some of the issues this statement raises in the next chapter, but it already shows us that Hades is not eternal. It is an intermediate state, and the souls of all who enter it at death will be forced to leave it in preparation for the Day of Judgment. It is at this point that God's final verdict on all of humanity is publicly announced, and Revelation says that this will be followed by death and Hades being "thrown into the lake of fire . . . the second death." They will have served their purpose. There will be no place for them in the "new heaven and . . . new earth" (Revelation 21:1) which God will bring into being. Just as death and Hades were joined together in their power over men—earlier in John's prophecy death is pictured as a horseman with "Hades . . . following close behind him" (Revelation 6:8)—so they are both discarded when they can serve no further purpose in God's plan.

John adds one further thing: "If anyone's name was not found written in the book of life, he was thrown into the lake of fire" (Revelation 20:15). Being thrown into this death beyond death—the "lake of fire"—is virtually the last thing the Bible has to say about the fate of the ungodly. A few verses later John calls it "the fiery lake of burning sulphur" (Revelation 21:8), but he gives no further details; his language leaves a terrible impression of finality.

GEHENNA

This brings us to the third of our "hell" words, *Gehenna*, and here we can get a much clearer picture of its origin and meaning by digging back into Jewish history. About 750 B.C., King Ahaz was ruler of Judah. A spineless idolater, he adopted some of the most revolting heathen practices of his day. Among the worst was the offering of human sacrifices—he even had his own sons burned to death. These atrocities were carried out in the Valley of Ben Hinnom, a place just south-west of Jerusalem and today called Wadi al-Rababi.

Ahaz paid dearly for his sin. His political alliances came unstuck, and in one battle alone he lost 120,000 men. His place was taken by the godly King Hezekiah, but he was succeeded in turn by his son Manasseh, who soon undid all the good his father had done. He rebuilt altars to heathen idols, reinstituted human sacrifices and, like Ahaz, burned his own sons to death, again in the Valley of Ben Hinnom. Manasseh was followed by his equally corrupt son Amon, who lasted only two years before being assassinated.

His eight-year-old son Josiah took his place, and by the time he was sixteen he had begun a program of vigorous reformation. Altars were torn down, images were smashed, and the pieces scattered over the graves of those who had bowed to them in worship. In his crusade, Josiah singled out the Valley of Ben Hinnom for particular attention. From being a place of idol worship, he turned it into a public rubbish dump in which all the offal and filth of Jerusalem were poured. Later, the bodies of animals and even the corpses of criminals were flung there and left to rot or to be consumed by the fire that was kept constantly burning to dispose of the stinking mass of garbage. As one writer comments, it was a place where "the fires never stopped burning and the worms never stopped eating."[13]

We can now see how this otherwise unimportant piece of land fits into the picture. The Hebrew place-name was originally Ge(ben)hinnom (the valley of the son(s) of Hinnom). The shortened form of the name was Ge-hinnom of which the Greek translation became Gehenna. The English word for Gehenna, with all its imagery of shame, disgrace, sin, guilt, judgment, and punishment is "hell."

The word Gehenna appears twelve times in the New Testament,

and because the three English versions of the Bible we have been comparing always translate it as "hell," we shall use the same word when quoting verses where it occurs. The most obvious thing to say about Gehenna is that of the three words we are examining, it is by far the most vivid in teaching the reality of eternal punishment. The second thing, which will surprise many people, is that eleven times out of the twelve that the word occurs it is Jesus who uses it. Nor does He mince His words. He speaks about a person's whole body being "thrown into hell" (Matthew 5:29), of those who will be "thrown into the fire of hell" (Matthew 18:9), and of hypocrites being "condemned to hell" (Matthew 23:33). When sending out His twelve apostles on their first mission, He warned them of the persecution they would face and added, "Do not be afraid of those who kill the body but cannot kill the soul. Rather, be afraid of the One who can destroy both soul and body in hell" (Matthew 10:28). Whatever "hell" means, Jesus taught that going there is a worse fate than being murdered. Elsewhere he spoke of it as being a place "where the fire never goes out" (Mark 9:43) and where "their worm does not die" (Mark 9:48).

We shall look more closely at these statements in a later chapter, as well as taking in other things Jesus said about punishment after death without using the word Gehenna, but we have already seen enough to make one thing crystal clear: to ignore the reality, the certainty, and the seriousness of hell is to reject the straightforward teaching of Jesus Christ, the Son of God. For example, when the Archbishop of York, Dr. John Habgood, told his diocese in 1991 that ideas of hell as a place of punishment "stem from Bible mistranslations" and that he believed hell is "an internal experience caused by people's unwillingness to open themselves to love,"[14] he was revealing more about his own beliefs and misunderstanding of Bible words than he was about what Jesus taught. By the same token, to treat hell in the trivial way that many people do today may seem amusing and clever, but in fact it is the height of stupidity. Hell can never be evaded or avoided by denying its existence.

RECAP

Before moving on, it may be helpful to give a very brief summary of what we have discovered in this chapter about the basis and background of the word "hell" as we find it in Scripture.

First, the Old Testament word Sheol is sometimes used to refer to death or the grave, mainly to the place to which all the dead go and occasionally to the place of punishment for the wicked. There are also the first glimmers of hope that God's people will be delivered from Sheol.

Secondly, the New Testament word Hades has a different emphasis, so that in most cases it refers to a temporary place of punishment for the wicked.

Thirdly, the New Testament word Gehenna is by far the clearest and most vivid of the three "hell" words and includes (as none of the others do) the punishment of both body and soul after the final Day of Judgment.

F O U R

The Forbidden Subject

At 6:21 A.M. on Tuesday, April 21, 1992, Robert Alton Harris became the first man in twenty-five years to be executed in a Californian gas chamber. Forty-nine witnesses, including the father of one of the two teenage boys Harris had killed, looked on as a packet of cyanide granules was lowered into diluted sulphuric acid in a reservoir below his chair in San Quentin Prison. Harris had been sentenced to death nearly fourteen years earlier, but his lawyers had succeeded in obtaining four stays of execution—the last at 4:00 A.M. that morning, when he was already strapped into the death chair. As the final appeal failed, Harris asked prison officials to make a note of his last words and to release them after his death: "You can be a king or a street-sweeper, but everybody dances with the Grim Reaper."[1]

In less traumatic circumstances, one theologian put the same simple truth like this: "Death is the most democratic institution on earth . . . It allows no discrimination, tolerates no exceptions. The mortality rate of mankind is the same the world over: one death per person."[2] When the Irish writer George Bernard Shaw had completed a detailed study on causes of death, he said that he had come to only one firm conclusion: one out of one dies. Another author, Laurence Sterne, called death "an inevitable chance . . . an everlasting act of parliament."[3] The American statesman Benjamin Franklin used to say that only two things in life were absolutely certain—death and taxes. The phrase became famous, but he got his facts wrong, because whereas taxes can be legally avoided and illegally evaded, death is a different matter. It is the most certain fact of life.

The Bible has its own way of putting it. One of the psalmists asks the rhetorical question: "What man can live and not see death, or save himself from the power of the grave?" (Psalm 89:48). More straightforwardly, we are told, "Like water spilled on the ground, which cannot be recovered, so we must die" (2 Samuel 14:14). The writer of Ecclesiastes says, "There is a time for everything, and a season for every activity under heaven: a time to be born and a time to die" (Ecclesiastes 3:1-2). Job tells God that in dying he will be going to "the place appointed for all the living" (Job 30:23) and one of the New Testament writers says bluntly, "Man is destined to die once" (Hebrews 9:27). Toward the end of his life, the nineteenth-century American statesman Daniel Webster told how he once attended a church service in a quiet country village. The minister, a simple, gentle old man, preached very earnestly about the brevity of life and the need to prepare for its end. His closing words were, "My friends, we can die but once." Commenting on the sermon years later, Webster said, "Fragile and weak as those words might seem, at once they were to me among the most impressive and awakening I had ever heard."

LIVING IS DYING

"On the 9th of February 1984, at 16 hours 50 minutes, because of heart and vascular insufficiency and cessation of breathing, death has come."[4] With that clinical statement by two leading members of the Soviet Medical Academy of Science, the world learned of the death of President Yuri Andorpov. But "Death has come" can be written at the end of every human life—and it comes in a bewildering variety of ways. Nearly 400 years ago the Puritan preacher Thomas Brooks wrote, "We carry about in our bodies the matter of a thousand deaths, and may die a thousand several ways every hour. As many senses, as many members, nay, as many pores as there are in the body, so many windows there are for death to enter at. Death need not spend all its arrows upon us; a worm, a gnat, a fly, a hair, the stone of a raisin, the kernel of a grape, the fall of a horse, the stumbling of a foot, the prick of a pin, the paring of a nail, the cutting of a corn; all these have been to others, and any one of them may be to us, the means of our death within the space of a few days, nay, of a few hours."[5]

Even today, in an age of organ transplants, micro-surgery, intensive care units, "wonder drugs," and other advances in medical science and technology, what Brooks wrote remains essentially true. All that the most gifted physician or the most brilliant surgeon can do is to postpone the inevitable; man is destined to die. The current death-rate is awesome. Three people die every second, 180 every minute, nearly 11,000 every hour, about 260,000 every day, 95,000,000 every year. Death comes to young and old, rich and poor, good and bad, educated and ignorant, king and commoner. No sex is spared, no age exempt and no color excused. The dynamic young businessman, the glamorous actress, the great athlete, the brilliant scientist, the television personality, the powerful politician—none of them can resist the moment when death will lay its hand upon them and bring all their fame and achievements to nothing. In the Bible's words, "No one has power over the day of his death" (Ecclesiastes 8:8).

Death is no respecter of time or place; it has neither season nor parish. It can strike at any moment of day or night, on land, on the sea or in the air. It comes to the hospital bed, the busy road, the comfortable armchair, the sports field, and the office; there is not a single spot on the face of the planet where it is not able to strike. The whole world is a hospital, and every person in it is a terminal patient. What we call living can be just as accurately called dying. As soon as a baby begins to live, it begins to die. One writer comments, "Death borders on our birth, and our cradle stands in the grave."[6]

On November 27, 1957, C.S. Lewis wrote to a friend about his wife Joy, who was seriously ill with cancer but seemed to be making something of a recovery: "The cancerous bones have rebuilt themselves in a way quite unusual and Joy can now walk . . . . Her general health and spirits seem excellent. Of course the sword of Damocles hangs over us. Or should I say that circumstances have opened our eyes to see the sword which really hangs always over everyone."[7] Whoever we are, we have an appointment with death, one we did not make and cannot cancel. We can take regular exercise, get into a keep-fit program, eat nothing but "health food," swallow dozens of vitamin pills a day, have a regular physical check-up and take the best medical advice we can afford—but we can never do more than delay the inevitable. In one modern writer's words, "Death is not a spectator sport."[8]

Yet man has an inner sense that death is unnatural, an intrusion, and he goes to amazing lengths to delay it—and even to overcome it. Recent years have seen a growth of interest in the science of cryonics, in which immediately after death, blood is drained from the corpse, which is then filled with freezer fluid, encased in aluminum and suspended in a bath of liquid nitrogen. Then (or so the scenario goes) when a cure has been found for the disease responsible for the death of the person concerned, the body can be thawed out and normal life resumed. The current going rate for this service is around 60,000 pounds sterling—but there is a bargain on offer. For a mere 20,000 pounds, only the head will be frozen, and when the necessary technology becomes available—in hundreds, or even thousands of years' time—the head will be unfrozen and a new body grown on to it, using the remaining supplies of DNA. The offer does not come with a guarantee!

Nor does human gullibility end with cryonics. In August 1992, a seventeen-day conference in Scottsdale, Arizona was attended by one thousand members of Flame Foundation, all of whom believe they are physically immortal. The movement's founder is Charles Paul Brown, who has in turn been a retail fashion buyer and a night-club singer, and also served in the United States Air Force. Brown made his startling discovery in 1960: "It was like a new intelligence flooding my body," he told *USA Today*.[9] Brown teaches that if you believe it strongly enough, you can think yourself into never dying. You might break a bone, or catch cold, but never encounter anything terminal. Truly believing this, Brown says, creates a "cellular awakening," a constant renewal of healthy cells. But what about death by accident, such as a fatal plane crash? Brown admits that even awakened cells cannot cope with this. Nor does the bad news end there: those wrenched into eternity in this way will have to diet and exercise in order to keep healthy!

The British affiliate of Flame Foundation is Together Forever, headed by Paul and Gemma Massey from their home in Wimbledon. When his *Daily Telegraph* interviewer reminded him that "people tended to die whether they wanted to or not," one member of the group blandly replied, "People expect to die. Either you're living to live or living to die. Most people don't know they have a choice. We're saying you do."[10] This does seem to push credibility to new limits.

THE KING OF TERRORS

People's sense that death is unnatural helps to explain why they try not only to delay it but to avoid having anything to do with the subject. The famous Austrian psychiatrist Sigmund Freud once wrote, "No one really believes in his own death."[11] Many people try not to think about it, nor even to talk about it directly or seriously. King

Louis XV of France is said to have forbidden his servants to mention the word "death" in his presence. Today there is the same reluctance to get to serious, personal grips with the subject. An article by the *Daily Telegraph's* feature writer Date Saunders provides a good illustration of this: "The grim reaper has begun winnowing among my friends. In the last three weeks, I have been to two funerals and received an invitation to a requiem mass . . . . One day, who knows when, it will be me under the pall." After discussing some of the arrangements she would like made ("Tea and whisky will be served afterwards, but no sandwiches, because it is always the saddest person who ends up making them") she adds, "If I am cremated, I don't intend to sit in a jar on the mantelpiece depressing my husband. What if my urn got broken? I don't much relish the thought of being Hoovered out of the carpet by his second wife. I have therefore decided that my ashes will be scattered in my favorite place—up the noses of certain former employers."[12]

As one modern preacher says, "If the nineteenth century tried to conceal the facts of life, the twentieth century tries to conceal the facts of death."[13] Today we have a whole battery of phrases we prefer to use instead of the "word"; we say that someone has "passed away," or "passed on," or is "no longer with us." More crudely (and to avoid being serious) people speak of someone "pushing up the daisies," or as having "kicked the bucket," "snuffed it," "bitten the dust," "given up the ghost," "cashed in his chips," "checked out," "dropped off the twig" or "conked out."

These slangy substitutes point to the fact that man is basically afraid of death; it baffles him, bothers him, frustrates him and frightens him. Why? Why does the Bible speak of people being "held in slavery by their fear of death" (Hebrews 2:15)? There are some obvious answers to the question. For some, it is the fear of the *pain* that might be associated with death. The British clergyman G. Studdert Kennedy used to say that if anyone is not disturbed by the problem of pain, it is for one of two reasons, hardening of the heart or softening of the brain. Nobody in their right senses can honestly look forward to the prospect of weeks, months, or even years of racking pain, knowing that things are always and only going to get worse.

For others, there is fear of *the unknown*. We are creatures of habit, comfort, and familiarity. We always feel more secure going into situations we have been in before; but by its very nature death does not come into this category. We know nothing about it at firsthand. Even if we have been intimately involved in someone else's dying, we have not shared in that person's death. When man dies he goes into unknown territory. Left to himself he has no landmarks, no signposts. The whole thing is dark, mysterious, and frightening—the kind of prospect that made American film producer Woody Allen say, "I'm not afraid of dying. I just don't want to be there when it happens."[14] But witty remarks do nothing to change the facts, and fear of the unknown is decidedly unfunny.

Thirdly, there is the fear of *meeting* God. While many people seem to give little or no thought to what may lie beyond the grave—and in that sense live and die almost like animals—many more than might care to admit it have a powerful instinct that one day they will have to give an account for their life on earth. When the British racing driver Stirling Moss was at the height of his career, with a reputation for great courage and daring on the racetrack, he told a newspaper reporter, "I am frightened of death, I know it means going to meet one's Maker, and one shouldn't be afraid of that. But I am." He was not making a religious comment but giving the honest expression of an inner instinct.

This was taken a little further by the writer and broadcaster Marghanita Laski. On an edition of the BBC radio program *Any Questions?* broadcast in March 1966, she was asked what were the most important issues any person had to face. She replied, "We are lonely, we are guilty and we are going to die." As an outspoken humanist, she was certainly not speaking from a religious perspective. Nevertheless, an inner instinct was coming through and at least suggesting fear, though without using the word. If death is associated with things like pain, mystery, loneliness, guilt, and the prospect of meeting one's Maker, it is hardly surprising to find the eighteenth-century French philosopher Jean-Jacques Rousseau saying that the person who pretends to face death without fear is a liar.

In one of the most moving passages in the Old Testament, one of Job's friends paints a devastating picture of death's approach for someone who has led an ungodly life:

> "The lamp of the wicked is snuffed out;
> the flame of his fire stops burning . . .
> the lamp beside him goes out.
> The vigour of his steps is weakened . . .

He is torn from the security of his tent
and marched off to the king of terrors"
(Job 18:5-7, 14).

Several thousand years later nothing has happened to change
death's image. For all his scientific, technological, and educational
progress, man still lives in the shadowed certainty that "Death will
one day put its terminating stamp upon every passion, position, possession and ambition."[15] But what exactly do we mean by "death"?
Why does it happen? What is the meaning and the cause of what the
sixteenth-century French Reformer John Calvin called "the violent
tyranny of death"?[16]

IN THE BEGINNING

The Bible's first mention of death comes very early in its account of
human history, but to get it in context we need to go right back to the
creation of man: "Then God said, 'Let us make man in our own
image, in our likeness, and let them rule over the fish of the sea and
the birds of the air, over the livestock, over all the earth, and over all
the creatures that move along the ground.'

"So God created man
in his own image,
in the image of God
he created him;
male and female
he created them"
(Genesis 1:26-27).

In the following chapter the Bible adds one other vital piece of information: "The Lord God formed the man of the dust of the ground and
breathed into his nostrils the breath of life, and the man became a living being" (Genesis 2:7).

These two statements tell us some very important things about the
nature of man, things which are crucial for us to understand in our
study of hell. The first is that man is not a chemical fluke or an atomic
accident. Nor is he an educated ape; He is as different from other animals as animals are from vegetables and vegetables from minerals. All
other living creatures are conscious; man is self-conscious. If a giraffe
could say, "I am a giraffe," it would cease to be a giraffe. Man is the

crown of God's creation, invested with a dignity and significance not given to any other creature. In the Bible's own language, man was created "in the image of God."

Being created in the image or likeness of God does not mean that man was made the same size or shape as God. "God is spirit" (John 4:24) and has neither "size" nor "shape." Nor does it mean that man was a miniature of God, possessing all His qualities in small quantities. What it does mean is that, without being divine, man was created with qualities which enabled him to be and to do in a finite way what God is and does in an infinite way. Man was not created "*with* the image of God" (as if this were something tacked on) but "*in* the image of God." "The image of God" is not telling us something about man's equipment about his identity. The Bible is clear on this, and even goes so far as to say that man "is the image . . . of God" (1 Corinthians 11:7), something said of no other part of creation. Being made in the image of God is what makes man man. To put it as simply as possible, man was created as an intelligent, rational, personal, moral and spiritual being, as a "visible replica of God."[17]

WHAT IS MAN?

Some of man's qualities tell us things that are particularly relevant to our present study. The most important thing is that man is *a spiritual being*. This is brought out by the statement that "God breathed into [man's] nostrils the breath of life, and the man became a living being." The word "being" is the Hebrew *nephesh*, which occurs over 750 times in the Bible and is translated by about thirty different words in our English version. In many cases, it means nothing more than an invisible life principle which animates the bodies not only of men but of all living creatures. With man, however, it sometimes means more, something usually referred to as the "soul." It is important to realize (and in a later chapter we shall see just how important) that man's body and soul are quite distinct. At one point in Genesis 2:7, the creation of Adam's body was complete, but it was motionless and lifeless. There was no *nephesh* until God breathed into his nostrils the breath of life. This tells us that it is the soul that enables the body to breathe, move, see, think—in fact, to live. One modern writer puts it like this: "The identity of a human being is not found merely by looking at the body as a physical object. I am who I am because of my thoughts, feelings, actions, memories and other rich elements of consciousness, which form my personal history." This writer goes on to say that to speak of a person's soul is to speak of the person himself (or herself)—"that essential core which makes us persons."[18] Dr. William Mayo, the surgeon who founded the renowned Mayo Clinic, once said, "This elegant penknife of mine may never discover the soul, this mysterious side of man. However, I know that it is there. I am as certain there is a soul in man as I am of the most basic principles of my medical science."[19]

This does not mean that man's body and soul are two unconnected parts or powers—something taught by some philosophers, such as Plato (c.428-347 B.C.) and Descartes (1596-1650). Nor is it right to think of the soul as being "inside" the body, a kind of ghost living inside a machine; nor that God injected something called "soul" into man in such a way that his physical and spiritual elements were amalgamated. The body is not identical with the soul, nor the soul with the body. We are on much more biblical ground if we think in terms of man being both body and soul rather than of his body and his soul as being two parts of a construction kit. Man is a psychosomatic unity; physically he is a body, spiritually he is a soul. The Bible reflects this by the way it sometimes uses the word "soul" to mean the whole person. For example, we are told of a man called Esau moving house with "all the members of his household" (Genesis 36:6). The word "members" translates the Hebrew *nepheshim* (the plural of *nephesh*) but nobody suggests that their souls moved on while their bodies stayed put! Elsewhere, the apostle Paul describes a shipwreck in which there were "two hundred and seventy-six persons" on board (Acts 27:37, NASB). Here "persons" translates the Greek word for "souls," but it would be just as ridiculous to think that the bodies of the persons were somewhere else as to imagine that if the captain had cried, "All hands on deck!" he would be calling for wholesale amputations.

Man is not a soul plus a body, nor a soul in a body; he is both soul and body. God created man, not as an amalgamation of bits and pieces which happened to work well together, but as an amazing unity which can function as God intended only when both the physical and spiritual elements do so. Man is not complete as a body without a soul, any more than he would be as a soul without a body. We can get a glimpse of the importance of this when we hear Paul praying that his readers may be made holy "through and through," something involving their "whole spirit, soul and body" (1 Thessalonians 5:23).[20] The additional word "spirit" in this verse does not mean that man has a third element in his make-up. The Bible often uses the words "soul" and "spirit" interchangeably. Where there is a difference, it is one of operation and not of substance. The term "soul" is generally used in terms of man's relationship with his body and his natural, physical environment, and "spirit" in terms of his relationship with God.

However, we must remember that body and soul are not identical. Nowhere in the Bible is this made clearer than when Jesus speaks of those who "kill the body but cannot kill the soul" (Matthew 10:28). These words establish beyond any shadow of doubt that the body and the soul are two separate entities.

The second thing we learn from the fact that man was created in God's image is that he was created both as *a moral being* and morally perfect. This was "the chief glory with which he was crowned."[21] As the American theologian J. Gresham Machen wrote, "Goodness was not something accidental, something that came in after man was created; but it was something that was stamped upon him in the very act of creation by the Creator's hand."[22] In other words, man was a true reflection of God's holy character. This is underlined by the fact that it was after the creation of man that "God saw all that he had made, and it was very good" (Genesis 1:31) and by the specific statement later in Scripture that "God made mankind upright" (Ecclesiastes 7:29). Man was not only innocent, he was positively good, "a finite reflection of God's moral perfections."[23] Immediately after the creation of Adam and Eve, our planet was a perfect environment inhabited by perfect people living in a perfect relationship with each other and with God.

Thirdly, we learn that man was created as *a rational being*, not merely having the ability to think, reason, draw conclusions, and make sensible decisions but also having the gift of freewill. He was not created as a puppet or machine but was free to do whatever he chose to do. He had both the ability to obey God and the freedom to disobey him. He was not like a mechanical toy which God had wound up and which had no option but to go in the direction already programmed in during the manufacturing process.

WHAT GAVE BIRTH TO DEATH?

But the gift of free will put man on probation; he was given a tremendous test of character. "The Lord God took the man and put him in the Garden of Eden to work it and take care of it. And the Lord God commanded the man, 'You are free to eat from any tree in the garden; but you must not eat from the tree of knowledge of good and evil, for when you eat of it you will surely die'" (Genesis 2:15-17). This means that man was not only given "a holy nature, but the responsibility of developing a holy character."[24] Adam and Eve (given to him by God as a life partner) were granted great liberty, being allowed to eat "from any tree in the garden." This speaks not only of freedom of choice but of an amazing variety of blessings from which to choose. They were surrounded by God's bounty and told to help themselves to whatever they wanted. As one modern theologian puts it, God gave them "the maximum freedom, authority and dominion possible for created beings."[25]

They were also given a strict but simple law: they were not to eat from "the tree of the knowledge of good and evil." Whatever the tree was, it provided a straightforward test of their willingness to obey God because God commanded them to do so. What is more, they were given a clear warning of what would happen if they failed the test: "When you eat of it you will surely die." In the words of that warning, we have the first mention of death in recorded human history.

They failed the test. The devil tempted them by suggesting that God either did not say what He meant, or did not mean what He said, and by promising that there would be great advantages in eating the forbidden fruit. In a fatal moment of weakness they caved in: "When the woman saw that the fruit of the tree was good for food and pleasing to the eye, and also desirable for gaining wisdom, she took some and ate it. She also gave some to her husband, who was with her, and he ate it" (Genesis 3:6). Whatever the detailed explanation of those words, the major point is clear: For the first time ever, man disobeyed God, and through that one act of disobedience sin entered human history. The result was catastrophic.

God had warned that the moment man ate from the forbidden tree he would "surely die"; yet both Adam and Eve lived for many years after their disastrous disobedience. Does this mean that God was wrong, or went soft on His warning, or decided to give them another chance, or let them off with "a slap on the wrist"? Far from it! God had said that the moment they sinned they would die—and they did.

What is more, their experience illustrates perfectly a vital biblical doctrine which is that death never means cessation but separation.

One of the clearest statements on this concerns the death of Rachel, wife of the Jewish patriarch, Jacob, when we are told that "her soul was departing" (Genesis 35:28, NASB). This is the Bible's consistent position. As Alec Motyer correctly concludes, "There are no biblical grounds for saying that 'death means the end.'"[26]

The sin of Adam and Eve did not annihilate their souls so that they were left as one-dimensional vegetables. It is obvious from what follows that in many ways they carried on living much as they did before, but their relationship with God gave way to a rift. The moment they sinned they lost the greatest blessing they possessed, their union with God. Before their sin, they had been in perfect harmony with their Creator; now, "They hid from the Lord God among the trees of the garden" (Genesis 3:8). Instead of being at peace in God's presence they were in a state of panic at the thought of meeting Him. When challenged by God about this, Adam admitted, "I was afraid" (Genesis 3:10). The entire divine-human relationship, which was dependent on man's unqualified obedience to God's perfect will, had been shattered, and the guilty pair were "banished . . . from the Garden of Eden" (Genesis 3:23). They were now in a state of living death. What they had forfeited was not their spiritual existence but their spiritual life. They retained personality and character; what they lost was communion with God.

But the death penalty incurred by human sin not only involved spiritual death (the separation of the soul from God) but physical death (the separation of the soul from the body), and God pronounced this part of the death sentence on Adam by telling him, "Dust you are and to dust you will return" (Genesis 3:19). From the moment he sinned, Adam's body became prone for the first time to decay, disease, and deterioration; and his physical death was a foregone conclusion. Many years later, Adam's life on earth came to its inevitable end, and the official announcement of it was even more abrupt than the one for Yuri Andropov: "Altogether, Adam lived 930 years, and then he died" (Genesis 5:5).

ADAM AND US

That may all sound like nothing more than very ancient history, but it is much more than that, because it changed the whole course of history. To put it very simply, the Bible teaches that because Adam stands as the head or representative of the human race, his guilt and corruption were passed on to every succeeding generation of mankind. Far from having a holy nature, perfectly attuned to that of his Creator, man is now a confused mess, retaining many traces of his glorious origin, yet distorted and misaligned. Blaise Pascal, the seventeenth-century mathematician, philosopher, and scientist had this comment on man in his fallen state: "What a monster, what a chaos, what a subject of contradiction, what a marvel! Judge of all things and imbecile earthworm; possessor of the truth and sink of uncertainty and error; glory and rubbish of the universe."[27] When Adam sinned, we sinned in him, and as a result we also share in the disastrous consequences of his sin. The clearest biblical statement of this is as follows: "Sin entered the world through one man, and death through sin, and in this way death came to all men, because all sinned" (Romans 5:12).

This tells us something crucially important about death, something that explains, as nothing else can, all the dark and dreadful images that surround the subject, and that is that death is not an accident but a judgment, a consequence not a cause. Death is not a part of what it is to be human; it is an unnatural intrusion, a foreign invader. Death, physical and spiritual, was never a part of human experience until man sinned; since then it has been "as much a part of life as life itself."[28] It is impossible to read the Bible and miss the connection between sin and death: "The truly righteous man attains life, but he who pursues evil goes to his death" (Proverbs 11:19). "The soul who sins is the one who will die" (Ezekiel 18:4). "The wages of sin is death" (James 1:15). This truth is so firmly embedded into the human experience that the Bible speaks of "the law of sin and death" (Romans 8:2). Death was not built into man's original make-up; God created man to live, not to die. In his original state, man was not subject to death, even though being given free will meant that he was exposed to the possibility of it. If Adam had not sinned he would not have died; God would simply (and that word is deliberate!) have sustained his body forever in an unfallen, uncorrupted state. As the American theologian Anthony Hoekema says, "Death in the human world is not an aspect of God's good creation but one of the results of man's fall into sin."[29]

All of this means that sin is the ultimate (but not necessarily immediate) cause of all human death. Man is destined to die because he is incurably infected with sin's deadly disease. In one sense, he is already dead; "dead in your transgressions and sins" (Ephesians 2:1) and "separated from the life of God" (Ephesians 4:18) is how the Bible puts it. In other words, all human beings now living on earth are in exactly the same condition into which Adam fell. They are already spiritually dead (their souls are separated from God) and nothing can prevent their physical death (their souls becoming separated from their bodies). None of this gives death a friendlier face, but it does mean that we can approach the rest of this study with our eyes open to the facts instead of being blinded by fantasies. One modern writer sums it up like this: "Death confronts us, as nothing else does, with our insignificance and weakness, and exposes the folly of our pretensions to greatness. Even when we attempt to face death with courage, we never succeed in finally overcoming it; it dominates us until at last we go to receive the wages of sin."[30]

TO SUM UP . . .

We can summarize this chapter by saying that we have discovered four things about death. Firstly, death is universal; we have an appointment with death and there is nothing we can do to cancel it. Secondly, death is terrible; for one reason or another it fills people with fear and dread. Thirdly, death is penal; it is a judgment, the righteous punishment by a holy God of unholy people. Fourthly, death is not final; the Bible nowhere teaches that death marks the end of a person's existence. Death is not a terminus; it is the point at which we switch tracks.

Is Anyone There?

The sixteenth-century German Reformer Martin Luther used to say that nothing in the world caused so much misery as uncertainty. If he was right, then the greatest misery of all must be caused by uncertainty about what happens after death. For thousands of years philosophers and theologians, to say nothing of countless people who are neither, have wrestled with the question. This is hardly surprising, because the issue is not merely some vague academic point that we can discuss at a distance or pick up and put down whenever we choose. It is inescapable and more important with every day that passes. As the nineteenth-century American scholar A.A. Hodge wrote, "Before any other knowledge attainable by us in the compass of the universe, it is most essential for us to know what our Creator and Sovereign Lord intends to do with us after death."[1] Nobody can casually disengage himself from the issue and ask, "Where does mankind go from here?", nor even, "Where do we go from here?"; he must eventually ask, "Where do I go from here?" Not only that, but there are other questions that touch any normal person's emotions. Sometimes the questions come home with dramatic impact.

In 1990 I stood on the bridge over the remains of the American battleship USS *Arizona* which lies a few feet underwater in Pearl Harbor, on the Hawaiian island of Oahu. Thousands of visitors were there that day and were reminded of the vicious Japanese air attack on December 7,1941, which caused devastation at Pearl Harbor and catapulted the United States into the Second World War. Some scattered flowers in memory of the men and women who had been slaughtered there nearly fifty years earlier. Many stood silently, lost in their private thoughts; some prayed; others took photographs—and beyond any doubt many looked at the rusted hulk of the *Arizona* and asked themselves, "What happened to the people who died there in 1941? Where are they now?"

But the questions are not reserved for famous (or infamous) historical sites. They are much more insistent, and come much closer to home: "Where are family members and friends who have already died? I know where their bodies are, but is that all there is to know? What has happened to them?" As this book goes along, we shall be examining some of the avalanche of theories that have been put forward, but we have already discovered enough to be able to dismiss two of them before going any further. The first can be dealt with very briefly; the second will take up the remainder of this chapter.

INTO THE UNKNOWN?

The first view that can be discarded is the one that says we have no way of knowing what happens to a person after death. This was the position taken by the sixteenth-century French philosopher Francois Rabelais. Although he had been both a Franciscan and a Benedictine monk in turn, his last words were: "I am going to the great Perhaps." William Shakespeare makes Hamlet say much the same kind of thing in his well-known "To be or not to be" speech, when he speaks of

> *... the dread of something after death—*
> *The undiscovered country from whose bourn[2]*
> *No traveller returns—puzzles the will,*
> *And makes us rather bear those ills we have*
> *Than fly to others that we know not of ...[3]*

The seventeenth-century political philosopher Thomas Hobbes spoke of taking "my last voyage, a great leap in the dark";[4] while his contemporary John Dryden, the first Poet Laureate, confirmed the truth of Martin Luther's comment:

> *Death in itself is nothing; but we fear*
> *To be we know not what, we know not where.[5]*

Toward the end of the nineteenth century, Robert Green Ingersoll was one of America's most eloquent agnostics (some people think his outspoken agnosticism prevented him from being nominated for the presidency). At his brother's graveside, Ingersoll said, "Life is a narrow vale between the cold and barren peaks of two eternities. We strive in vain to look beyond the heights. We cry aloud and the only answer is the echo of our wailing cry."[6]

A few years ago John Betjeman (like Dryden, a Poet Laureate) wrote these words in a poem describing his thoughts when listening to the bells of St. Giles Church, Oxford, while lying in hospital waiting for an operation:

> *Intolerably sad, profound*
> *St. Giles' bells are ringing round . . .*
> *Swing up! and give me hope of life,*
> *Swing down! and plunge the surgeon's knife.*
> *I, breathing for a moment, see*
> *Death wing himself away from me*
> *And think, as on this bed I lie,*
> *Is it extinction when I die?*[7]

Sometimes, agnosticism has a more cheerful face. In the last chapter of his book *Around the World in 81 Days*, the British comedy actor Robert Morley wrote, "If, as I have always thought, life is a party, I should be leaving quite soon. Mustn't outstay my welcome . . . I'll just collect my shroud and be off. Where to exactly? Is there another party just up the road?"[8]

But agnosticism is not only unsatisfactory (it provides no answers to any of our questions), it is also unnecessary. It is true that left to ourselves there is nothing we could know about existence (or nonexistence) after death—but we are not left to ourselves. God has spoken. Scripture has revealed truth we could never otherwise have discovered. This is why the psalmist is able to tell God, "Your word is a lamp to my feet and a light for my path" (Psalm 119:105). The beam of that light penetrates beyond the cemetery; in fact, the Bible's message is far more about eternity than it is about time. Only a few verses are about man's origin; the rest is about his destiny. While the Bible may not tell us everything, it does tell us something. The view may not be very clear in some areas, but it is by no means pitch dark. Nobody can be an honest agnostic on the subject while he has the Bible in his hand.

THE BIG ZERO?

The second idea that can be dismissed at this stage is that human beings are annihilated at death. This is the most basic form of annihilationism (we shall look at important variations of it in a later chapter) and the theory has been around for a very long time. The Greek philosopher Aristotle, who died in 322 B.C., said that death was "the most to be feared of all things . . . for it appears to be the end of everything."[9] His fellow Greek philosopher Epicurus, who died in 270 B.C., wrote to one of his friends, "Death, the most dreaded of evils, is therefore of no concern to us; for while we exist death is not present, and when death is present we no longer exist."[10] The Roman writer Seneca, who died in New Testament times, said much the same thing: "There is nothing after death, and death itself is nothing."[11]

In the present century, the British philosopher Bertrand Russell was an eloquent spokesmen for this idea. In 1938 he asserted, "Man is . . . the outcome of an accidental collocation of atoms. No fire, no heroism, no intensity of thought or feeling can preserve an individual life beyond the grave; all the noonday brightness of human genius is destined to extinction . . ."[12]

Russell recognized that at a personal level that kind of thinking could lead to only one conclusion: "When I die I shall rot."[13] In a modern play by Tom Stoppard, one of his characters says, "Death is not anything . . . It's the absence of presence, nothing more . . . the endless time of never coming back . . . a gap you can't see, and when the wind blows through it makes no sound."[14]

This bleak picture is the logical outcome of four major philosophies that have influenced millions of people over the centuries.

The first is *atheism*, which can be summed up in three words by the nineteenth-century German philosopher Friedrich Nietzsche: "God is dead." But the idea that God is dead (which implies that He never existed) not only rules out the supernatural, it degrades humanity by denying it ever had a Creator and, at least by inference, rules out the possibility of human existence after death.

The second is *materialism*, which says that only physical matter is "real" and which is one of the most pervasive philosophies of our day. The contemporary British preacher John Benton explains: "At school, we are taught materialism. No, we do not have any lessons in it, but it is taught in every class. We are taught from an early age that the only things which matter, the only things which exist, are the things you can taste, touch, smell, hear and see. Death is the end, and therefore we must adopt the philosophy of 'eat, drink and be merry, for tomorrow we die.'"[15]

The third is *existentialism*, which says that individual experience is everything, but that it has no explanation. The modern British author Colin Wilson summarizes existentialism's conclusions by saying, "Man is a useless passion. It is meaningless that we live, and it is meaningless that we die."[16]

The fourth is *secular humanism*, which puts man at the center of everything. Its view of man's future was clinically outlined by a director of the British Humanist Association: "On humanist assumptions, life leads to nothing, and every pretence that it does not is a deceit."[17] The speaker went on to add this chilling illustration to emphasize what he meant: "If there is a bridge over a gorge which spans only half the distance and ends in mid-air, and if the bridge is crowded with human beings pressing on, one after another they fall into the abyss. The bridge leads nowhere, and those who are pressing forward to cross it are going nowhere. It does not matter where they think they are going, what preparations they have made, how much they may be enjoying it all." This ties in exactly with the following official statement issued by the American Humanist Association in 1973 as part of its "Humanist Manifesto II": "Promises of immortal salvation or eternal damnation are both illusory and harmful . . . There is no credible evidence that life survives the death of the body."[18]

What can be said in response to all this? There are basically two ways to confront annihilationism. One is to play it at its own game, in other words, to come to our own conclusions without divine revelation to guide us—the kind of "do-it-yourself" approach made up of our observations, experience, thoughts, and emotions. What kind of arguments do they bring to bear on the subject? Here are three of the most powerful.

VOICES FROM THE PAST

Firstly, there is the argument from *history*. However popular annihilationism has been in some circles, it has never been held by the majority of people. The ancient Egyptian *Book of the Dead* is among the oldest pieces of literature in the world—and life beyond the grave is one of its main themes. The coffins of those buried in the great pyramids were called "the chests of the dead" and contained a map to guide the deceased on his journey. In ancient Greek religion, a silver coin was placed in the dead person's mouth to pay the fare across the River Styx to Hades. Many other cultures have shown their belief in an afterlife by burying certain items with their corpses. Indians laid arrow-heads and earthen vessels by the side of the dead body to help the person concerned cope in the next world; Norsemen buried a horse and armour, believing that the deceased was going on a triumphant journey; Laplanders buried flint and tinder to provide heat and light; in the case of a child, Greenlanders buried a dog to act as a guide. Buddhism and Hinduism are two of the oldest surviving religions in the world, and both have a firm belief in the afterlife.

Some of these customs may seem faintly ridiculous, but even today we have symbols that are saying the same kind of thing. Candles placed at the head of the coffin have been called "the modern representatives of the primitive man's fire which was to light the way of the soul on its dark journey."[19] Whatever we may think of some of the cultures and religions I have mentioned, it is impossible to deny that belief in an afterlife has been around as long as man himself. As one modern writer confirms. "The evidence of this belief can be found in abundance in every culture as far back as archaeologists have been able to uncover traces of human life."[20] We can also say that belief in an afterlife has been the norm, not something held by just a relatively few people here and there, or at certain times over the centuries. The Canadian scientist Arthur Custance observes, "In every culture, and apparently throughout history, it has been normal for man to assume that he has some continuance beyond the grave."[21]

What do we make of all this? It can hardly be a fluke, because by definition a fluke is accidental or occasional, and belief in life after death is neither. Nor is it something that has ebbed and flowed over the centuries. It has been embedded in humanity from the very beginning, and nothing has been able to remove it. Rather than calling it accidental, it would be more honest to admit that it is constitutional, part of the whole business of being human. The American author Dave Hunt puts it like this: "At the same time that death is acknowledged to be inescapable, there is an equally universal and overpowering conviction that death does not end human existence. That man is a spiritual being, who survives the death of his physical body, is a basic human instinct which is denied only with the greatest effort."[22]

THE GOOD, THE BAD AND THE ULTIMATE

Secondly, there is the argument from *morality*. This is based on the fact that man has a conscience, a moral sense of right and wrong. The human conscience is not itself a law but a faculty by which the intellect and emotions respond to a law. Our intellect makes an assessment of issues in relation to that law (in terms of whether things are right or wrong), and our emotions tell us what we ought or ought not to do.

Yet the law to which the conscience relates is an external law, something which man can neither create nor control. We can no more change the moral law than we can change the law of gravity. Nor can we get rid of it; it is there. Even if no reference is made to it, it is the basis of all the laws by which we try to govern, improve, and develop human society. When people complain that certain laws are unjust, they are helping to prove the existence of an external law that is permanent and perfect. This is why, even in his fallen state, man has a sense of rightness, fairness and justice. Daniel Webster went so far as to say, "Justice is the great interest of man on earth."[23] That may be overstating it, but it is obvious that a sense of justice is ingrained into human life. Even though we are sometimes tempted to bend the rules when it suits us, we generally want justice "done, and seen to be done."

The problem is that too often what we find is exactly the reverse: Not only is justice not seen to be done, it is seen not to be done. People "get away with murder" (literally and otherwise), the good die young, the innocent suffer, the cheat prospers, crime does pay. All the cozy clichés stand on their heads—not always, but often enough to make them seem a mockery—and the thought that they will stand on their heads forever is more than we can take.

The only satisfying alternative to the injustices of this life is perfect justice in the next one; the only remedy for the present triumph of evil over good is the future triumph of good over evil. In a moral universe all bills must be paid and all accounts settled; but annihilationism throws these hopes out of the window. For the annihilationist, there is no possibility of perfect justice or the righting of wrongs. Good will remain unrewarded and evil unpunished. The serial murderer and the tiny child, the rapist and the kindly old lady, the ruthless dictator and the gentle nurse, everything they are and everything they have been and done will be wiped out of existence.

Dabbling with annihilationism may be fascinating, but carrying it to its logical conclusions is frightening, because without eternal standards man loses his ethical moorings—and there is no limit to how far he can drift. To take an obvious example: if death leads to nothing, this life is everything, and the smart thing to do is to squeeze out of life as much pleasure and "success" as possible, regardless of how it affects other people.

But that is only the beginning. Annihilationism authorizes anything—killing included. In the 1930s, Adolf Hitler's atheism accommodated an argument that led him to exterminate millions of Jews in the Second World War. Today, issues like abortion and euthanasia should hardly cause the annihilationist to bat an eyelid. Some have gone much further. An American university professor is quoted as saying, "Mental defectives do not have a right to life, and therefore might be killed for food—if we should develop a taste for human flesh—or for the purpose of scientific experimentation."[24] At the same conference, another speaker took much the same line: "Humans without some minimum of intelligence or mental capacity are not persons . . . Idiots, that is to say, are not human."[25]

Even that is not the end of the line. In the early 1980s, a professor of anthropology wrote, "Surely there can be no special pride in the practice of letting millions of soldiers rot on the battlefield because of a taboo against cannibalism. One can even argue that, nutritionally, the best source for human beings is human flesh because the balance of amino acids is precisely that which the body requires for its own proper functioning."[26]

Revolting as some of these things will sound, they are the logical outcome of a philosophy that limits man's existence to the here and now.

HUMANLY SPEAKING . . .

Thirdly, there is the argument from humanity. Man has always had a self-conscious sense of the special worth and dignity of the human race. This is what lies behind his humanitarianism, his instinct to care for the sick, help the poor, comfort the sorrowing, and do a thousand other kindnesses to those in need. Forced to choose between saving the life of a human being or a dog, only an eccentric would choose the dog. When the Scottish poet Robert Burns wrote his famous words about "man's inhumanity to man"[27] he was saying something very significant: When people act toward each other with kindness, care and compassion (in other words, when they treat each other with dignity), they are behaving in a human manner, they are functioning as they were intended to. As one contemporary author has said, "A society's maturity and humanity will be measured by the degree of dignity it affords to the disaffected and the powerless."[28]

But what does man's dignity amount to if it is buried with him? Of what use are pious platitudes at a funeral if the person concerned has no more dignity then than a few kilograms of potassium permanganate? There is not much dignity in fertilizer! There is a powerful link between this conviction about man's dignity and annihilationism, as the well-known American theologian Francis Schaeffer explains: "All men . . . have a deep longing for significance, a longing for meaning . . . It is quite clear: no man—no matter what his philosophy is, no matter what his era or his age—is able to escape the longing to be more than merely a stream of consciousness or a chance configuration of atoms now observing itself by chance. In an extreme form the longing for significance expresses itself most clearly in *the fear of non-being*. It has been obvious for centuries that men fear death, but depth psychologists tell us that such a fear, while not found in animals, is for man a basic psychosis: no man, regardless of his theoretical system, is content to look at himself as a finally meaningless machine which can and will be discarded totally and for ever."[29]

To put it more simply, annihilationism squeezes out of human existence on earth every drop of meaning or purpose. I remember speaking at a school for seriously disabled children, some of them so badly deformed that they were strapped into what looked to me like mechanized high chairs. Carefully trained teachers tended to their needs with amazing devotion and patience. Specially adapted vans ferried them from home to school and back again. But why bother to go to such a huge expense of money, energy, and manpower on children who were unlikely to make any contribution to society? Why not have them quietly exterminated and concentrate on projects that would yield some return? The answer is obvious: because we have an inbuilt sense that every human being in the world, however sick, or deformed, or incapable, has dignity and meaning which go far beyond his physical or mental condition.

The British preacher David Watson made the same point: "I remember talking to a medical student who just that morning had dissected his first human corpse. The body had been there in front of him on the bench and he had cut away different parts of the anatomy. It was like a lifeless wax model. He said to me, shaken a little from his first experience, 'If this is all that we become at death, what is the point of anything?'"[30]

These are some of the arguments against the theory of annihilation. It would be too much to claim that they are proof of life beyond the grave, but they are certainly powerful pointers in that direction. However, the greatest evidence lies elsewhere.

BACK TO THE BIBLE

The whole notion that the human personality is annihilated at death collapses as soon as we open the pages of Scripture. The evidence is everywhere, but the two subjects around which most of it is concentrated are man's creation and his death. The opening chapter of Genesis reveals three aspects to creation, each introduced by the Hebrew word *"bara"*—a word used exclusively "for an act of divine production which brings into existence something entirely new."[31] It is used first about the creation of all material existence: "In the beginning God created the heavens and the earth" (Genesis 1:1). Secondly it is used of the beginning of all living existence: "God created . . . every living and moving thing with which the water teems . . . and every winged bird . . . and all the creatures that move along the ground" (Genesis 1:21, 25). The third use of the word is reserved exclusively for the creation of humanity, which marked the beginning of all spiritual existence on earth, and as if to give this particular aspect of creation special emphasis, the word *"bara"* is used three times in one sentence:

"So God created man
in his own image,
in the image of God
he created him;
male and female
he created them"
(Genesis 1:27).

Just as the animal world was set apart from the material world, so Adam and Eve were set apart from the rest of creation. This is what gives humanity its unique identity and dignity. As Francis Schaeffer says, "It is not that God has not made both man and the great machine of the universe, but that he has made man different from the rest of the universe. And that which differentiates man from the machine is that his basic relationship is upward rather than downward or horizontal. He is created to relate to God in a way that none of the other created beings are."[32]

The Bible says not only that man was made "in the image of God," but more specifically that "The Lord God formed the man from the dust of the ground and breathed into his nostrils the breath of life, and the man became a living being" (Genesis 2:7). This means much more than that God gave man something we call "life"; we are not told that God "breathed into" any of the other living beings He created. This was something different, something infinitely more, something which constituted man as a spiritual being. As the British theologian Ernest Kevan commented, "His is the life that has come from the breath of God."[33]

When we combine the creation of man's body from the dust of the ground and the direct divine creation of his soul we get a profile of man which time and space can neither contain nor destroy. The human body is a part of the material universe, and it has long been established that no material object in the universe can be destroyed in the sense of being wiped out of existence. Even if it disappears, it is immediately reconstituted either as matter or energy. As this is a law which operates everywhere in nature, the human body is literally indestructible, and that being the case the extinction of the soul would be out of character with everything else that God has created. The American theologian Emery Bancroft states the case very clearly: "Unending existence is an inescapable part of man's heritage as a creature made after the image and likeness of God. He is indestructible. He cannot be annihilated."[34]

Dr. Bancroft's better-known contemporary, Louis Berkhof, came at the same truth from another angle by saying, "God does not annihilate his work, however much he may change its form. The biblical idea of death has nothing in common with annihilation."[35] Perhaps this is what is being said in the statement that "[God] has . . . set eternity in the hearts of men" (Ecclesiastes 3:11). Later in the same Old Testament book we are told that at a person's death "The dust returns to the ground it came from, and the spirit returns to God who gave it" (Ecclesiastes 12:7). Even without drawing conclusions from what we know about the indestructibility of physical matter, how can the human spirit return to God if it has been extinguished at death? The author of a religious work written around 40 B.C. had no doubt about the meaning of the Old Testament's teaching on the subject: "God created man for eternity, and made him in the image of his own immortality."[36]

In his moving little book *A Severe Mercy*, Sheldon Vanauken writes of the way in which to man "time" is so precious yet never satisfactory, whereas animals seem unaware of time, untroubled by it, and act as if time was their natural environment. He then goes on to speak of these wonderful experiences when "time stands still" as times of revealing "a kind of appetite for eternity . . . It suggests that we have not been or will not always be temporal creatures. It suggests that we were created for eternity. Not only are we harried by time, we seem unable, despite a thousand generations, ever to get used to it. We are always amazed at it—how fast it goes, how slowly it goes, how much of it is gone. Where, we cry, has the time gone? We aren't adapted to it, not at home in it. If that is so, it may appear as proof, or at least a powerful suggestion, that eternity exists and is our home."[37]

This understanding of creation has tremendous impact on the whole of human life, especially in giving it purpose and direction. Dave Hunt explains it well: "If there is no God who created us for his eternal purposes, then human life is not only a meaningless accident, but a crude practical joke perpetrated by an impersonal cosmos that has somehow spawned beings who inexplicably long for meaning and purpose when there can be none. Life has no ultimate meaning unless it continues, not temporarily, but eternally, beyond both the grave and the passing existence of this physical universe.'[38] This leads us to a second way in which the Bible contradicts annihilationism.

THE MOMENT THAT MATTERS

Nobody needs to ask, "Is there death after life?" The real issue is whether there is life after death—and the best way to find out is to discover from Scripture the nature and the meaning of death. Until comparatively recently, determining the moment of a person's death was fairly straightforward. A person was said to be dead when the heart stopped beating or the lungs stopped functioning. But in the sophisticated world in which we now live, the literal application of such simple definitions can have bizarre results. Some years ago, when California had a law which defined death as the heart no longer beating, a man accused of murder defended himself on the grounds that according to state law his victim was not dead because his heart had been transplanted and was beating away quite normally in another body![39]

Since then, medical science has done a considerable amount of fine-tuning in this area, and the moment of death is now said to be when there is no longer any brain wave function. But whatever current biochemical opinion may be, there is a much more satisfactory definition of death which comes straight from the pages of Scripture, and never has to be amended to keep up with advances in medical science. Put as simply as possible, the Bible says that just as life comes to the body when the spirit enters it, so death comes when the spirit leaves it.

One of the clearest statements of this is that "The body without the spirit is dead" (James 2:26)—words written 2,000 years before we knew anything about brain wave function. Centuries earlier one of the psalmists wrote much the same thing, and said of moral men that "When their spirit departs, they return to the ground" (Psalm 146:4). The Bible also has several narratives to illustrate this principle. In the Old Testament, Jacob's wife Rachel was said to be dying "when her soul was departing" (Genesis 35:18, NASB). In the New Testament, the death of Jesus is pinpointed as the moment when he "gave up his spirit" (John 19:30). It would be difficult to know how to make the point in fewer or clearer words.

THE UNIVERSAL ABNORMALITY

Yet as well as identifying the moment of death and confirming that death is universal, the Bible also makes it clear that death is not normal. Strictly speaking, nobody dies from "natural causes." Death is neither natural nor part of human nature. Death is "the terrible and unnatural ripping of the soul out of a man's body. Death tears a man in half. Man was made to live, not to die."[40]

To say that death is universal but not normal sounds nonsensical until we realize that death is a biological event with a theological meaning. It has to do with God, man, and their relationship to each other. Specifically, it is the outcome of that relationship being broken. God's original purpose for man was that he should live a life of perfect obedience, reflecting God's glory in all that he was and all that he did, and as a result enjoy an unbroken and eternal relationship with his Creator. That scenario was wrecked by man's rebellion, in spite of God's warning that any disobedience would be punished by death. God kept His word to the letter, and the moment man sinned, the first installment of the death penalty came into effect, Man's relationship with God was severed, his likeness to God shattered; he was no longer what God wanted him to be. But he was not reduced to nothing, nor was he shunted off into one of the other categories of creation and turned into an animal or a lump of cosmic substance. He remained a human being, body and soul. Every part of him became *alienated*, but no part of him was *annihilated*. This fact is accurately emphasized in the New Testament. For example, Paul writes of certain people as having once been "dead in your transgressions and sins" (Ephesians 2:1).

It is not even true to say that when man sinned the image of God in him was destroyed. Man still bears the image of God in the sense that he remains a personal, rational, moral being. He still possesses reason, will, and conscience. Above all, he has the capacity to know and love God. This has important implications for the way we behave toward our fellow men. One of the New Testament writers illustrates it like this: "With the tongue we praise our Lord and Father, and with it we curse men, who have been made in God's likeness . . . My brothers, this should not be" (James 3:9-10). The whole basis of James's charge of inconsistency is that man, fallen though he is, still bears God's likeness. It may be obscured, but it has not been obliterated.

This underlines a bedrock biblical truth which is the key to the whole issue being examined in this chapter: In Scripture, the fundamental meaning of death is not annihilation but *separation*. One has only to examine the effect of man's rebellion in Genesis 3 to see that it has separation written all over it. Adam became separated from himself (guilt and fear were his first psychological problems); he became separated from the only other human being alive at the time (he immediately rounded on Eve and blamed her for what had happened); and above all he became separated from God. Those who deny the relevance of Genesis in today's world have to explain why every one of modern man's psychological, moral, social and religious problems is directly linked to these three aspects of the separation caused by Adam's sin.

There is also a link between spiritual death and physical death. Physical death is the second installment of the one penalty which a holy God imposed as the result of human sin—and just as with spiritual death, physical death means separation, not annihilation. In spiritual death the soul is separated from God; in physical death the soul is separated from the body; in neither case does the Bible even hint at annihilation.

The Greek theologian Spiros Zodhiates makes two very clear points here. Firstly, he says that death "does not put an end to man's existence; it simply brings about a change from bodily existence to bodiless existence."[41] Secondly, he says, "Since it is not the body but the spirit that thinks, wills, plans, remembers, and is related to God, it follows that the conscious existence of man after death does not depend on the body. Man's spirit continues to function separately from the body after death."[42]

As Stephen, the first Christian martyr, sank to his death under a hail of stones, he cried out, "Lord Jesus, receive my spirit" (Acts 7:59). How could he ask the Lord to receive something that was on the brink of being annihilated? The significance of Stephen's words was not lost on John Calvin, one of the most influential theologians in history: "This verse clearly testifies that the soul of man is not a vanishing breath, as some people foolishly suggest, but that it is an essential spirit, and survives death."[43]

THE GOD OF THE LIVING

The Bible's evidence against annihilation is powerful and could be developed in many other ways, but we must settle for just one further point. When discussing the afterlife with a group of religious leaders, Jesus told them that their basic error was ignorance of the meaning of Scripture. When the subject turned to the resurrection of the dead, Jesus reminded them of an incident 1,500 years earlier when God had identified Himself to Moses as "the God of Abraham, the God of Isaac, and the God of Jacob" (Matthew 22:32, quoting Exodus 3:6). This was not so much saying that these great leaders belonged to God, but that God "belonged" to them—in the sense that David was able to say, "The Lord is my rock, my fortress and my deliverer" (Psalm 18:2) and "The Lord is my shepherd" (Psalm 23:1). To emphasize the reality of life after death, Jesus suddenly switched to the present tense and told them "[God] is not the God of the dead but of the living" (Matthew 22:32). But how could God belong to Abraham, Isaac, and Jacob if they had been annihilated at death? Jesus' words would have had even greater impact on His hearers because they all knew that the remains of the three men concerned were lying in the cave of Machpelah at Hebron, about twenty miles down the road.

Scripture is united and conclusive on the subject. Even on the shadowy pages of the Old Testament, "The great assumption . . . is that life continues beyond the grave."[44] In the New Testament, it is difficult to find a single page where a future life is not stated or implied. Man is not "all dressed up and nowhere to go." The Bible annihilates annihilationism.

This raises an obvious and inescapable question.

Where Do We Go from Here?

So far we have set aside two theories about what happens to a person after death. We have seen that agnosticism (saying there is no way of knowing) is ruled out because the Bible does give us a certain amount of information, and that annihilation is ruled out because the Bible says that after we die there is something that follows. Its teaching goes beyond the grave; in fact, the Bible's center of gravity lies not in this life but in the life to come. Many people think of Christianity as being nothing more than a moral code, a set of rules and regulations to help people live a decent life in peace and harmony with their fellow men. Yet that is light years away from the truth. The Bible sees man as much more than a social animal; it sees him as being made in God's image and given a significance that goes far beyond the few years he spends on this planet. In this chapter, we shall begin to examine what the Bible says about the other side of death.

A pastor friend of mine had just finished conducting a burial service when a woman ran to the edge of the grave, looked down on her father's coffin and screamed, "Where is he now?" Even in her uncontrollable agony she was pointing to something we discovered earlier, that man is both body and soul, and that these two are separate entities. The woman concerned was obviously not asking, "Where is my father's body?"; she knew it was just six feet away from her. What her mind shrieked to know was "Where is his soul?" After all, we know what happens to the human body after death. If it is buried, it slowly decomposes; if it is cremated, it is quickly reduced to ashes. Even if a body is disposed of in some other way, God's word to Adam remains meticulously accurate: "Dust you are and to dust you will return" (Genesis 3:19).

Elsewhere, the Bible underlines the same simple fact. In speaking to God of His dealings with men, one writer says, "When you take away their breath, they die and return to the dust" (Psalm 104:29), while another adds, "When their spirit departs, they return to the ground; on that very day their plans come to nothing" (Psalm 146:4). Incidentally, notice that only a man's plans are said to "come to nothing," not his body. This is not talk of annihilation here. A man's body is degraded, but it is not destroyed. Just as spiritual death does not mean the extinction of the soul, so physical death does not mean the extinction of the body. Adam still exists, as do Pontius Pilate, Shakespeare, Napoleon, and every one of the billions of human beings who have ever been born.

PASSING STRANGE

When someone dies, our immediate concern is naturally and obviously focused on what happens to the body and, for so long as we can, we treat it with reverence and care. Even afterwards we consider the remains to be important, although this sometimes produces bizarre results. In May 1990, one of our national newspapers carried the following story. As a young man, Arthur Strange had played soccer for Dorchester Town FC, and when his playing days were over had remained a loyal supporter for the rest of his life. When he died, his family carried out his wish that his ashes be scattered in the center circle of the club's home ground. Some time later, the club moved to a new venue to make way for a supermarket. This brought a huge profit for the club, but a great deal of heart-searching over what to do with the remains of Mr. Strange and those of at least five other fans. Eventually some soil was taken from the old football pitch and placed in a symbolic cross in the center circle of the new one. After officiating at a short ceremony, the club's chaplain, the Rev. David Fayle, told the press, "What people did not want was their relatives under the fish counter at Tesco's."[1]

This story emphasizes the fact that we know what happens to the body after death; it may also suggest that the only thing left to discover is what happens to the soul. We could even get that impression from the Old Testament statement that when someone dies, "The dust returns to the ground . . . and the spirit returns to God who gave it" (Ecclesiastes 12:7). But we have already seen that the Bible never says the body is irrelevant. If we put together the facts that man is not truly man unless body and soul are united, and that the human soul survives the moment of death, it becomes obvious that if man has an eternal future as man it must be as body and soul. Francis Schaeffer makes an important point here: "Watch a man as he dies. Five minutes later he still exists. There is no such thing as stopping the existence of man. He still goes on. He has not lost his being as a human being. He has not lost those things which he intrinsically is as a man. He has not become an animal or a machine."[2] This is where the Bible's teaching cuts right across the ancient, pagan idea that the body was "at best worthless and at worst essentially sinful"[3] while the soul was virtually divine. The Bible no more teaches that the disembodied human soul exists endlessly and alone after death than it does that it never had a beginning. Those pagan ideas are firmly rejected by Scripture, as are all the products of human imagination and tradition.

On December 29, 1890, near the reservation town of Pine Ridge, South Dakota, some 200 Sioux Indians—men, women and children— were massacred by troops of the American Seventh Cavalry. This incident is still known (at least to the white man) as the Battle of Wounded Knee. The massacre left deep scars in the memory, and North American Indians mourned their dead kinsmen for exactly one hundred years until, on December 29, 1990, a solemn ceremony brought the official period of mourning to an end, and it was announced that "Their spirits are now free."[4] One can understand the Indians' grief, and admire their dignity, but the idea that after death the human spirit undergoes a period of imprisonment before being released has no foundation in Scripture, and must therefore be rejected.

THE OTHER SIDE OF DEATH

As we have already seen, the Old Testament speaks about the body returning "to the dust" and the spirit "to God who gave it." The New Testament is more specific. It says that "Man is destined to die once, and after that to face judgment" (Hebrews 9:27). But taken in isolation, that statement hides a great deal, because elsewhere the New Testament teaches that while the final judgment occurs eventually, it does not take place immediately. Instead, there is what has become known theologically as "the intermediate state," to which we made a brief reference in chapter 3.

What does the Bible tell us about it? Not nearly as much as we would like to know! A well-known modern theologian says that the most information we have on the subject is "the clear whispering of the New Testament."[5] However, as that whispering is from God, it is infinitely more reliable than the shouted guesses of those with no biblical basis for what they say.

SLEEPING SOULS?

The first thing we can establish about the intermediate state, as we listen to the New Testament's "clear whispering," is that it is a state in which the souls of those who have died are alive and conscious. The first part of this point emphasizes what we saw at the end of the previous chapter about life continuing beyond the grave; the second point counters the theory that when a person dies the soul goes either permanently or temporarily into unconscious hibernation.

Those who promote this idea of "soul sleep" (including sects like Jehovah's Witnesses and Mormons) say that there are places in Scripture which link dying to the idea of falling asleep—and superficially this might seem to give them a case. The Bible says that when King Jehoash of Israel died, "He slept with his fathers" (2 Kings 14:16, NASB) and the same kind of phrase is used about forty times in the Old Testament. In the New Testament, we are told that when Jesus heard that His friend Lazarus had died, He said he had "fallen asleep" (John 11:11). When Stephen was stoned to death, he "fell asleep" (Acts 7:60). Later, when Paul was preaching in Pisidian Antioch, he reminded his hearers that "When David had served God's purpose in his own generation, he fell asleep" (Acts 13:36). Elsewhere, in writing about dying believers, he called them "those who have fallen asleep" (1 Thessalonians 4;13). At first glance, these and similar statements seem to give some kind of credence to the idea of "soul sleep," but there are powerful arguments against it.

Firstly, Scripture never teaches that either the soul or the body fall asleep as separate entities. What falls asleep is the person, in the sense that he or she is taken out of operation as far as earthly activities are concerned—which, of course, is what happens when someone does fall asleep.

Secondly, the fact that the Bible nowhere speaks of the soul falling asleep points to the fact that when using "sleep" in connection with death it is employing it as a picture and not to make a theological statement. After all, a dead person gives every appearance of being asleep, and there are times when just for a few seconds it is difficult to make the distinction. Moments after my stepmother died, nurses came into the hospital ward and began to change her position to make her more comfortable before they realized she was no longer alive.

Thirdly, there are many places in Scripture which indicate that the soul is not unconscious after death. As far as the Old Testament is concerned, we have already noted that at death, "The dust returns to the ground it came from, and the spirit returns to God who gave it" (Ecclesiastes 12:7). This is a graphic way of expressing the fact that death is essentially the separation of soul and body, though not, as we saw in the last chapter, the annihilation of either. As far as the soul is concerned, it "returns to God who gave it"—a phrase the inspired writer would surely not have used if what he meant was that it lapsed into a state of unconsciousness, unaware of either its whereabouts or its company?

ALIVE AND ALERT

In the New Testament, as we should expect, the picture becomes much clearer. When Jesus was being crucified, one of the thieves being put to death at the same time cried, "Jesus, remember me when you come into your kingdom" (Luke 23:42). He had apparently become convinced that Jesus was the Messiah, and believed that at some distant time He would establish a glorious and eternal kingdom that would finally replace all the passing kingdoms of this present world. The reply Jesus gave promised much more than he asked: "I tell you the truth, today you will be with me in paradise" (Luke 23:43). As "paradise" is one of the Bible's words for heaven, a place of eternal bliss in the presence of God, the promise Jesus made to the dying thief rules out the idea that the soul becomes unconscious at death. As Anthony Hoekema comments, "Surely soul-sleep is here excluded, for what would be the point of saying these words if the thief after death would be totally unaware of being with Christ in Paradise?"[6] Unconsciousness would obviously be better than experiencing the agony of crucifixion, but if this is what Jesus was promising then his own spirit was also about to be rendered unconscious because the promise was that "You will be with me."

There can be no serious doubt as to what Jesus meant: the penitent, believing thief was to be in God's blissful presence the moment crucifixion had done its deadly work. It would seem impossible even to attempt any other interpretation of Jesus' words but, almost unbelievably, there are those who do. In a desperate bid to make His words fit in with their teaching, Jehovah's Witnesses and others have produced a novel form of punctuation, which makes Jesus say, "I tell you the truth today, you will be with me in paradise." But when else could Jesus have spoken the words but "today"? He could hardly have spoken them the previous day (before the question had been asked) or the following day (when both men were dead). The attempt to twist the meaning of Christ's promise owes more to ingenuity than to integrity.

The parable of the rich man and Lazarus provides further evidence against the idea of soul sleep. Whatever the difficulties in interpreting some of its details, it is impossible to deny that both the rich man (in Hades) and Lazarus (in paradise) were alive, even though at that stage their bodies remained in their graves.

Another important New Testament passage on the subject is where Paul gives a very moving testimony about his readiness to live or to die: "For to me, to live is Christ and to die is gain. If I am to go on living in the body, this will mean fruitful labor for me. Yet what shall I choose? I do not know! I am torn between the two: I desire to depart and be with Christ, which is better by far, but it is more necessary for you that I remain in the body" (Philippians 1:21-24). Paul's phrase "better by far" could literally be translated "much rather better," meaning "by far the best." As we know from what we wrote elsewhere, Paul had no doubt that when he died he would go to heaven; here, he puts the phrases "to depart" and "to be with Christ" alongside each other, making it crystal clear that there was to be no "gap" between dying and being in the immediate presence of his God and Savior. And as Paul had led such a dynamic, eventful and satisfying life, how could he have meant that a state of spiritual limbo would be "better by far," even if that limbo was to be shared with Christ?

The same kind of truth comes across in words Paul wrote to the Christians in Corinth: "Therefore we are always confident and know that as long as we are at home in the body we are away from the Lord. We live by faith, not by sight. We are confident, I say, and would prefer to be away from the body and at home with the Lord" (2 Corinthians 5:6-8). Paul paints two pictures here. He says that the Christian believer living on earth is "at home in the body" but "away from the Lord"; however close a Christian's fellowship with Christ, he still lives "by faith, not by sight." The second picture makes it clear that as soon as the believer is "away from the body" (in other words, as soon as he dies) he is "at home with the Lord." It is this living, dynamic, joyful experience of Christ's presence that Paul says he would prefer, and he tells the Corinthian Christians that this will be his the moment he dies.

There are several other New Testament references that eliminate the idea of "soul sleep." One speaks of "thousands upon thousands of angels in joyful assembly" being joined by "the spirits of righteous men made perfect" (Hebrews 12:32), an activity which would be impossible if they were sleeping or unconscious. The same kind of picture emerges in Revelation, where John describes believers who had been persecuted on earth but whom he now says "before the throne of God and [who] serve him day and night in his temple" (Revelation 7:15). How can one square this activity with unconsciousness?

The idea of "soul sleep," or any other kind of post-mortem hibernation, is nowhere to be found in the pages of Scripture.

THE DIVIDING LINE

The next thing we discover about the intermediate state is that it is not the same for everyone. When the French leader Charles De Gaulle looked at the dead body of his young mongoloid daughter he said, "Maintenant elle est comme les autres" ("Now she is like the others"). We can see what he meant—or hoped—but the Bible says that even in the intermediate state, all are not alike, and the deciding factor is the spiritual condition of the person concerned. At this point we need to notice that the Bible divides mankind into two categories, "the righteous" and "the wicked" (Psalm 1:6). It also uses many other words which effectively make the same distinction. For example, "the righteous" are also called "the people of God" (Hebrews 4:9), "Christians" (Acts 11:26), and "the elect" (Romans 11:7), and are said to be "saved" (Romans 8:24); while "the wicked" are also called "the children of the devil" (1 John 3:10), "unbelievers" (Luke 12:46), and "the unrighteous" (2 Peter 2:9) and are said to be "lost" (Luke 19:10). The contrasts could hardly be greater. But who are "the righteous" and "the wicked"? Although this is a tremendously important question (in some ways the most important of all) the right place to answer it is not here but toward the end of this book. For the remainder of this chapter I will use the words "righteous" and "wicked" as far as possible.

What happens to the souls of the righteous? As we saw earlier in this chapter, one New Testament writer describes the intermediate state of the righteous as being "the spirits of righteous men made perfect" (Hebrews 12:23). The souls of the righteous are not wandering around in space, hovering around cemeteries, or languishing in limbo; they are alive and well and living in God's presence. In Paul's phrase they are "away from the body" and "at home with the Lord" (2 Corinthians 5:8). This emphasizes not only that death means separation, but that the souls of the righteous go immediately into God's presence, and as nothing unholy can exist in God's company we can be sure that they are morally perfect. Even though, as we shall see in the next chapter, their joy is not complete, their souls are "in happiness and in safe keeping."[7] The American preacher Vance Havner once told me that his stock reply to people who expressed their sorrow that he had lost his wife was, "But I haven't lost her. I know where she is!"

What happens to the souls of the wicked? One of the clearest answers to this question comes in the story Jesus told about the rich but godless man who died and went immediately to "hell, where he was in torment" (Luke 16:23). As we say in chapter 3, Jesus used the Greek word *Hades*, which in most cases in the New Testament means the place of punishment for the wicked, as it obviously does here. If the man's soul was "in torment" he was clearly conscious, able to feel all that "torment" implies. The other relevant clue about Hades in this story is that the man cried out, "I am in agony in this fire" (Luke 16:24), but there are others elsewhere. When Judas betrayed Jesus and then committed suicide, the Bible says that he went "where he belongs" (Acts 1:25) and Jesus had said earlier that he was "doomed to destruction" (John 17:12), a word meaning loss and ruin. Elsewhere, Peter said that God "did not spare angels when they sinned, but sent them to hell,[8] putting them into gloomy dungeons to be held for judgment", and a little later wrote that "The Lord knows how to . . . hold the unrighteous for the day of judgment, while continuing their punishment" (2 Peter 2:4, 9).

Pulling these statements together we see that Hades is a place of imprisonment, ruin, torment, fire, and darkness. The picture is grim, but even this is not the final state of the wicked, because they have yet to be brought to judgment. Some may suggest that it is unjust to imprison anyone at that state, but this is not the case. People are often remanded in custody because the judge decides that in the circumstances this would be the right thing to do, even thought they have not been found guilty. In holding the souls of the wicked in Hades, God is rightly detaining those He knows to be guilty. There can surely be no complaint about that?

The condition of the righteous and the wicked after death and before the Day of Judgment has been well summarized by the nineteenth-century American theologian, W. G. T. Shedd: "The intermediate state for the saved is heaven without the body, and the final state for the saved is heaven with the body . . . the intermediate state for the lost is hell without the body, and the final state for the lost is hell with the body."[9]

ESCAPE ROUTES?

The next point to be made is that paradise and Hades are the only intermediate states mentioned in the Bible. There are no other places or conditions to which human souls go at death. This is vitally important to grasp, especially as it rules out two theories that have been taught by many and believed by millions.

In 1439, the Council of Florence proclaimed as an article of faith the doctrine of purgatory, and this decision was confirmed by the Council of Trent in 1548. It lists no fewer than five potential destinations for the human soul immediately after death, four of them currently said to be in operation. These are as follows:

1. Unbaptized infants go the *Limbus Infantum*, located on the outskirts of hell, and where they endure no suffering but have no vision of God.

2. Old Testament believers went to the *Limbus Patrum*, also on the outskirts of hell and with the same conditions as the *Limbus Infantum*. Between His death and resurrection, Jesus released these believers from the *Limbus Patrum* (which presumably is now empty or no longer exists) and took them with Him in triumph to heaven.

3. All unbelieving adults and those not at peace with the Roman Catholic Church go straight to hell.

4. All Christian martyrs and believers who are in a state of moral perfection go straight to heaven.

5. All others who are at peace with the church but not yet perfect go to a place called purgatory, where they are punished and purified until they are fit to be transferred to heaven. This process can take from a few hours to thousands of years, depending on how much purging is needed, but it can be short-circuited by the prayers and gifts

of believers on earth, and in particular by the saying or singing of masses on their behalf.

It is a fascinating scenario but fatally flawed and, not surprisingly, has given rise to many unholy practices. One of the most odious is the financial trafficking in indulgences (the reduction of time in purgatory) which led to the doctrine of being described as "the goldmine of the priesthood."[10] The completion of St. Peter's Cathedral in Rome was financed to a large extent by indulgences granted by Pope Leo X. The chief salesman was a Dominican friar by the name of Johann Tetzel who became so brazen that he claimed to be able to manipulate the exact moment when a soul would be released from purgatory and used to end his sales pitch with the couplet:

As soon as the coin in the coffer rings
The soul from purgatory springs.[11]

Indulgences were often associated with the veneration of relics, said to be such items as pieces of Jesus' cross, parts of His crown of thorns, nails used to crucify Him, the Virgin Mary's wedding ring, locks from her hair and vials of her milk. John Calvin once said that so many churches claimed to have pieces of Jesus' cross that "If all the pieces . . . were collected in a single heap . . . it would take more than three hundred men to carry."[12] At Wittenberg in Germany, 17,443 relics were eventually on display, and it has been calculated that those who prayed before them stood to gain the equivalent of 127,709 years and 116 days of indulgences.[13]

Although indulgences are no longer hawked around, the principle remains. Purgatory is still said to be "a wholesome doctrine," and it remains part of the Roman Catholic Church's teaching that not to believe in it is to be accursed. But the whole principle is offensive both to common morality and biblical theology. The American scholar Loraine Boettner shrewdly comments: "If any one of us actually had the power to release souls from purgatory and refused to exercise that power except in return for payment of money, he would be considered cruel and unchristian—which indeed he would be. By all Christian standards that is a service that the church should render freely and willingly to its people. No decent man would permit even a dog to suffer in the fire until its owner paid him five dollars to take it out."[14]

The doctrine of purgatory clashes with Scripture at one point after another, as we shall see in the following paragraphs.

Firstly, it distinguishes between sins which are mortal ("any great offense against the law of God" which kills the soul and subjects it to eternal punishment) and those which are venial ("small and pardonable sins against God or our neighbor"). The Bible makes no such distinction. It does say that some sins are greater than others, but also makes it clear that all sin is mortal (that is, fatal): "Sin . . . gives birth to death" (James 1:15). There are no "small sins" in the Bible, because "sin is lawlessness" (1 John 3:4), a rebellious offense against God.

Secondly, it says that there is hope of recovery and restoration after death, something the Bible emphatically denies. In a brilliant illustration from nature, the Bible pictures death as a storm uprooting a tree, and adds that "Where it falls, there it will lie" (Ecclesiastes 11:3).

Thirdly, it insists that man's good works have saving merit, whereas the Bible declares that "All our righteous acts are like filthy rags" (Isaiah 64:6) and that if anyone is to be saved it must be "by grace . . . through faith . . . the gift of God—not by works" (Ephesians 2:8-9).

Fourthly, it implies that the church holds the keys to the place of punishment in the afterlife, whereas the Bible says that Christ alone holds "the keys of death and Hades" (Revelation 1:18).

Fifthly, it also implies that we need to make sacrifices for sins, when the Bible teaches that when Christ died on the cross he "offered for all time one sacrifice for sins" (Hebrews 10:12).

As there is no biblical foundation for it, how did the doctrine of purgatory take root? The main basis for it is in a book called II Maccabees, written around 110 B.C. and part of a collection of similar books called the *Apocrypha*, which was added to the Roman Catholic Bible by the Council of Trent in 1546—though only after a strong protest by some of the council members. To put it in a wider context, this means that II Maccabees was only accepted by a majority decision of a few representatives of a single church over 1,300 years after the Bible was written. As if that were not flimsy enough, the book is said to be full of "palpable exaggerations"[15] and the passage on which the doctrine of purgatory is based actually proves too much because it teaches the possible salvation of soldiers who died in the mortal sin of idolatry, which would mean that they went straight to hell without ever going to purgatory!

One supporter of the doctrine has argued that it was one of those things that had developed from "a small scriptural germ," but in a major article on purgatory in the *New Catholic Encyclopedia* R. J. Bastian is forced to admit that "In the final analysis, the Catholic doctrine on purgatory is based on tradition not Scripture."[16] Loraine Boettner fine-tunes the flaw by saying that "It is an instance of the development from a germ that was never there to begin with."[17] After a major study of the subject, one church historian came to an even more serious conclusion: "In every system except that of the Bible the doctrine of purgatory after death, and prayers for the dead, has always been found to occupy a place. Go wherever we may . . . we find that paganism leaves hope after death for sinners, who, at the time of their departure, were consciously unfit for the abodes of the blest."[18] Regardless of how many millions believe in it, purgatory is not a doctrine to be found in the Bible.

Incidentally (but not unimportantly) the fact that purgatory is non-existent means that prayers for the dead are pointless, because the dead are either in paradise, where they do not need our prayers, or under God's judgment, in which case our prayers will achieve nothing.[19]

SNAKES AND LADDERS?

Another persistent and equally unbiblical theory is that of reincarnation. Beliefs about reincarnation go back a very long way, forming an essential part of religions as ancient as Hinduism and Buddhism, though with a number of complex variations. In Hinduism—from which Buddhism later developed—the picture is of a cycle of lives (*samsara*) in which a man's destiny is decided by his deeds (*karma*) from which he can seek release through various disciplines such as yoga. If he fails, he must go through as many reincarnations as are necessary to become absorbed into Brahma, a universal and all-embracing spirit. Karma is the keystone, the law which governs the whole universe and which determines the nature of the next life. This means that any good or evil that comes to us in the present life is exactly what we deserve because of our actions during previous incarnations. However, rather like shares on the stock market, past performance is apparently no guarantee of something similar in the future and, should our present performance deserve it, we may return to earth as someone in the gutter of society, or even as an animal, a bird, a reptile, or an insect.

Reincarnation, or transmigration of souls as it is sometimes called, has more recently been taken up in one form or another by Theosophists, Anthroposophists, and Rosicrucians, as well as by many occultists and some spiritualists. The theory received a boost in the late nineteenth century with the formation of the Society for Psychical Research, whose membership included Sir Arthur Conan Doyle, the creator of Sherlock Holmes, and Lewis Carroll, author of *Alice in Wonderland*, but interest later waned until the recent resurgence of occultism. A survey by *The Times* in 1980 suggested that twenty-nine percent of its readers believed in reincarnation, and a Gallup Poll conducted in the United States in 1982 said that nearly twenty-five of those interviewed did so.[20] The New Age Movement, which has grown rapidly in recent years and has links with Transcendentalism, Spiritism, Theosophy, New Thought, and Christian Science, and, above all, Hinduism, is a bewildering cocktail of beliefs and includes the idea of repeated incarnations in order to reach the awareness of one's own higher nature or divinity.

In 1991 David Icke, one-time professional soccer player, BBC sports presenter, and political spokesman for the Green Party, wrote a book entitled *The Truth Vibrations*. In it, he informed his readers that he originated in another solar system, made his first appearance on earth at the beginning of the Atlantis civilization and, in the course of a long-running series of reincarnations, was married in ancient Greece to a lady called Lucy, became the brother of the seventeenth-century philosopher Francis Bacon, served as one of Napoleon's generals, and was a North American Indian chief. Mr. Icke's claims did not attract significant endorsement, and he has subsequently revamped his resumé.

If reincarnation theories have been around for a long time, so has Christian opposition to them. Within a few years of the completion of the New Testament, Irenaeus, Bishop of Lyons, and one of the most significant theologians of his time, wrote five volumes exposing popular heresies of the time—and reincarnation was among them: "Souls not only continue to exist [after death], not by passing from body to body, but that they preserve the same form."[21] We can make an even stronger point by going back beyond Irenaeus to the New Testament itself. If reincarnation is true, it is obviously tremendously important, as it concerns man's eternal destiny, and we should therefore expect Jesus to make it an integral part of His teaching, but as a recent writer comments, "Nothing is more remarkable than the silence of Jesus Christ on the subject."[22]

This is particularly significant because He was given at least one golden opportunity to introduce it. When He met a man blind from birth, His disciples asked Him, "Who sinned, this man or his parents, that he was born blind?" Instead of confirming that some sinful actions in a previous incarnation had led to the man's condition, or that it was punishment for his parents' sins, Jesus replied, "Neither this man nor his parents sinned . . . but this happened so that the work of God might be displayed in his life" (John 9:2-3).

In direct contrast to the doctrine of reincarnation, the Bible teaches that "He who goes down to the grave does not return. He will never come to his house again; his place will know him no more" (Job 7:9-10) and that "Man is destined to die once" (Hebrews 9:27). Just as wrongly, reincarnation teaches that a person's evil is purged by his own efforts throughout a series of lives, whereas the Bible says that the testimony of those made right with God is that "The blood of Jesus, [God's] Son, purifies us from every sin" (1 John 1:7). Reincarnation is equally flawed at a wider level, where its claim to be the solution to this world's injustices is denied by Scripture's teaching that God alone is the one who will establish "a new heaven and a new earth, the home of righteousness" (2 Peter 3:13).

After a major study of the subject, the contemporary American writer Robert Morey came to this conclusion: "When one examines all of the arguments that the reincarnationists use in order to support their position, one finds that these arguments are totally devoid of any historic, scientific, philosophic or religious merit."[23] We can emphasize the last of those points by saying that it is clearly condemned in Scripture, which asserts that at death the souls of the righteous go immediately into God's blissful presence, while the souls of the wicked go to the painful prison of Hades, where they are remanded in custody awaiting the next stage of God's dealings with them. It is to that stage that we must now turn our attention.

The Moment of Truth

In the dome of the Capitol building in Washington D.C., these words are written:

> *One God, one law, one element;*
> *And one far off, divine event*
> *To which the whole creation moves.*

These lines are not taken directly from the Bible, but the message is certainly biblical. Scripture tells us that history is not an endless succession of meaningless circles, but an ordered movement toward an eternal goal which God in His sovereign wisdom has established and which nothing can set aside:

> "His dominion is an eternal dominion;
> his kingdom endures from generation to generation . . .
> He does as he pleases
> with the powers of heaven
> and the peoples of the earth.
> No one can hold back his hand
> or say to him: 'What have you done?'"
> (Daniel 4:34-35).

As far as human destiny is concerned, we have already seen that immediately after death the body begins to decay and the soul goes either to paradise (in the case of the righteous) or Hades (in the case of the wicked). But this is only an intermediate state. "Man is destined to die once, and after that to face judgment" (Hebrews 9:27); when a person has reached the intermediate state, death is past, but judgment still lies ahead. No doctrine is more plainly taught in Scripture than that of a final day of judgment. In every section of the Old Testament—the Law, the Prophets, and the Writings—the note of judgment is loud and clear. Moses says that ultimately "Judgment belongs to God" (Deuteronomy 1:17). Malachi delivers God's warning, "I will come near to you for judgment" (Malachi 3:5). And David emphasizes that "There is a God who judges the earth" (Psalm 58:11). When we turn to the New Testament, the issue is not clouded but clarified. Jesus warns about a coming "day of judgment" (Matthew 10:15). Paul says that "We will all stand before God's judgment seat" (Romans 14:10). John the Baptist speaks of "the coming wrath" (Matthew 3:7). James warns that "The Judge is standing at the door!" (James 5:9). Peter says that God is "ready to judge the living and the dead" (1 Peter 4:5). Even a superficial scanning of the evidence confirms the assessment of the well-known British preacher J. I. Packer that "The entire New Testament is overshadowed by the certainty of a coming day of judgment."[1] But before judgment takes place, two other important events must occur.

THE MAN WHO IS COMING BACK

The first of these events is the personal return of Jesus Christ to the earth, usually called the Second Coming of Christ. Of all biblical doctrines, this may be the most ridiculed or neglected, not least because centuries of foolish and futile guesswork about when it might happen have given the doctrine a bad name. As the year 1000 approached, many people argued that this would be the time when Christ would return (because they felt that God would be likely to deal in round numbers?). For quite different reasons, later pundits suggested 1260. A Roman Catholic priest wrote a book suggesting 1847; he was given permission to have the book published in 1848! Cults and heretical sects have often majored on their interpretation of events surrounding the Second Coming, as well as joining in the guesswork as to when it might happen. The Jehovah's Witnesses have backed a whole string of losers, including 1874, 1914, 1915, and 1975. In 1988, an American by the name of Edgar Whisenant listed eighty-eight reasons why he believed Christ's return was imminent—and even nominated September 11, 12, or 13 as the likely date. Amazingly, his book became a best seller—although sales did go into serious decline from September 14 onwards!

Yet in spite of such continued abuse, the fact remains that the Second Coming of Christ is one of the most pervasive doctrines on the pages of the New Testament. It is mentioned over three hundred times, an average of once for every thirteen verses from Matthew to Revelation. When His disciples became depressed at the prospect of His arrest and execution, Jesus told them, "Trust in God; trust also in me. In my Father's house are many rooms; if it were not so, I would have told you. I am going there to prepare a place for you. And if I go and prepare a place for you, I will come back and take you to be with me that you also may be where I am" (John 14:1-3). As soon as Jesus had ascended into heaven, an angel appeared to the disciples and promised them, "This same Jesus, who has been taken from you into heaven, will come back in the same way you have seen him go into heaven" (Acts 1:11). Paul wrote about "the appearing of our Lord Jesus Christ" (1 Timothy 6:14). Peter said that "The day of the Lord will come" (2 Peter 3:10). John spoke of tremendous changes that would come about "when he appears" (1 John 3:2). Jude wrote, "The Lord is coming" (Jude 14). James mentioned "the Lord's coming" (James 5:7-8).

After American and Filipino troops were forced to surrender the Philippines to the invading Japanese in May 1942, General Douglas MacArthur, who commanded the Allied Forces in the Southwest Pacific, vowed to retake the Islands. To underline his promise, he had the words "I will return" printed on tens of thousands of leaflets and other items which were then scattered all over the country. Toward the end of 1944, he kept his promise; by July 1945 the country was liberated, and a month later the war was over. In the same way, Christ's promise to return was not an isolated or impulsive statement made on the spur of the moment; it is scattered so widely all over the New Testament that it is virtually impossible to open it anywhere without seeing it. In the words of Anthony Hoekema, "The faith of the New Testament is dominated by this expectation."[2]

The Second Coming of Christ will be something unique in the history of the world. As Scottish author Bruce Milne writes, "It will . . . transcend all events in space and time hitherto experienced."[3] His first coming was in poverty and obscurity; his second will be "with power and great glory" (Matthew 24:30). Although the Bible lists certain signs of His coming (ecological disturbances, international tensions, and widespread concern over world events among them) nobody on earth knows when it will happen. When Jesus was questioned about this He replied, "No one knows about that day or hour" (Matthew 24:36). Paul confirmed this by saying that it will catch everyone by surprise, like "a thief in the night" (1 Thessalonians 5:2). But the most important thing about the Second Coming in the context of our subject is this: it will bring history to a close and be the prelude to mankind's final destiny. In the Bible's words, "Then the end will come, when he hands over the kingdom to God the Father after he has destroyed all dominion, authority and power" (1 Corinthians 15:24).

THE GRAY AREAS

The day when Jesus returns to the earth will begin like any other day—and end like no other day. Thousands of people will be born, thousands get married, and thousands die. Some will fall in love, others get divorced; some will get promotion, others be made redundant; some will be admitted to hospitals, others be discharged. It will be a day when some women will discover they are pregnant, while others will decide to have an abortion. It will be a day when life on earth goes on as usual—and during which it will end forever.

Some of the details surrounding the Second Coming are complex and controversial. Even scholars who submit to the authority of the Bible as the Word of God have come to different conclusions about the exact meaning of certain events, and about the order in which they will take place. The identity of the "antichrist" (1 John 2:18), the significance of the nation of Israel in God's plan, the fulfillment of particular prophecies, the meaning of a period of a thousand years (sometimes called the millennium) and the battle of Armageddon, both mentioned in the book of Revelation, are just some of the issues that have spawned whole libraries of books over the centuries, but we will not allow ourselves to get sidetracked into examining any of them, because they have no direct bearing on our subject.

Much more to the point for us is the fact that "Every eye will see him" (Revelation 1:7), a statement which rules out the false claims of the Jehovah's Witnesses who say that Christ has already returned but has so far remained invisible.[4] The personal return of Jesus Christ to earth will be visible to all and hidden from none. Many will be surprised at his return, but nobody will be in any doubt about it. His return will be dynamic and dramatic, "with a loud command, with the voice of the archangel and with the trumpet call of God" (1 Thessalonians 4:16)—and that trumpet call will summon the whole of humanity to judgment.

The fact that Christ's return is linked to the day of final judgment has tremendous implications for each one of us. In one of his broadcast talks, C. S. Lewis made the point in this way: "But I wonder whether people who ask God to interfere openly and directly in our world quite realize what it will be like when he does. God's going to invade all right. When that happens, it's the end of the world. When the Author walks onto the stage, the play's over. For this time, it will be something so overwhelming that it will strike either irresistible love or irresistible horror into every creature. It will be too late then to choose your sides . . . It will be the time when we discover which side we have really chosen, whether we realize it or not.'[5]

This brings us to the second tremendous event which will take place before the Day of Judgment.

UP FROM THE GRAVE

On the face of it, bringing the whole of humanity to judgment would seem to raise an insuperable problem because, as we saw earlier, a person is fully human only when body and soul are joined. Yet until Jesus returns, humanity is fragmented in four directions. There are those who are integrated (body and soul) and living on earth, there are millions of bodies (or at least the atoms which made up those bodies) scattered over land and sea all around the world, the souls of the righteous are in paradise and the souls of the wicked in Hades. What does the Bible tell us about the logistics of bringing all of humanity to judgment? Without going into details, it outlines a number of things that will happen.

Firstly, the bodies of all those who have died during the course of world history will be raised from the dead. Jesus made this very clear. Speaking of Himself as the Son of God, He said, "A time is coming when all who are in their graves will hear his voice and come out— those who have done good will rise to live, and those who have done evil will rise to be condemned" (John 5:28-29). What an awesome statement that is! J.C. Ryle, the first Bishop of Liverpool, said that these words "ought to sink down very deeply into our hearts and never be forgotten."[6] People may be "dead and buried," but they are never "dead and gone." The day is coming when all the dead will "hear" Christ calling them from the grave and summoning them to appear at the bar of God's judgment—and not one will be able to refuse. People from every race, every culture, and every century, from the greatest figures in history to those of whom history knows nothing, will respond to Christ's voice. Those who die a moment before Christ returns will instantly obey His command—and so will Adam!

Secondly, in his vision of the Day of Judgment, John adds another important face: "The sea gave up the dead that were in it, and death and Hades gave up the dead that were in them, and each person was judged according to what he had done" (Revelation 20:13). By linking death and Hades, John shows that death (by which he obviously means the grave) gives up the body and Hades the soul, so that body and soul can be joined together to stand before God in judgment. It is not just the soul that will be judged, nor just the body, but the whole person. Man was created body and soul, he lives on earth as body and soul, and he will be judged body and soul. Before this can take place, his body and soul must be reintegrated—and the Bible makes it clear that this is precisely what will happen at the Second Coming of Christ.

Thirdly, the Bible tells us something of what will happen to those people living on earth when Jesus returns. To show that His return would be sudden and unexpected, and to illustrate how it would affect a believer and an unbeliever who were together at the time, Jesus reminded His hearers of the massive flood recorded in Genesis: "As it was in the days of Noah, so it will be at the coming of the Son of Man. For in the days before the flood, people were eating and drinking, marrying and giving in marriage, up to the day Noah entered the ark; and they knew nothing about what would happen until the flood came and took them all away. That is how it will be at the coming of the Son of Man. Two men will be in the field; one will be taken and the other left. Two women will be grinding with a hand mill; one will be taken and the other left" (Matthew 24:37-41).

On another occasion, He made the same point but with an interesting addition: "I tell you, on that night two people will be in one bed; one will be taken and the other left. Two women will be grinding grain together; one will be taken and the other left; (Luke 17:34-35). This not only underlines the suddenness of Christ's return, it also shows that it will be universal and instantaneous. In one part of the world, it will be night, with people in bed; in another part of the world, it will be day, with people at work. The Second Coming of Christ will not be some kind of spiritual movement that will spread from one country to another, so that some people will be able to get reports of it happening elsewhere and prepare for it to reach them. It will be unexpected, instantaneous, universal, and decisive. In a split second, everyone in time will be in eternity.

It may have been to emphasize this point that Jesus added nothing further, but later in the New Testament Paul gives us a little more detail, and it is worth quoting the whole section to include the background to what he says: "Brothers, we do not want you to be ignorant about those who fall asleep, or to grieve like the rest of men, who have no hope. We believe that Jesus died and rose again and so we believe that God will bring with Jesus those who have fallen asleep in him. According to the Lord's own word, we tell you that we who are still alive, who are left till the coming of the Lord, will certainly not precede those who have fallen asleep. For the Lord himself will come down from heaven, with a loud command, with the voice of the archangel and with the trumpet call of God, and the dead in Christ will rise first. After that, we who are still alive and are left will be caught up together with them in the clouds to meet the Lord in the air" (1 Thessalonians 4:13-17).

Christians in Thessalonica were grieving over the deaths of fellow believers and anxious about what would happen to them at the Second Coming, but Paul reassures them that they have nothing to be concerned about. Their dead friends will not be forgotten or left behind. In fact, they will be raised from the dead (their bodies and souls reunited) first, then Christians still living will be caught up from the earth to join them. Trying to construct a more detailed timetable of what will happen when Christ returns is pointless—but at least this gives us one part of the scenario, though things will happen so quickly that we shall be unable to think in terms of sequence and timing.

Paul was writing to, for, and about Christians and added nothing about unbelievers; what he does say elsewhere is that "There will be a resurrection of both the righteous and the wicked" (Acts 24:15) and that "God . . . will judge the living and the dead" (2 Timothy 4:1). The Bible is unanimous on this. In the Old Testament, one of the clearest statements comes from the prophet Daniel: "Multitudes who sleep in the dust of the earth will awake: some to everlasting life, others to shame and everlasting contempt" (Daniel 12:2). Hundreds of years later Jesus confirmed the truth of Daniel's prophecy by saying that "A time is coming when all who are in their graves will hear [the voice of the Son of God] and come out—those who have done good will rise to live, and those who have done evil will rise to be condemned" (John 5:28-29). At God's irresistible command all those who have died before Christ's return and all those still alive on earth at the time will be brought before Him to give account. This gives us only a sketchy outline of what will happen, but it is all we need in order to understand that nothing—not even death—can enable us to escape the day of reckoning when "Each of us will give an account of himself to God" (Romans 14:12). Trying to keep God at a distance is the most ridiculous thing that anyone can do, because the day when He must be faced is getting closer all the time.

IMPOSSIBLE? TO WHOM?

Not surprisingly, people raise all kinds of questions to try to blur the issue or to make the idea of universal resurrection seem absurd. A favorite line is to ask how the bodies of the dead can themselves be reconstructed, let alone be reunited with their souls. What about bodies lost at sea, buried in avalanches, blown to pieces in mid-air, or vaporized in the atomic blasts at Hiroshima and Nagasaki? What about someone who lost a limb years before dying, or who had an organ transplant? Questions like these are fascinating, but fatuous, for one simple reason that John Benton puts very well: "To die is not to be beyond God. A teacher may write a word with his chalk on the blackboard and then rub it off. But that does not preclude him from writing that same word again. It should not surprise us that God is able to rewrite that bundle of genetic and psychological information which is us and draw us again on the blackboard of life after we have died."[7] The Bible gives no detailed explanation of this process and tells us merely that human bodies, which were created to live in time, will be modified in some way to live in eternity, while retaining their individual and unique identities.

All this teaches that after their resurrection all people will have bodies identifiable with those they had on earth, yet dramatically changed to fit their new environment, whatever that may be. As far as Christians are concerned, Paul says that the change will be from a body that is "perishable" (liable to decay and death) to one that is "imperishable"; from one that is "sown in dishonor" (buried as a corpse) to one that is "raised in glory"; from one of "weakness" to one of "power"; and from one that is "natural" (suitable to life on earth) to one that is "spiritual" (suited to life in heaven) (1 Corinthians 15:42-44).

The Bible gives us very little detail about the exact nature of the Christians' resurrection bodies, but we have a kind of model in the person of Christ, who in His resurrection became "the first-fruits of those who have fallen asleep" (1 Corinthians 15:20). When Christ rose from the dead, He was recognizable as the one who had lived and been put to death, and His body was certainly physical, with the marks of the nails and spear clearly visible in His hands and side. Yet at the same time His body was radically different and free from normal human limitations so that He was able to appear and disappear at will; for instance, He suddenly materialized at a gathering of His disciples, even though they were meeting "with the doors locked" (John 20:19).

As far as unbelievers are concerned, they too will be reintegrated and possess material, physical bodies identifiable with those they had on earth, yet dramatically changed to fit their ultimate environment. In their new, reconstituted form they will be taken from their intermediate punishment in Hades to face their Maker and receive their final sentence.

There is a second reason why questions about the reassembling of the bodies of the dead are foolish. As God created the entire universe out of nothing in the first place—He simply "spoke, and it came to be" (Psalm 33:9)—why should it be any problem to Him to do whatever will be necessary to raise from the dead as living beings bodies that had disintegrated and to all intents and purposes disappeared? As John Calvin wrote, "Since God has all the elements at his disposal, no difficulty can prevent him from commanding the earth, the fire and the water to give up what they seem to have destroyed."[8] Nothing, not even death, will enable us to avoid the moment when every one of us, including the writer and reader of these words, stands body and soul before our Maker and Judge.

The Great Day

To many people the word "judgment" has an ominous ring, whereas "justice" sounds much less threatening; they are in favor of the second but in fear of the first. This is hardly surprising, because there are times when it seems that the only place where the words are close together is in a dictionary. Even in the renowned system of British justice, with appeals against conviction or sentence allowed right up to the House of Lords and beyond, there is always the possibility of some miscarriage of justice which would lead to the guilty going free, the innocent being punished, or the wrong penalty being imposed. Many factors contribute to this. With the exception of murder, judges have no perfect yardstick by which to assess the right penalty; even the finest judges and fairest of juries can be misled and make mistakes; vital evidence may be missing or be suppressed; witnesses may commit perjury and the law can never take account of attitudes that fall short of being crimes.

The fact that I can write those words is part of the evidence that mankind has an instinct for justice. Even though we are fallen sinners we remain moral beings, with an innate, God-give sense of right and wrong; one theologian has said, "The whole of recorded history is one great longing for justice."[1] That longing was part of man's make-up when he was created as a moral and responsible being, with the result that these factors are part of the very fabric of human society. As David Watson notes, "The idea of accountability is built into the very framework of life. The whole of society would collapse without it. Everywhere we must give an account of our work, time or money to someone."[2] We instinctively feel that people should get what they deserve; right should be rewarded and wrong should be punished.

That being the case, surely it ought to be the most natural thing in the world to accept that our greatest accountability is to our Creator? When we read that "The Lord is a God of justice" (Isaiah 30:18) it should ring a bell—because God put the bell there. When a person is in his right mind, the judgment and justice of God produce praise, not panic. Notice how this comes across in the Bible:

"The Lord reigns, let the earth be glad;
let the distant shores rejoice . . .
righteousness and justice are the foundation of his throne"
(Psalm 97:1-2).

"I will sing of your love and justice;
to you, O Lord, I will sing praise"
(Psalm 101:1).

"Give thanks to the Lord . . .
Sing to him, sing praise to him . . .
He is the Lord our God;
his judgments are in all the earth"
(Psalm 105:1-2, 7)

These statements tell us that God's judgment and justice are operating in the world here and now. Paul emphasizes the punishment of evil by saying that "The wrath of God is being revealed from heaven against all the godlessness and wickedness of men" (Romans 1:18). God is not an idle spectator of world events. From the moment He expelled Adam and Eve from the Garden of Eden He has been actively expressing His holy anger against human sin. Sometimes there have been devastating demonstrations of this, such as when He overwhelmed the world with a massive flood, destroyed the cities of Sodom and Gomorrah, wasted Egypt with a series of plagues and allowed Jerusalem to be demolished by its enemies. At other times, the Bible concentrates on the way God's righteous anger punished individuals rather than nations, but the same principle applies: "God is a righteous judge, a God who expresses his wrath every day" (Psalm 7:11).

One Bible scholar makes this excellent summary of the point: "To read the Bible seriously and to open one's eyes to the chronicle of history is to be awed and terrified. God has declared Himself the Judge of sinners and his judgments crowd the pages of the Bible and shout at us in every segment of human life. His temporal judgments are seen in individuals and in society and in the whole human race."[3] Another writer is more graphic: "Judgment does not sit twiddling its thumbs until the end of the age."[4] As I write these very words, 72,000 people are attending a concert in Wembley Arena, about fifteen miles away, in memory of Freddie Mercury, the one-time lead singer of the rock band Queen. Those taking part in the concert—which is also being seen on television by upwards of one billion people in 100 countries around the world—said they were organizing the event to "celebrate" Freddie Mercury's life. But Mercury died in November 1991 when he was just forty-five years old—not by accident, but of AIDS, the direct result of the persistently immoral lifestyle of which he boasted.

Yet there are times when the principle seems to fail in practice. Where is God's justice when people are killed in natural disasters such as earthquakes, drought, floods, or tornadoes? Where is it when civilians are maimed or massacred in war, or when people are making fortunes by rampant dishonesty, or children deprived of a stable home life because of their parents divorce, or others thrown on to the streets and forced to live rough and fend for themselves? It is about 3,000 years since one of the Old Testament writers complained about "righteous men who get what the wicked deserve, and wicked men who get what the righteous deserve" and found it "meaningless" (Ecclesiastes 8:14)—and many today would agree. Some have rejected the whole idea of God being in control, and say that "Even those who challenge God escape" (Malachi 3:15). Even many of those who believe that God is in control have been driven by circumstances to ask Him anguished questions: "How long will my enemy triumph over me?" (Psalm 13:3). "O Lord, how long will you look on?" (Psalm 35:17). "How long, O Lord? Will you hide yourself forever?" (Psalm 89:46). "Why does the way of the wicked prosper?" (Jeremiah 12:1). "Why do you make me look at injustice? Why do you tolerate wrong?" (Habakkuk 1:3).

The Bible has a threefold response to these and similar questions. Firstly, God tells us that His ways are beyond our understanding: "As the heavens are higher than the earth, so are my ways higher than your ways and my thoughts than your thoughts" (Isaiah 55:9). Secondly, as we are His creatures and He is our Creator, we have no right to argue with either His actions or His intentions: "But who are you, O man, to talk back to God?" (Romans 9:20). Thirdly, while God's judgments here on earth are often hidden, or partial, or delayed, the day is coming when He will call the whole of human history to account:

"The Lord reigns for ever;
he has established his throne for judgment.
He will judge the world in righteousness;
he will govern the peoples with justice"
(Psalm 9:7-8).

Things are not out of control. History is not swirling around in chaos. As surely as the world is a moral creation, it will come to a moral conclusion. The judgments of God fall often enough in this world to let us know that God judges, but seldom enough to let us know that there must be a judgment to come. God is not always a God of immediate justice, but He is a God of ultimate justice. Nothing less than the character of God is at stake here. Theologian Leon Morris says, "It is unthinkable that the present conflict between good and evil will not be disposed of authoritatively, decisively, finally"[5]— and the reason why it is unthinkable is because God is God and has committed Himself to seeing that it will be done.

Nor is He in a hurry. In the seventeenth century, the British preacher Thomas Watson wrote, "As long as there is eternity, God has time enough to reckon with his enemies."[6] And reckon with them He certainly will. Judgment Day is coming for the whole of humanity, and that stark, simple fact ought to get our attention and concentrate our minds. An anonymous seventeenth-century hymn writer put its reality and relevance like this:

Great God, what do I see and hear!
The end of things created:
The Judge of mankind doth appear
On clouds of glory seated;
The trumpet sounds, the graves restore
The dead which they contained before:
Prepare, my soul, to meet him!

The certainty of universal and personal judgment immediately raises at least seven very important questions, which every thinking person will want to ask: When will it be? Who will be the judge? What is its purpose? Who will be judged? On what basis? What will be taken into account? What will be the verdict? The remainder of this chapter will unearth the Bible's answers.

THE UNKNOWN CERTAINTY

Nothing is more plainly taught in Scripture than that there will be a final and universal judgment. Two-thirds of the parables Jesus told were related to the subject. It is so basic a truth that one New Testament writer lists "the resurrection of the dead" and "eternal judgment" as being among the Bible's "elementary teachings" (Hebrews 6:1). Elsewhere, Paul says, "[God] has set a day when he will judge the world" (Acts 17:31). The word "set" comes from a verb meaning "to single out." The final judgment is not an option that God is considering. With all of time at His disposal He has singled out "a day" when humanity's account will be settled once and for all. What is unknown to us is a certainty to God, and nothing will change His determination to meet His own schedule.

The Bible gives us two clues as to when it will be: it will come after Jesus returns to the earth and after the great resurrection of all who have died before then. Jesus supplies the first clue by saying that the Day of Judgment will be "when the Son of Man comes in his glory, and all the angels with him" (Matthew 25:31). The second clue comes in a remarkable Old Testament prophecy we noted in the last chapter. "Multitudes who sleep in the dust of the earth will awake: some to everlasting life, others to shame and everlasting contempt" (Daniel 12:2). These two pieces of evidence give us a picture in which the return of Christ to the earth, the resurrection of the dead and the final judgment take place in that order, yet there seems to be a sense in which all three events take place at the same time. It is impossible (and unnecessary) for us to be dogmatic about the details in the timetable, but what is perfectly clear is that man's final judgment does not take place at the moment of death, nor during the intermediate state (in Hades or paradise). It is only after these that men are brought, body and soul, to give their final account. This is what makes the whole subject not only important but urgent. Our earthly lives will be brought to an end by death or by the Second Coming of Christ—and as either one could take place at any time, we live every moment on the very brink of what Jude calls "the great Day" (Jude 6).

THE MAN IN CHARGE

The simple and straightforward answer to our second question, "Who will be the judge?", is that "Judgment belongs to God" (Deuteronomy 1:17). J. I. Packer rightly points out that "As our Maker, he owns us, and as our Owner, he has a right to dispose of us."[7] The fact that God is the supreme Judge can be found throughout the Bible. He is "the Judge of all the earth" (Genesis 18:25). "The Lord is a God of justice" (Isaiah 30:18). "It is God who judges" (Psalm 75:7). However, the New Testament adds that the final judgment will be carried out by God the Son, the Lord Jesus Christ. Jesus Himself said, "The Father judges no one, but has entrusted all judgment to the Son" (John 5:22). Linking this with his Second Coming, He told His disciples. "The Son of Man is going to come in his Father's glory with his angels, and then he will reward each person according to what he has done" (Matthew 16:27-28).

This teaching became an essential part of the apostles' message. As Peter once said, "He commanded us to preach to the people and to testify that he is the one whom God appointed as judge of the living and the dead" (Acts 10:42). Paul declared that "[God] will judge the world with justice by the man he has appointed. He has given proof of this to all men by raising him from the dead" (Acts 17:31); he also wrote that "We must all appear before the judgment seat of Christ" (2 Corinthians 5:10). Mankind will be judged not by an invisible, unfeeling spirit, but by *the man* to whom God the Father has given absolute authority. The one who will act for the Godhead in pronouncing judgment on humanity knows what it is to be human. From personal experience He knows all about facing the pressures of living in sinful human society. He was not insulated from those pressures, but was "tempted in every way, just as we are—yet was without sin" (Hebrews 4:15). The man who came to be the world's Savior will be its judge: He alone has all the necessary qualifications.

THE UNVEILING OF GOD

What is the purpose of the final judgment? The instinctive answer to that question goes something like this: to reward good, punish evil, and ensure that everyone gets what they deserve. But this sees the final judgment as being primarily concerned with man's welfare, with God as a celestial loss-adjuster, or a magistrate in a claims court. This shows how self-centered people have become, even to the point of thinking that God exists merely to service their needs, make sure they get their rights and tidy up all the loose ends at the end of their earthly lives. That is not the case. God, not man, is at the center of the universe, and we shall never have a clear view of anything until we acknowledge that fact. What, then, is the primary purpose of the Day of Judgment? It is to display to the entire universe the glory of God's character.

It will display *His authority*. At the dedication of the temple in Jerusalem, David used these words at the beginning of his prayer:

"Praise be to you, O Lord,
God of our father Israel,
from everlasting to everlasting.
Yours, O Lord, is the greatness and the power
and the glory and the majesty and the splendor,
for everything in heaven and earth is yours.
Yours, O Lord, is the kingdom;
you are exalted as head over all"
(1 Chronicles 29:10-11).

On the Day of Judgment God's majestic authority as the one who is "head over all" will be revealed in such an awesome way that the whole universe will recognize it. Even those who denied God's existence or doubted His power will be forced to acknowledge them. As God told one of His Old Testament prophets,

"Before me every knee will bow;
by me every tongue will swear.
They will say of me, 'In the Lord alone
are righteousness and strength'"
(Isaiah 45:23-24).

It will display *His holiness*. A modern theologian has rightly said, "In a world created by a sovereign and holy God, there must be a judgment, or else the very fabric of the spiritual universe is torn to shreds."[8] The Day of Judgment will be a dazzling demonstration that God is not only sovereign but holy. The Bible says that "The Lord our God is holy" (Psalm 99:9) and that "God is light, in him there is no darkness at all" (1 John 1:5). These statements tell us not only that God is morally perfect, but that His perfection separates Him from everything else in the universe. In Alec Motyer's words, "Holiness expresses all that makes God distinct."[9] On the Day of Judgment all creation will see the truth of this as never before.

It will display *His justice*. Psalm 51 is one of the most moving passages in Scripture. King David had committed adultery with Bathsheba and then arranged for her husband, one of his best army officers, to be killed in battle. Some time later, crushed by the realization of what he had done, he confessed his sin to God:

"Against you, you only, have I sinned
and done what is evil in your sight,
so that you are proved right when you speak
and justified when you judge"
(Psalm 51:4).

David's sins were so blatant that condemning them was straightforward, but there is a principle here that goes far beyond open and shut cases. God is *always* justified (the word here means "pure") when He judges. His own character guarantees that. Every decision He makes is right, just, and perfect, and on the Day of Judgment "His righteous judgment will be revealed" (Romans 2:5).

Because "The Lord is righteous in all his ways" (Psalm 145:17) He has never dealt unjustly with a single person in all of human history, and because He "does not change like shifting shadows" (James 1:17) His impeccable justice will be revealed in all its glory on the final Day of Judgment. Millions of people (some, ironically, who had previously said they were atheists) have complained at God's dealings with them, but not a single complaint has ever been valid. The same will be true on the Day of Judgment.

It will display *His anger*. Earlier in this chapter we saw that God has been expressing His anger throughout human history, though His judgments are often hidden or partial. That will all change on what one of the Old Testament prophets calls "the great and dreadful day of the Lord" (Joel 2:31). Elsewhere, the Bible calls it "the day of God's wrath" (Romans 2:5), the day when His righteous anger will be seen in all its terrifying fury. One writer has illustrated the point by saying that expressions of God's anger in the lives of people here on earth are like light or moderate showers which "will one day become a cloudburst falling on all unbelievers."[10] That is hardly overstating the case. In one of the most telling statements in Scripture, an Old Testament writer warns us:

"That day will be a day of wrath,
a day of distress and anguish,
a day of trouble and ruin,
a day of darkness and gloom,
a day of clouds and blackness"
(Zephaniah 1:15).

To some people, the idea that God could be angry seems like a contradiction in terms. Their view of God is so distorted that if they think of Him at all they think only in terms of His love, His mercy, His kindness, or His forgiveness. But this kind of thinking leads to a caricature of God rather than an accurate picture, because as the modern writer A. W. Pink has pointed out, "There are more references in Scripture to the anger, fury and wrath of God than there are to his love and tenderness."[11] It is impossible to make any sense of Scripture without accepting God's holy opposition to all sin. As one writer puts it, "God's wrath is a central piece in the biblical jigsaw puzzle; if we have made the other pieces fit without it, doesn't it suggest we have forced them into a pattern God never intended?"[12]

The Bible's teaching could not be clearer: it says that all the members of the human race are "by nature objects of [God's] wrath" (Ephesians 2:3). That can hardly be an irrelevant statement when we are all hurtling toward the final judgment! The contemporary American theologian R. C. Sproul says that if people would think soberly for five seconds, they would realize their error in imagining that God is not a God of holy anger: "If God is holy at all, if God has an ounce of justice in his character, indeed if God exists as God, how could he possibly be anything else but angry with us? We violate his holiness, we insult his justice, we make light of his grace. These things can hardly be pleasing to him . . . But a God of love who has no wrath is no God. He is an idol of our own making, as much as if we carved him out of stone."[13] On the final Day of Judgment God's blazing, glorious anger will be seen in all its terror and power.

It will display *His love*. In the light of what we have just seen about God's anger, this seems to raise an obvious problem, but if we find it impossible to imagine how a God of such terrifying anger can also be a God of amazing love, it is because God is utterly beyond the reach of our finite understanding. The Bible has no such problem, and tells us to consider both "the kindness and severity of God" (Romans 11:22, NASB).

One of the Bible's titles for Jesus is "the Lamb of God" (John

1:29)—a reference to His gentleness and meekness when He was sacrificed for the sins of others—but in His picture of the Day of Judgment, John tells of those who will be terrified at "the wrath of the Lamb" (Revelation 6:16). The same Scriptures that speak so often of God's anger also say that "God is love" (1 John 4:8) and that "God demonstrates his own love for us in this: While we were still sinners, Christ died for us" (Romans 5:8).

The voluntary death of the Son of God in the place of sinners is the most amazing act of love in history, and the one who sits in judgment on humanity will be the one who died on the cross of Calvary. Those who rejected His love will recognize Him with horror. Those who accepted it will recognize Him with joy. Everyone in the human race will be filled with awe as they come face to face with God's stupendous love.

PRESIDENTS AND PEASANTS

Our fourth question is "Who will be judged?" The first part of the answer is often overlooked: the Bible tells us that there will be a judgment of *fallen angels*. As we saw in a note to chapter 3, "God did not spare angels when they sinned, but sent them to hell, putting them into gloomy dungeons to be held for judgment" (2 Peter 2:4). This is underlined elsewhere: "The angels who did not keep their positions of authority but abandoned their own home— these [God] has kept in darkness, bound with everlasting chains for judgment on the great Day' (Jude 6). We are not told who these angels were, nor of the nature of their sin, but they are a solemn warning to us that no created being is so great as to be beyond the reach of God's justice.

Secondly, *all of humanity* will stand before God on the Day of Judgment. The Bible confirms this in a number of ways. In a global sense, the Bible calls God "the Judge of all the earth" (Genesis 18:25) and says that He will judge "all the nations on every side" (Joel 3:12). Jesus said that when He sits on the throne of judgment, "All the nations will be gathered before him" (Matthew 25:31). Paul taught that Christ "will judge the world" (Acts 17:31) and that those judged would include "the living and the dead" (2 Timothy 4:1). Then the Bible specifically says that God's people will be judged. God told Moses, "The Lord will judge his people" (Deuteronomy 32:36), and in writing to Christians at Corinth, Paul said, "For we must all appear before the judgment seat of Christ" (2 Corinthians 5:10). Notice how much is packed into these words. "We" means that Paul includes himself, even though he occupied one of the highest positions in the church at that time. He then goes on to say that "we *must* all appear . . ." God has issued a summons, not an invitation, and we have no option but to be present. Paul reinforces this by saying, "we must *all* appear . . ." There are no exceptions; even the most godly and faithful of believers must answer the summons. As David Watson put it, "When it comes to a man's rights before God, the only thing we can say is that we have the right to be judged."[14]

Finally, the Bible makes it clear that *the summons to judgment is personal and individual*. Not only will we "all stand before God's judgment seat," but "Each of us will give an account of himself to God" (Romans 14:10, 12). Humanity will not be judged as nations, cultures, or ethnic groups, or in categories of any kind. Instead, everyone who has ever lived will be judged as an individual person. One of our national newspapers used to tell its readers, "All the world is here." That was journalistic license, but on the Day of Judgment that statement will literally be true. All the world *will* be there; kings and commoners, presidents and peasants, nobility and "nobodies," great and small; those from every religion and those with no religion; those who loved God and those who loathed Him; those who died in infancy and those who lived for a century; everyone from Adam to a baby drawing its first breath as Jesus returns to earth: and every single one will stand alone before the God "to whom we must give account" (Hebrews 4:13).

The point was powerfully made by the nineteenth-century American theologian J. L. Dagg: "Every one will be brought to judgment as if he were the only creature present, and every one will give account of himself, and receive sentence for himself, with as much discrimination and perfection of justice as if the judge were wholly absorbed in the consideration of his single cause."[15]

Anyone who does not find this sobering is not being serious. The fact that we have an inescapable appointment with our Maker means that trying to avoid Him is both foolish and futile. Trying to run away from God is as ridiculous as trying to run away from death, because every moment spent doing so brings us closer to the moment we are trying to avoid. The Bible spells out the only sensible response: "Prepare to meet your God" (Amos 4:12).

REVELATION AND RESPONSE

Before answering the next question—"On what basis will we be judged?"—we need to understand that when we appear before God on the Day of Judgment we shall not be on trial. In a trial, the judge has to hear the evidence (or a plea of guilty) before he can decide on a verdict, let alone on any sentence; but God is not in that position. The Day of Judgment will not enable God to discover anything, but to declare what he already knows and announce the verdicts and sentences He has already determined. No evidence will be offered, because none will be needed. There will be no witnesses, no plea bargaining, no jury, and no exhibits. Nor will anybody be found guilty or not guilty. All of this is obvious from the language the Bible uses. It says that "[God's] righteous judgment will be revealed" (Romans 2:5), in other words, that there will be a public unveiling of His decisions. An earthly trial is a process of investigation; the last judgment is a moment of declaration by a Judge who has perfect knowledge of the character and history of everyone who stands before Him.

When Job was concerned about injustice and oppression that was going unpunished, and wondered why God did not intervene and "set times for judgment" (Job 24:1), his friend Elihu told him, "God has no need to examine men further, that they should come before him for judgment" (Job 34:23); the same principle will hold good at the last judgment. In the course of a trial, virtually all evidence is given as a result of questions being asked, but it is very significant that in everything the Bible tells us about the final judgment, there is no record of God asking even one question. Elihu gives us the simple reason for this:

> "His eyes are on the ways of men;
> he sees their every step.
> There is no dark place, no deep shadow
> where evildoers can hide"
> (Job 34:21).

The evidence for God's omniscience runs throughout Scripture, and is summed up by John when he says that "God is greater than our hearts, and he knows everything" (1 John 3:20).

With that in mind, we can turn to the question of the basis on which we shall be judged. The Bible teaches that this will be related to the revealed will of God and makes provision for the fact that this has not been the same for everyone. God will not condemn anyone for failing to respond to light they have not received. Some have received the full light of the Christian gospel—what the Bible calls "the light of the knowledge of the glory of God in the face of Christ" (2 Corinthians 4:6)—and will be judged accordingly. Jesus made this very clear: "For God did not send his Son into the world to condemn the world, but to save the world through him. Whoever believes in him is not condemned, but whoever does not believe stands condemned already because he has not believed in the name of God's one and only Son" (John 3:17-18). Paul emphasized this by saying bluntly, "If we disown him, he will also disown us" (2 Timothy 2:12). Those who have heard the gospel, yet refuse to respond to God's love by putting their trust in Christ, have to reckon with the fact that the day is coming when the one they have rejected will finally and fatally reject them.

Others have received only the dimmer light of Old Testament teaching, and the Bible says that "All who sin under the law will be judged by the law" (Romans 2:12). Jesus once summarized Old Testament teaching in two sentences: "Love the Lord your God with all you heart and with all you soul and with all you mind and with all your strength," and "Love your neighbor as yourself" (Mark 12:30-31). If these commandments are the only light certain people have received, God will judge them on that basis, but as the Bible says that "Whoever keeps the whole law and yet stumbles at just one point is guilty of breaking all of it" (James 2:10) this is hardly a soft option.

THE UNEVANGELIZED

But what about those who have heard neither the New Testament gospel nor the Old Testament law? This raises a very important issue which, although not central to the subject of this book, is currently receiving a lot of attention, pinpointed in a recent book by Peter Cotterell, Principal of London Bible College.[16] In it, he expresses his concern that to insist that people must hear the Christian gospel before they can get right with God "must necessarily condemn [all these] myriads to an eternal separation from God." Against this background, and using the shanty-dwellers of Bombay and Calcutta as examples of those who "are unlikely to be able to see God in the utter meaninglessness of their existence," he comes to the conclusion that it must be possible for such people to get right with God without ever hearing what the Bible has to say.

His argument is based in part on the premise that "To any reasonable person it would appear to be unjust to condemn people to an eternal hell for failing to avail themselves of a medicine of which they have never heard, and moreover, of which they could not have heard." Another writer who takes this line argues that God will not abandon "those who have not known and therefore have not declined his offer of grace."[17]

Peter Cotterell makes his case warmly and in an admirable spirit, but in the end he moves outside the boundaries of Scripture and into the realm of speculation. On such an important issue, we must make doubly sure that our touchstone is not what will fit neatly into the thinking of "any reasonable person," but what God has revealed in his Word. We dare not fall into the trap of weaving our theology into a pattern determined by what is emotionally acceptable and intellectually reasonable—yet this is what Peter Cotterell seems to have done.

For example, one of his ten theses suggests that the Bible "has nothing at all to say about the position of those who, for whatever reason, are not aware of God's self-revelation in creation, and are never brought to the point of hearing the proclamation of the Good News." Yet the Bible does have something to say about them: "The wrath of God is being revealed from heaven against all the godlessness and wickedness of men who suppress the truth by their wickedness, since what may be known about God is plain to them, because God has made it plain to them. For since the creation of the world God's invisible qualities—his eternal power and divine nature—have been clearly seen, being understood from what has been made, so that men are without excuse" (Romans 1:18-20). When Paul wrote those words, he made no concession to those living in pitiless slavery; he has no "bias to the poor," such as some modern theologians like to preach. Instead, his statement takes in all of humanity, and it still applies today. Nobody can plead ignorance of God's existence, because we are all surrounded by evidence that He exists. As one contemporary writer puts it, "It can be clearly seen that there is an Unseen."[18]

Then can people be saved on the basis of what God has revealed in nature? Peter Cotterell maintains that they can and suggests that some may even seek Him and find Him without this revelation, let alone any knowledge of Christ, but again he is wandering into wishful thinking. Sinners are promised salvation if they truly seek God but, as Paul makes clear, this is exactly what they fail to do: "There is no one righteous, not even one; there is no one who understands, no one who seeks God . . . There is no fear of God before their eyes . . . for all have sinned and fall short of the glory of God" (Romans 3:10-11, 18, 23). Later, after promising that "Everyone who calls on the name of the Lord will be saved," he adds these very significant words: "How, then, can they call on the one they have not believed in? And how can they believe in the one of whom they have not heard?" (Romans 10:13-14). This seems a long way from the idea that people can be saved without hearing about Christ!

Peter Cotterell's arguments also run aground on the fact that the sinner's problem is deeper than the question of his response, or lack of response, to what he sees around him; it goes back to his own creation. Man is made in the image of God, with an instinct which tells him that he is answerable to his Maker. A contemporary British preacher has made the point well: "All men have an inner sense that they ought to love God. Men are 'naturally' religious. All men have an inner sense of duty toward their fellow humans. They have a concept of 'natural' justice, 'natural' affection . . . . Even cannibals usually refuse to eat close relatives and friends! There is an inner duty to God and man that is very hard to erase. We are not naturally irreligious and amoral."[19]

The Bible says that even those with no written law to guide them have "the requirements of the law written on their hears, their consciences also bearing witness" (Romans 2:15). The theologian Cornelius Van Til calls this "the point of contact."[20] This moral consciousness was damaged when man fell into sin, but it was not destroyed. The pagan who has never heard of God's law (or even of God) still has some sense of law. He has some conception of the difference between right and wrong; he approves of honesty; he responds to love and kindness; he resents it if someone steals his goods or tries to injure him. In other words, he has a conscience which passes judgment on his behavior and the behavior of others, something the Bible calls a law written on his heart.

To quote Van Til again, "The most depraved of men cannot wholly escape the voice of God."[21] But man does not always obey that law. He violates it again and again, and anyone who *knows* more than he *does* is guilty in the sight of God and rightly liable to condemnation. Many an offender has been told by a magistrate or judge that "Ignorance of the law is no excuse"; exactly the same applies in the matter of human sin and God's right to execute judgment.

As one contemporary writer says, "There is sufficient knowledge for each person after all to be criminally liable for sin . . . they have suppressed the truth they have both received and understood."[22] We shall all be judged according to the light we have received, and it will be useless for us to claim that we needed more light, because we have all abused the light God has given us. Every one of us has received the law of God in one form or another, and every one of us has broken it in one way or another. That is the problem facing us as we move toward the Day of Judgment. The Swiss theologian Rene Pache has expressed it very well: "God does not allow any of his creatures to be eternally lost without, in his own way, seeking to win them. Thus when the time comes to leave the world, every man has had enough light to have accepted or rejected God, so that he is fully responsible to him."[23]

CHILDREN AND OTHERS

This admittedly leaves some gray areas. What about the baby who dies before it can have any grasp of right or wrong, or someone who is a congenital imbecile or who for some other reason has never been capable of understanding anything? As far as infants are concerned, one Old Testament incident may give a glimmer of light. When his baby boy was taken ill, King David was distraught, weeping, refusing to eat, and lying on the floor all night; yet when the child died he quickly recovered his composure. When his servants asked him to explain this, the king answered, "While the child was still alive, I fasted and wept. I thought, 'Who knows? The Lord may be gracious to me and let the child live.' But now that he is dead, why should I fast? Can I bring him back again? I will go to him, but he will not return to me" (2 Samuel 12:22-23). The phrase "I will go to him" may mean no more than "I will join him in the grave," or "I will join him in the place of departed spirits," but there may be a hint of something more, an assurance that the child was now safely in God's blissful presence and that he, as a believer, would eventually join him there.

The *Westminster Confession of Faith* has this to say on the subject: "Elect infants dying in infancy are regenerated and saved . . . . So also are all other elect persons who are incapable of being outwardly called by the ministry of the Word." Wisely, the Confession goes no further. Those saved in these situations may be very few or very many;

what it makes clear is that all who are saved are saved by God's gracious choice. Salvation is entirely by grace, and God is free to grant it to all or some, few, many, or none, and whatever He chooses to do is certain to be "in conformity with the purpose of his will" (Ephesians 1:11). One writer makes these careful comments on the Confession's statement: "If infants dying in infancy are human, they are also such as sinned in Adam, and they are therefore guilty and liable to damnation. If they are to be saved it can never be 'because it would be unjust for God to condemn them', but only because he has elected them to eternal life which they do not deserve."[24]

As far as other cases are concerned we must tread even more carefully. No sensible person will deny that there are areas in connection with the fate of the unevangelized about which we must settle for reverent, silent agnosticism; there are details which God in His wisdom has chosen not to reveal to us at this stage. What we dare not do is make unwarranted assumptions based on supposition rather than Scripture. Then how should we feel about the issue? An evangelist tells of visiting Francis and Edith Schaeffer in L'Abri, Switzerland. After dinner one night, the conversation ranged over a number of profound theological issues. Suddenly, somebody asked Dr. Schaeffer, "What will happen to those who have never heard of Christ?" Everyone around the dinner table waited for the great theologian to deliver a weighty, intellectual answer. None came; instead, he bowed his head and wept.

One final comment needs to be made on this complex question, and that is that, for all the gray areas, we are not left floundering in the dark about the whole issue, because the Bible does lay down one bedrock principle that covers not only these cases but any others that could be imagined—and that is that "[God] will judge the world in righteousness" (Psalm 9:8); "God's judgment . . . is based on truth" (Romans 2:2). The glory of God's character will ensure the perfection of his judgment. It is impossible to invent any permutation of problems that will baffle God's wisdom, righteousness, justice, and love. Abraham once asked God, "Will not the Judge of all the earth do right?" (Genesis 18:25). There is only one answer to that question— and it is the answer to all others.

THE BOOKS

If there were gray areas in answering that question, there are none in answering the next one: "What will be taken into account?" The

Bible's teaching on this is as clear as daylight, and is summarized in this dramatic Old Testament prophecy of the Day of Judgment:

"As I looked,
thrones were set in place,
and the Ancient of Days took his seat.
His clothing was as white as snow;
and the hair of his head was white like wool.
His throne was flaming with fire,
and its wheels were all ablaze.
A river of fire was flowing,
coming out from before him.
Thousands upon thousands attended him;
ten thousand times ten thousand stood before him.
The court was seated,
and the books were opened"
(Daniel 7:9-10).

About seven hundred years later God revealed the same picture to John: "Then I saw a great white throne and him who was seated on it. Earth and sky fled from his presence, and there was no place for them. And I saw the dead, great and small, standing before the throne, and books were opened" (Revelation 20:11-12).

These "books" are God's complete and infallible knowledge of every detail of our lives. They confirm that "Nothing in all creation is hidden from God's sight" and that "Everything is uncovered and laid bare before the eyes of him to whom we must give account" (Hebrews 4:13). The opening of these books is the ultimate moment of truth, when every detail of our lives will be brought out into the open and be seen to have determined our destiny. But the Bible not only states this in general terms, it goes into specifics.

Our words will be taken into account. Jesus could not have been clearer about this: "But I tell you that men will have to give account on the day of judgment for every careless word they have spoken. For by your words you will be acquitted, and by your words you will be condemned" (Matthew 12:36-37). If even our careless words are carefully recorded, how can we bear the thought that our calculated ones—including the downright lies, the clever half-truths, the boastful claims, the cutting criticisms, the off-color jokes, and the unkind comments—will also be taken into account? Even our whispered asides and words spoken in confidence or when we thought we were "safe" will be heard again. As Jesus put it, "What you have said in the dark will be heard in the daylight, and what you have whispered in the ear in the inner rooms will be proclaimed from the roofs" (Luke 12:3).

I was once in a BBC studio for a live television interview. Months later, the friend who had arranged the interview embarrassed me by reciting several things I had said in the studio before and after the broadcast. Unknown to me, every word I had spoken in that studio had been tape-recorded elsewhere in the building. My friend had got hold of a copy of the tape, and then had great fun in replaying it at my expense. It is no laughing matter to realize that God's tape recorder is running all the time, and that one day we shall be condemned by every wrong word we have ever spoken.

Our deeds will be taken into account. In one sense "deeds" cover every activity in our lives, but singling them out in this way helps us to make an important point. If we think of God's knowledge of our words in terms of a tape recorder, we can think of His knowledge of our deeds in terms of a video camera, running twenty-four hours a day and never missing a single moment from the day of our birth to the day of our death. The relevance of our deeds is so clearly taught in the Old Testament that even the smallest of its thirty-nine books summarizes it in one sentence:

"The day of the Lord is near
for all nations.
As you have done, it will be done to you;
your deeds will return upon your own head"
(Obadiah 15).

As usual, Jesus confirmed and clarified what the Old Testament said: "For the Son of Man is going to come in the Father's glory with his angels, and then he will reward each person according to what he has done" (Matthew 16:27). But it is something Paul wrote which highlights the important point I want to make: "For we must all appear before the judgment seat of Christ, that each one may receive what is due to him for the things done while in the body, whether good or bad" (2 Corinthians 5:10).

Even trying to summarize God's "videotape" here would be pointless, because it contains everything we have ever done. The crucial thing to notice is that these deeds are done "in the body," and as they can be performed in the body only when it is energized by the spirit (in other words, when we are alive) Paul's statement confirms that our destinies are settled at death. There is to be no second chance, no opportunity to rectify mistakes, make amends for our failures, or overcome sinful tendencies. Someone has illustrated it like this: "With physical death, human destiny is fixed irrevocably. No person can any longer influence that destiny any more than the runner who has finished the mile race can continue the race when the mile is completed . . . When the soul leaves the body it has already taken all the decisions it could have taken."[25]

This means that nothing changes after death, when body and spirit are separated. The moment of death is a kind of provisional judgment, yet our external destiny is already sealed and settled. The final judgment does not reopen the case to see whether we have made any better use of a second chance during the intermediate state. There is no second chance; God's final judgment takes into account all our deeds, and they will all have been done "in the body."

Our thoughts will be taken into account. God's knowledge of us goes far beyond our words and deeds. The Bible says that "The Lord knows the thoughts of man" (Psalm 94:11). God knows not only what we are saying and doing, but what we are thinking. His judgment extends as far as His knowledge; the Bible specifically says that "God will judge men's secrets through Jesus Christ" (Romans 2:16). We are told that "He will . . . expose the motives of men's hearts" (1 Corinthians 4:5). This may be the most penetrating statement we have seen so far in this section of our study. How much time we spend covering up what we really think! We live in what someone has called "a world of deceptions."[26] Things are seldom what they seem, because most of what goes on is written in the invisible ink of our thoughts, which indelibly records all the ducking and weaving, all the wriggling and rationalizing. It is our thoughts that also produce what in international trading terms would be called our "invisible exports," things like jealousy, envy, greed, self-seeking, pride, hatred, impurity, and covetousness. These are not crimes, and we can hide them from most people most of the time. But the day is coming when even our deepest and darkest thoughts will be blazoned across the heavens.

The good we fail to do will be taken into account. People who cling to the hope that their lives are good enough to see them safely through the Day of Judgment have never realized that God requires us to keep His law in every part. We brushed against this earlier when we read that "Whoever keeps the whole law and yet stumbles at just

one point is guilty of breaking all of it" (James 2:10). A little later the
same writer adds this: "Anyone, then, who knows the good he ought
to do and doesn't do it, sins" (James 4:17). As with the question of
"deeds," it is pointless trying to list our sins of omission, because the
list is virtually endless, and in any case one or two questions should
be enough to let us know where we stand. Have we always done
everything we knew to be right? Have we always fulfilled our responsibilities as members of our families? Have we always given as much
help as we should to those in need? Have we always been as generous, as helpful, as kind, as gracious as was humanly possible?

Even the person whose conscience is so deadened and ego so
inflated that he claims to pass these tests has to face the fact that there
is one sin of omission which guarantees a person's condemnation and
that is the sin of not trusting the Lord Jesus Christ as Savior. Having
said that God did not send His Son to condemn the world but to save
it, Jesus added, "Whoever believes in him is not condemned, but whoever does not believe stands condemned already because he has not
believed in the name of God's one and only Son" (John 3:18). We
came across this statement earlier, but the last part is particularly relevant here, because the damning indictment is not anything the person has done but something he has not done. No virtue of any kind,
no amount of respectability or religion can take the place of personal
commitment to Christ. Failure to make that commitment is fatal.

Our characters will be taken into account. Writing from a different perspective, the American psychologist William James once said,
"Sow a thought, reap an action; sow an action, reap a habit; sow a
habit, reap a character; sow a character, reap a destiny."[27] The Bible
puts it more bluntly: "Do not be deceived: God is not mocked. A man
reaps what he sows" (Galatians 6:7). Our character, our inner being,
will determine our destiny. When the Bible says that "We must all
appear before the judgment seat of Christ" (2 Corinthians 5:10) it
means more than putting in an appearance! The verb "to appear" is
taken partly from a word meaning "to cause to shine,"[28] and to
"appear" before the judgment seat of Christ means to have the very
core of our personalities brought out into the open, so that we are
revealed for what we truly are rather than for what we would like
people to think we are. We will be turned inside out. All the things we
had so carefully hidden from others will be revealed. More impor-
tantly, they will be seen to form the very fabric of our character, and
it is our character that will count. J.C. Ryle made the point with his

usual crispness and clarity: "Characters on earth will prove an ever-lasting possession in the world to come. With the same heart that men die, with that heart they will rise again."[29]

THE VERDICTS

This brings us to the last of our seven questions about the Day of Judgment: "What will be the verdict?" The first thing to say is that in every one of the billions of cases involved the Judge's pronouncement will be clear-cut; there will be no partial verdicts. Nobody's case will be adjourned or postponed for any reason, and as there will be no jury or bench there will be no majority verdicts. Instead, Christ the Judge will make a decisive announcement which will bring unspeakable joy to some and unspeakable anguish to others.

Jesus often spoke of this moment in the course of His ministry, but it may help if we concentrate on just one of the pictures He used: "When the Son of Man comes in his glory, and all the angels with him, he will sit on his throne in heavenly glory. All the nations will be gathered before him, and he will separate the people one from another as a shepherd separates the sheep from the goats. He will put the sheep on his right and the goats on his left. Then the King will say to those on his right, 'Come, you who are blessed by my Father; take your inheritance, the kingdom prepared for you since the creation of the world . . .'" (Matthew 25:31-34).

It will be helpful if we interrupt the illustration at that point so that we can determine the identity of the "sheep." Jesus said that these are the people who will go to heaven; they receive the great blessing of entering into the full inheritance of the kingdom of God. Yet it is important to notice that this is not because they deserve it. They receive the kingdom of God as an inheritance, and, by definition, an inheritance is not something one can earn. It is a gift, graciously bestowed by one person on another. The words Jesus used make this absolutely clear: He told the "sheep" that the kingdom of God was "prepared for you," not "earned by you." The next phrase reinforces the point by saying that their place in His kingdom was something that God the Father had set aside for them "since the creation of the world"—which rules out any possibility that they could have contributed to it.

The vital question still remains: who are the "sheep"? There is an important clue in the first word Jesus spoke to them: "Come . . ." He was not sending them to heaven, but taking them there, to continue the relationship they had already had with Him on earth. This is confirmed throughout the New Testament, but two references will be sufficient to make the point. The first is where we are told that "To all who received [Christ], to those who believed in his name, he gave the right to become children of God" (John 1:12). The second is where Paul tells fellow-Christians that as "God's children . . . we are heirs—heirs of God and co-heirs with Christ" (Romans 8:16-17). The link is clear: heaven is the eternal destiny of those who inherit it by being God's heirs; God's heirs are those who are His children; and His children are those who have trusted Christ as their Savior and acknowledged Him as their Lord.

This all confirms that the Day of Judgment is not ultimately an investigation but a declaration. There is no possibility that any of God's children will be condemned on that day and fail to receive their inheritance. None of their sins will count against them, but all will be seen to have been atoned for by the death of Christ on their behalf. They will not see their sins as threatening accusers; instead, they will rejoice in the assurance that they have been eternally saved by Christ, who bore the penalty for their sins in His death on their behalf.

What is more, it will be a day of vindication, when every sin committed against God's people will be seen to have been committed against God. The millions of Christians who have been slandered, ridiculed, despised, rejected, persecuted, tortured, or martyred in this world will be honored by God. Jesus promised this in the Sermon on the Mount: "Blessed are you when people insult you, persecute you and falsely say all kinds of evil against you because of me. Rejoice and be glad, because great is your reward in heaven, for in the same way they persecuted the prophets who were before you" (Matthew 5:11-12).

As far as their good deeds are concerned, we are told in other parts of Scripture that while these will contribute nothing to their salvation, they will be taken into account and graciously rewarded over and above the gift of eternal life. This will be part of their joy in heaven, a place so glorious as to be beyond our ability to imagine. The Bible does give us some glimpses of glory, and perhaps none is more wonderful than this summary of what it will mean to those who are there: "God himself will be with them and be their God. He will wipe every tear from their eyes. There will be no more death or mourning or crying or pain, for the old order of things has passed away" (Revelation

21:3-4). This description opens up some amazing concepts, but as this is not a book about heaven we dare not stop to develop them here.

So much for the "sheep"; what about the "goats"? In their case, the King's sentence will be equally clear and concise—but disastrously different: "Then he will say to those on his left, 'Depart from me, you who are cursed, into the eternal fire prepared for the devil and his angels'" (Matthew 25:41). The contrast between these words and those spoken to the righteous could not possibly be greater. Instead of being on the King's "right hand," the place of honor, they will be put "on his left," the place of shame; instead of an invitation to "Come . . . ," they will be given an instruction to "Depart . . ."; instead of being told they are "blessed," they will be told they are "cursed"; instead of being welcomed into a "kingdom," they will be sent into a "fire."

These contrasts are well summarized by the Scottish theologian John Murray, when he says, "The fact that Jesus will sit upon the throne of Judgment will be the consternation of his enemies and the consolation of his people."[30] Later in his illustration Jesus added that immediately after the verdicts have been announced the righteous "will go away . . . to eternal life" while the unrighteous will go away to "eternal punishment."

Suddenly, in one moment, the sentences are executed. There is no delay, no remand, no appeal. The King's decision will be final and irreversible. For the righteous, it is the moment when they join their Father in His eternal, heavenly home. For the rest, it is the moment when they join the devil and his angels in "the eternal fire."

The Bible calls it hell.

The Ultimate Horror

Virtually every major religion in the world teaches some form of punishment after death for sins committed here on earth.

One strand of Islamic doctrine says that each individual is questioned by two angels, Munkar and Nakir, before walking a bridge that stretches over hell. The faithful cross safely into paradise, while unbelievers fall into a place with seven grades of punishment, including being roasted, boiled, and afflicted with pus. Other Islamic teaching says they will be turned until their skins are destroyed, at which point they will be given new skins so that the process can be repeated.[1]

Buddhism mentions many hells to be endured on an unpleasant journey toward Nirvana, a kind of blissful non-existence. Classical Buddhist teaching has seven "hot hells," each surrounded by torture chambers which include fiery pits and quagmires, while other versions speak of "cold hells" in addition to less traumatic punishment for minor offenders. According to certain Chinese Buddhists, devils in human form inflict all kinds of gruesome torture, including pulling out slanderers' tongues with red-hot wires and pouring molten lead down liars' throats.[2]

In Taoism, the God of walls and moats sends the wicked to one of several hells, where they are punished for a fixed period of time.

Hinduism has twenty-one hells, tailor-made to match a person's behavior on earth: "If you failed to feed the hungry while you were living, you might be chained to a rock where birds come to eat your stomach."[3] An adulterer might be forced to embrace a beautiful woman whose temperature is white-hot, while the worst offenders face incarceration in a series of lower hells where they are scorched in hot sand, boiled in jars, or eaten by ravens. Jainism, a spin-off from Hinduism, has no fewer than 8,400,000 hells, as well as a bottomless abyss where the worst sinners are kept forever.

In an earlier chapter we saw that people have in innate sense of ultimate justice, a gut feeling that on the other side of the grave wrongs will be righted and good will eventually triumph over evil. The grotesque guesses we have just looked at are a long way from biblical truth, but they do point to the fact that human beings feel themselves to be eternally accountable for the way they live. This stubborn instinct is welded to religion's insistence that after death there is such a thing as punishment for sin. What does Christianity say on the subject?

FANTASY OR FACT?

"The little child is in this red-hot oven. Hear how it screams to come out. See how it turns and twists itself about in the fire. It beats its head against the roof of the oven and stamps its little feet upon the floor. God was very good to this little child. Very likely God saw that it would get worse and worse and never repent, so it would have been punished more severely. So God in his mercy called it out of the world in early childhood."[4] Those blood-curdling words come from a nineteenth-century tract written by a Roman Catholic priest (for Sunday school children!) to warn them of the reality and nature of hell. This kind of appeal was very popular at the time, though the priest's words are a model of moderation when compared with those of earlier writers.

In the *Apocalypse of Peter*, written just after New Testament times, the author described the wicked as "hanging by their tongues, while the flaming fire torments them from beneath," adulterous women suspended by their hair over bubbling mire, and murderers thrown into "a pit full of evil reptiles."

In the Middle Ages, there was a resurgence of interest in post-mortem punishment, and no let-up in the lurid language used to describe it. The Venerable Bebe (673-735), who became the Bishop of Hexham and is sometimes known as "the Father of English history," described a vision in which he saw a man suffering such torments in hell that "The flames of fire gushed out from his ears and eyes and nostrils and at every pore."[5] Others embellished this idea and spoke of these hideous effects being produced by demons blowing trumpets into the ears of those who had used music for evil purposes.

The most famous of all the visions of hell during this time was that of the Italian poet Dante Alighiere (1265-1321). In *La Davina Commedia (The Divine Comedy)* he pictured himself being lost in a dark forest when Virgil, the Roman poet who died in 19 B.C., offered to guide him to paradise through hell and purgatory. On the evening of Good Friday, they reached hell, a vast pit shaped like an inverted cone, with its lowest point at the center of the earth. Nine circles, each filled with thousands of people being tortured by monsters and devils, led down to its lowest point, a frozen lake where the devil personally administered the punishment. Here is part of Dante's vision, taken from his description of what he saw when he reached the seventh circle:

> *Enormous herds of naked souls I saw.*
> *Lamenting till their eyes were burned of tears;*
> *They seemed condemned by an unequal law,*
>
> *For some were stretched supine upon the ground,*
> *Some squatted with their arms about themselves,*
> *And others without pause roamed around and around.*
>
> *Most numerous were those that roamed the plain;*
> *Far fewer were the souls stretched on the sand,*
> *But moved to louder cries by greater pain.*
>
> *And all over that sand on which they lay*
> *Or crouched, or roamed, great flakes of flame fell slowly*
> *As snow falls in the Alps on a windless day.*[6]

Elsewhere in the poem he tells of "infinite wailings" and of souls being battered by an "infernal hurricane" and describes hell's victims as shrieking and moaning, and tearing each other piecemeal with their teeth. Not surprisingly, the most famous words Dante ever wrote were those he pictured over the gate of hell: "Abandon all hope ye who enter here."[7]

One of Dante's contemporaries, the English mystic Richard Rolle de Hampole, wrote an essay entitled *Stimulus Conscientiae*, in which 1,000 lines were taken up with a gruesome description of the torments of hell. Three hundred years later the English poet John Milton

(1608-1674) wrote *Paradise Lost,* in which he described God hurling Satan and his angels into hell "with hideous ruin and combustion, down to bottomless perdition" where they "lay vanquished, rolling in the fiery gulf, confounded, though immortal."[8]

Speaking on BBC Radio in 1992, a leading humanist dismissed the idea of fiery punishment in hell by saying, "I have no fear of being confined to an eternal shish kebab."[9] Is that the right response? What are we to make of the vivid descriptions of monsters and reptiles, boiling mud, red-hot ovens, people hanging by their hair, and others with blood gushing out of every pore? Are these things fantasy or fact? Are we meant to laugh or cry? Should we mock these statements, or take them seriously?

The straightforward answer is that we can safely set aside every one of these grisly images because none of them accurately reflects the teaching of Scripture. This is true not only of the teachings of the non-Christian religions, but in specific terms the same applies to the writings of Dante, Milton, and others. They had Scripture in mind when they wrote, but they did not pretend to be making exact theological statements. They had an idea and allowed themselves poetic license in developing it. In other words, they let their imagination run riot. But human imagination is no substitute for divine revelation, which is our only reliable source of information on the subject. Only God can tell us the truth about the punishment of the wicked after death.

THE PARAMOUNT PRINCIPLE

The modern theologian Reinhold Neibuhr has written, "It is unwise for Christians to claim any knowledge of either the furniture of heaven or of the temperature of hell."[10] Technically speaking, he is correct, yet though the Bible is very restrained when speaking of life after death, it says enough to enable us to come to some settled convictions and, if we are sensible, take radical and urgent action.

For instance, the Bible tells us a number of specific things about heaven. It is "not a part of this creation" (Hebrews 9:11); it is "a high and holy place" (Isaiah 57:15), which shines "with the glory of God" (Revelation 21:11). It is called "a better country" (Hebrews 11:16); it is God's eternal dwelling place: "The Lord is in his holy temple; the Lord is on his heavenly throne" (Psalm 11:4). Those who go there will be "richly rewarded" (Hebrews 10:35), receive a "crown of righteousness" (2 Timothy 4:8), and enter a state of never-ending joy:

"There will be no more death or mourning or crying or pain" (Revelation 21:4). In heaven, "They will not need the light of a lamp or the light of the sun, for the Lord God will give them light. And they will reign for ever and ever" (Revelation 22:5). Heaven is where Christian believers will spend eternity with their Lord and Savior, Jesus Christ, as "heirs of God and co-heirs with Christ" (Romans 8:17).

These scriptural statements may not throw much light on heaven's "furniture," but they hardly leave us in the dark as to its environment and atmosphere. In introducing a radio program on Easter Day 1992, the well-known humanist Ludovic Kennedy said that he had no fear of death and hoped to be spared "the tedium of everlasting life."[11] One assumes the remarks were honest; they also betrayed total and tragic ignorance of what heaven is like.

What then can we know about hell, which someone has called "the ultimate horror of God's universe"?[12] As with heaven, we are locked in to what Scripture says, and we must resist the temptation either to soften the subject by trying to explain away its meaning or to embellish the Bible's statements with our own enthusiastic interpretation of what they mean. The first mistake can be made very simply, but not honestly. The second can be made very easily and understandably, as the following two examples show.

Isaac Watts (1674-1748) is widely acknowledged as one of the greatest hymn writers in the history of the Christian church, but in a work entitled "The Day of Judgment," he wrote:

Hopeless mortals! How they scream and shiver while
Devils push them into the pit wide yawning;
Hideous and gloomy to receive them headlong
Down to the center.[13]

There are glimmers of truth in these lines, but as Scripture nowhere says that devils push the damned into a wide pit, Watts is also guilty of some distortion.

The second example concerns Charles Haddon Spurgeon, arguable the greatest Christian preacher of the nineteenth century. Here is an extract from one of his sermons: "There is a real fire in hell, as truly as you have a real body—a fire exactly like that which we have on this earth, except this: that it will not consume though it will torture you. You have seen asbestos lying amid red hot coals, but not consumed. So your body will be prepared by God in such a way that

it will burn for ever without being desensitized for all its raging fury
. . . the acrid smoke of the sulfurous flames searing your lungs and
choking your breath. . . ."[14]

A great deal of that statement is truly biblical, but to speak of
"flames searing your lungs and choking your breath" is over the top,
because nowhere does the Bible say this will happen. Although
Spurgeon remains one of my great heroes, I am not prepared to follow him when he goes beyond Scripture.

As we move into the next crucial sections of our subject we dare
not stray an inch from what the Bible says about hell. To help in main-
taining this principle we shall quote directly from Scripture about 150
times in the next two chapters alone. Sometimes, to highlight the
point under discussion, we shall have to repeat certain verses several
times, and this will help us to keep our attention focused on what God
says in His Word. Every step we take needs to be guided by one clear
principle: "What does the Scripture say?" (Romans 4:3). As often as
possible, we shall simply allow the Bible to speak for itself. This will
leave us none the wiser as to hell's "temperature," but as well
informed as we need to be about its nature and purpose.

THE BIBLE SAYS . . .

Comparatively little of what Scripture says about hell is found in the
Old Testament. Much earlier in this book we noted that biblical revelation is progressive, often giving a fuller picture of a subject in the
New Testament than in the Old; and this is certainly true with regard
to hell. Now come several surprises.

The first is that most New Testament teaching on hell comes from
the lips of Jesus. It has been calculated that of 1,870 verses recording
words which Jesus spoke, thirteen percent are about judgment and
hell.[15] Jesus spoke more about these two topics than about any other
(angels came second and love third).

The second surprise is that of about forty parables Jesus told, more
than half of them related to God's eternal judgment of sinners.

Again, of the twelve times that the word *Gehenna*, the strongest
biblical word for "hell," appears in the New Testament, there is only
one occasion when Jesus was not the speaker.

The final surprise comes to those who try to deflect the New
Testament's teaching about hell by saying, "My idea of Christianity
is the teaching of Jesus in the Sermon on the Mount." This provides

no escape whatever, because it was in that sermon that Jesus did some of His straightest talking on the subject, warning people of "the fire of hell" (Matthew 5:22), the danger of being "thrown into hell" (Matthew 5:29) and the need to turn from "the road that leads to destruction" (Matthew 7:13). When the liberal theologian Nels Ferré suggested that "Whether Jesus taught eternal hell or not is uncertain,"[16] he was at odds with the evidence!

It is impossible to read the New Testament in general, and the words of Jesus in particular, without facing the fact that hell is not a figment of religious imagination but a terrifying reality. What does the Bible tell us about it? The remainder of this chapter will be taken up with the "environment" of hell and the following chapter with the experience of those who go there, though there will be points at which the two subjects cross over from one chapter to the other.

WHAT AND WHERE

The Bible gives many different descriptions of hell and consistently refers to it as a specific place. Peter told his fellow disciples that Judas Iscariot (who committed suicide after betraying Jesus) had gone "to his own place" (Acts 1:25, NASB). This does not mean that hell is a building or a tract of land that we could measure with a yardstick or a theodolite. The Bible says nothing about its square mileage or the distances between any of its features. Hell is something beyond our time-and-space understanding. Yet it is clearly more than a state of mind or a philosophical concept because, as we shall see, Jesus taught that the whole resurrected person—body and soul—is punished in hell, and for this to happen there must be a place where it can be done. A body can hardly be said to enter a state of mind or a philosophical concept. What we can say with certainty is that hell is a place in every sense of the word that can properly be used of something that is totally beyond our earthly ideas of time and space.

As to its location, we are given no details—though perhaps there is at least one important clue. Jesus told a parable in which the wicked are depicted as a guest who appeared improperly dressed at a wedding reception for the king's son. The king was grossly offended and ordered his servants, "Tie him hand and foot, and throw him outside, into the darkness" (Matthew 22:13). This word "outside" is the one that Jesus used frequently when speaking about hell and almost certainly lays to rest the notion that hell is located somewhere in the center of the earth.

This idea has been around for a long time and recently got some excited attention when a Finnish newspaper supposedly reported that scientists in Siberia had drilled a hole nine miles deep and, with an ultra-sensitive listening device, had picked up the sound of millions of human voices screaming in agony from a massive subterranean cavern with a temperature calculated by the scientists to be over 1000 degrees Celsius. The whole report turned out to be an elaborate hoax, and the scientists' "findings" have no substance in Scripture. As far as its location is concerned, we have almost nothing to go on. Not even statements which say that heaven is "above" and hell "beneath" tell us very much. The clearest clue we have is that hell is "outside."

THE RUBBISH DUMP

As we saw in chapter 3, the Valley of Hinnom was notorious in Jewish history as the place where idolatrous kings had offered human sacrifices to pagan gods. In New Testament times, it had become the city's permanent rubbish dump. Every kind of garbage was thrown there, along with the corpses of criminals. Worms bred and fed in the filth, and smoke from the fires kept burning there added to the stench created by rotting rubbish. The Jewish name for this place was *Ge Hinnom*, the Greek form of which is Gehenna. The English translation is "hell," and Jesus used this word no fewer than eleven times when speaking about the eternal destiny of the wicked.

In the Sermon on the Mount, He spoke of those whose behavior put them "in danger of the fire of hell" (Matthew 5:22), adding that it would be better to lose a part of the body "than for your whole body to be thrown into hell" (Matthew 5:29). He said almost the same thing a moment later and placed such importance on this particular principle that He underlined the same truth on four other occasions.

Jesus used even stronger language when speaking to religious leaders who made a great pretense of their religion, but were self-righteous hypocrites: "You snakes! You brood of vipers! How will you escape being condemned to hell?" (Matthew 23:33). Warning His disciples of the opposition they would face, He added this encouragement: "Do not be afraid of those who kill the body but cannot kill the soul. Rather, be afraid of the One who can destroy both soul and body in hell" (Matthew 10:28). He was obviously not referring to corpses being thrown on Jerusalem's rubbish dump but to the terrible truth that there are those whose eternal fate will be to have God toss them aside, body and soul.

Whenever I use the local council rubbish dump, I find being there a strange experience. Everything I see is an item no longer considered by its owner to be of any value. There is paper, metal, wood, pottery, and glass; refuse from people's gardens and rubbish from their homes; everything from chromium to cardboard, plastic to polystyrene—and all of it thrown away. The dump is a wasteland. Even when full, it has a feeling of emptiness. Whenever I am there, I never take a deep breath or stop to admire the scenery; instead, I unload and leave, glad to turn my back on it.

That dump often makes me think of hell—and the link is not far-fetched. Speaking of those whose religion was a formal pretense, Jesus compared them to salt which had lost its saltiness, then added, "It is fit neither for the soil nor for the manure heap; it is thrown out" (Luke 14:35). However much we wince at the thought, hell is God's cosmic rubbish dump, and all who go there become the garbage of the universe—wasted and worthless. C.S. Lewis has a telling comment along the same lines: "To enter heaven is to become more human than you ever succeeded in being on earth; to enter hell is to be banished from humanity. What is cast (or casts itself) into hell is not a man; it is 'remains.'"[17]

THE PRISON

One of the clearest pictures Jesus gave of hell was that of a prison. He told a parable of a king's servant who was sent to jail for cruel and unforgiving behavior, then added this warning: "This is how my heavenly Father will treat each of you unless you forgive your brother from your heart" (Matthew 18:335). On another occasion, in urging people to get right with God while they still had opportunity, He likened this to settling a lawsuit out of court, warning His hearers that if they failed to do so, they would be dragged before the judge who would "turn you over to the officer, and the officer throw you into prison" (Luke 12:58).

Sometimes, Jesus used other related pictures. He spoke of the wicked as weeds, and said that the day was coming when God would order His angels to "tie them in bundles to be burned" (Matthew

13:30). In the story of the wedding reception for the king's son, the king told his attendants, "Tie him hand and foot, and throw him outside . . ." (Matthew 22:13).

Other New Testament writers also spoke of the lost as being imprisoned. Peter said that "God did not spare angels when they sinned," but put them "into gloomy dungeons to be held for judgment" (2 Peter 2:4). Jude said much the same thing: "And the angels who did not keep their positions of authority but abandoned their own home—these he has kept in darkness, bound with everlasting chains for judgment on the great Day" (Jude 6). These two references are to angels, not human beings, and to imprisonment before the Day of Judgment rather than after it, but there are three reasons why there is no comfort from either of those facts. Firstly, Peter added that "The Lord knows how to . . . hold the unrighteous for the day of judgment, while continuing their punishment" (2 Peter 2:9)—which means that during the intermediate state, they share the fallen angels' punishment in Hades. Secondly, we are told that after the final judgment all those in Hades will be "thrown into the lake of fire" (Revelation 20:14); and thirdly, Jesus made it clear that the wicked will be condemned to "the eternal fire prepared for the devil and his angels" (Matthew 25:41).

When I was a teenager, on the Channel Island of Guernsey, I lived only a few hundred yards from the island's prison. Whenever I walked past those grim, granite walls, I experienced a strange feeling, even though I had done nothing that deserved imprisonment. Several years later, as Secretary to the States of Guernsey Prison Board, I went into the prison regularly in the course of my duties, and my emotions were always heightened at seeing men and women whose behavior had locked them away from society and into that miserable place.

Earthly prisons vary in their conditions and amenities, from the primitive, and even barbaric, to those with more creature comforts (and sometimes better food!) than their inmates would normally enjoy outside. Some people have even been known to commit crime in order to get back "inside." As we assemble the Bible's profile of hell, we shall see that the contrast between earthly prisons and the eternal prison of hell could not be greater. In hell, there will be no comforts, pleasures, or friendships, nor will there be any facilities for rest or recreation. Hell will make the worst earthly prison seem like a holiday camp.

There is another radical difference. Earthly prisons confine only the body; the spirit can still be free—to worship, create, imagine, anticipate, hope. When Paul and his companion Silas were in Philippi, the magistrates ordered them to be stripped, flogged, and thrown into prison. Under instructions to guard them carefully, the jailer "put them in the inner cell and fastened their feet in the stocks"—yet in the middle of the night "Paul and Silas were praying and singing hymns to God" (Acts 16:24-25). Neither pain nor prison could stifle their joy.

Sixteen centuries later, Madame Guyon, a religious mystic who spent ten years in French prisons, wrote of having an inner sense of liberty during her imprisonment:

> My cage confines me round;
> Abroad I cannot fly;
> But though my wing is closely bound,
> My heart's at liberty.
> My prison walls cannot control
> The flight, the freedom of the soul.[18]

Things are very different in hell, where the prisoner is incarcerated "soul and body" (Matthew 10:28); his spirit is as crippled and confined as his body, with no instinct to worship god and no interest in doing so. An imprisoned spirit is stilted, stale, and sterile.

Earthly prisoners also have opportunities to work, achieve, influence, be a means of inspiration and help to others, and gain some dignity for themselves. Paul wrote long sections of the New Testament while in prison; at one point he called himself "an ambassador in chains" (Ephesians 6:20). In the seventeenth century John Bunyan was often imprisoned for the same "offense" as Paul, that of preaching the gospel, but while he was incarcerated he produced *Pilgrim's Progress*, one of the greatest Christian books ever written. Other prisoners have learned a trade, developed useful skills, passed examinations, even earned university degrees. In the United Kingdom local council elections in 1992, one candidate conducted his campaign from his prison cell in Glasgow and won a seat on Glasgow District Council.

Drawing together what the Bible says about hell as a prison, it seems that its inmates have neither the instinct nor the opportunity to achieve anything but that they are helpless, hopeless, and powerless, utterly drained of all ideas and inspiration.

THE PIT

There is a related picture in the Old Testament which speaks of sinners falling or being thrust into a pit. There are times when the language may be purely figurative and confined to some form of earthly retribution, but there are cases where this clearly does not exhaust the meaning. David says,

> "He who is pregnant with evil
> and conceives trouble gives birth to disillusionment.
> He who digs a hole and scoops it out
> falls into the pit he has made'
> (Psalm 7:15).

The picture is worse than it first seems: David sees the whole life of the ungodly person as a process of "scooping out" the pit into which he will eventually fall. In that sense, hell is self-made, and the more sin a person commits, the deeper that person's pit becomes. Yet God is also involved in the sinner's doom; David says elsewhere, "But you, O God, will bring down the wicked into the pit of corruption" (Psalm 55:23), words with all the vile connotations of Gehenna (one Greek version of the Old Testament actually uses *Gehenna* to translate David's phrase). The prophet Isaiah, foreseeing God's final and terrible judgment on the wicked, makes their fate clear: "Terror and pit and snare await you, O people of the earth" (Isaiah 24:17). It would be difficult for Isaiah to compress greater horror into fewer words, and his warning is a sobering reminder to all who read them that, as John Calvin put it, "God has an endless variety of scourges for punishing the wicked."[19]

In the Authorized, or King James, Version of the Bible, there are several references in Revelation to "the bottomless pit" (Revelation 9:1-2; 11:7; 17:8; 10:1) and many Christian preachers and writers over the years have spoken inaccurately about hell in these terms. The "bottomless pit" (modern Bible versions tend to call it "the Abyss") is the temporary home and headquarters of Satan and his demonic angels. There is a hint of this early in the New Testament when Jesus was about to cast demons out of a man and "They begged him repeatedly not to order them to go into the Abyss" (Luke 8:31).

It is from this "bottomless pit"—not hell—that Satan masterminds his operations. Hell is still unoccupied, either by Satan, demons, or human beings and will remain so until after the judgment when all evil beings will be "thrown into the lake of burning sulfur" and be "tormented day and night for ever and ever" (Revelation 20;10). Hell is certainly a "pit"; the Bible does not tell us that it is "bottomless." However, in the light of all the other things we are told about hell, the absence of the adjective is no consolation.

DARKNESS

Another aspect of hell's environment is that of darkness. One of the fullest expressions is in the Old Testament, where Job speaks of "the land of gloom and deep shadow . . . the land of deepest night, of deep shadow and disorder, where even the light is like darkness" (Job 10:21-22).

Centuries later, Jesus warned of the fate awaiting those Jews who rejected him in spite of their special privileges and said that they would be "thrown outside, into the darkness" (Matthew 8:12). In a parable, we noted earlier the king's attendants were told to take the improperly dressed wedding guest and "throw him outside, into the darkness" (Matthew 22:13). In another parable, a slave owner gave similar instructions: "And throw that worthless servant outside, into the darkness" (Matthew 25:30).

Elsewhere, Peter writes of those who "follow the corrupt desire of the sinful nature and despises authority," who have "eyes full of adultery" and are "experts in greed," and then pronounces their doom: "Blackest darkness is reserved for them" (2 Peter 2:10, 14, 17). Another New Testament writer uses a similar expression in condemning those whose sinful lifestyles included the rejection of authority: he says they were those "for whom blackest darkness has been reserved for ever" (Jude 13).

The Bible gives no explanation of what this "darkness" means, but as "God is light" (1 John 1:5) and as darkness is the opposite of light, the description could not possibly be more negative. What is significant is that Jesus did not describe hell as "darkness" but as "the darkness," as if to emphasize that it will be infinitely worse than any physical, moral, mental, or spiritual darkness ever experienced here on earth. It is almost impossible for us to imagine a place with no dawns, no mornings, no ray of sunshine, no clear sky, and where every day is night.

THE FIRE

The Bible's most frequent description of hell is that of fire, and perhaps nothing will make the point more impressively than to list—with

a minimum of comment—twenty-one of the places where this particular picture is used.

David indicates how God will deal with those who reject His rule
in their lives: "On the wicked he will rain fiery coals and burning sulfur" (Psalm 11:6).

The prophet Isaiah speaks to God about "the fire reserved for your
enemies" (Isaiah 26:11).

Later, in a message aimed particularly at the godless King of
Assyria but applying equally to all the wicked, he says,

> "Topheth has long been prepared;
> it has been made ready for the king.
> Its fire pit has been made deep and wide,
> with an abundance of fire wood;
> the breath of the Lord,
> like a stream of burning sulfur,
> sets it ablaze"
> (Isaiah 30:33).

Topheth (the name probably comes from an Arabic word meaning "a
fire-place") was where the child sacrifices were offered to pagan gods
in the Valley of Ben Hinnom. It therefore carried with it all that place's
shameful associations.

In another message, again in connection with the punishment of
pagan Assyria, Isaiah prophesies that when wicked people living in
Zion (that is, Judah) see God's power at work in the destruction of
His enemies, they will realize the danger they are in:

> "The sinners in Zion are terrified;
> trembling grips the godless:
> 'Who of us can dwell with the consuming fire?
> Who of us can dwell with everlasting burning?'"
> (Isaiah 33:14).

In its immediate contest, this verse obviously refers to God's righteous
judgment on the wicked of that time. But the earliest translators of
the Old Testament into Aramaic had no hesitation in borrowing this
wording when speaking of eternal punishment.[20]

At the very end of Isaiah's prophecy God has a sobering message
for all those who rebel against His authority: He says that "Their

worm will not die, nor will their fire be quenched, and they will be loathsome to all mankind" (Isaiah 66:24).

The prophet Nahum uses similar language and says of God, "Who can withstand his indignation? Who can endure his fierce anger? His wrath is poured out like fire . . ." (Nahum 1:6).

In the final chapter in the Old Testament the prophet Malachi records this warning: "'Surely the day is coming; it will burn like a furnace. All the arrogant and every evildoer will be stubble, and that day that is coming will set them on fire,' says the Lord Almighty" (Malachi 4:1).

Early in the New Testament, John the Baptist warns that Jesus would take decisive action against sinners: "His winnowing fork is in his hand, and he will clear his threshing-floor, gathering his wheat into the barn and burning up the chaff with unquenchable fire" (Matthew 3:12).

In the Sermon on the Mount Jesus warns, "Anyone who says, 'You fool!' will be in danger of the fire of hell" (Matthew 5:22). Lifted out of context, that sounds like an exaggeration. After all, we sometimes use the phrase "You fool!" in a light-hearted way that hardly implies criticism, let along anything more sinister. However, the word "fool" in Jesus' statement probably comes from the Hebrew *moreh*, a very strong word of moral condemnation. To call a person "You fool!" would amount to character assassination and imply "a murderous hatred"[21]—and as Jesus uses this illustration to show that murder could be committed with the mind as well as in the flesh His warning is right in line with New Testament teaching.

The illustration of hell as fire also appears in several of the parables Jesus told. In one, relating to the way in which a farmer would deal with weeds in his fields. Jesus explains its meaning: "As the weeds are pulled up and burned in the fire, so it will be at the end of the age. The Son of Man will send out His angels, and they will weed out of his kingdom everything that causes sin and all who do evil. They will throw them into the fiery furnace, where there will be weeping and gnashing of teeth" (Matthew 13:40-42).

In another parable, He speaks of fishermen throwing away bad fish caught in their net and added: "This is how it will be at the end of the age. The angels will come and separate the wicked from the righteous and throw them into the fiery furnace, where there will be weeping and gnashing of teeth" (Matthew 13:50).

On another occasion Jesus says, "If your hand or your foot causes you to sin, cut it off and throw it away. It is better for you to enter life maimed or crippled than to have two hands or two feet and be thrown into eternal fire. And if your eye causes you to sin, gouge it out and throw it away. It is better for you to enter life with one eye than to have two eyes and be thrown into the fire of hell" (Matthew 18:8-9). The passage is about the dangers of being lured into sin, and means that if something we choose to do ("your hand"), somewhere we choose to go ("your foot") or something we choose to look at ("your eye") becomes an avenue of temptation, we are to take drastic action by cutting certain things out of our lives. Jesus is not advocating amputation, but insisting on radical moral surgery. In our present context, the other pictures in this passage are as clear as crystal— "life" means heaven and "eternal fire" is the same place as "the fire of hell."

The last time Jesus uses the metaphor of fires is in His teaching about the day of final judgment, when He warns that He will tell the wicked, "Depart from me, you who are cursed, into the eternal fire prepared for the devil and his angels" (Matthew 25:41).

Later in the New Testament we read that if people persist in living sinful lives in open rebellion against the truth their prospects are bleak—"a fearful expectation of judgment and of raging fire that will consume the enemies of God" (Hebrews 10:27).

Another writer reminds us that centuries beforehand the cities of Sodom and Gomorrah, which had steeped themselves in sexual immorality and perversion, had been destroyed by catastrophic divine judgment, and then adds, "They serve as an example of those who suffer the punishment of eternal fire" (Jude 7). The writer chose these two cities because they were destroyed when "The Lord rained down burning sulfur on Sodom and Gomorrah" (Genesis 19:24). This catastrophe may have been caused by an earthquake which ignited the inflammable gasses produced by the huge deposits of petroleum, bitumen, and sulfur which characterized the Valley of Siddim in which Sodom and Gomorrah were located. Even if this were the case, the Bible makes it clear that the occurrence and timing of the disaster were not accidental but that it was an act of God.

The remaining passages all come from Revelation and concern events related to the final Day of Judgment and beyond. In the first, John says that "if anyone worships the beast and his image and receives his mark on the forehead or on the hand" he will be "tormented with burning sulfur in the presence of the holy angels and of the Lamb" (Revelation 14:10). The message is stark and simple: those who plunge themselves into sin will pay a terrible price for their wickedness.

Later on, John speaks about "the beast" and "the false prophet" who had "deluded those who had received the mark of the beast and worshipped his image" and goes on to tell us of their fate: "The two of them were thrown alive into the fiery lake of burning sulfur" (Revelation 19:20). Whatever the exact identity of 'the beast' and "the false prophet," they will suffer the same disastrous consequences as those they eluded and destroyed.

John then tells us of Satan's own fate, and says that he too will be "thrown into the lake of burning sulfur, where the beast and the false prophet had been thrown," where they will all be "tormented day and night for ever and ever" (Revelation 20:10).

Next, John speaks specifically about the final Day of Judgment when "death and Hades" will be "thrown into the lake of fire," something he describes as "the second death" (Revelation 20:14). The meaning is clear: when neither physical death nor Hades (the remand prison for the souls of the wicked prior to the final judgment) have any further part to play in God's purposes they will be thrown away.

John then adds that the same fate awaits everyone who has not got right with God during his lifetime: "If anyone's name was not found written in the book of life, he was thrown into the lake of fire" (Revelation 20;15).

Finally, John identifies some of those who will be condemned to spend eternity in hell: "But the cowardly, the unbelieving, the vile, the murderers, the sexually immoral, those who practice magic arts, the idolaters and all liars—their place will be in the fiery lake of burning sulfur" (Revelation 21:8).

In the Authorized Version, the word "sulfur" in these verses in Revelation is translated "brimstone" (hence the common use of the phrase "fire and brimstone"). The Greek word is based on *theia*, places touched by lightning, which leaves a sulfurous smell. It was sometimes associated with God's judgment on the wicked, such as in the destruction of Sodom and Gomorrah.

Whatever the precise meaning of "fire" when used as a description of hell, these twenty-one references make it clear that hell is a place of terrible pain and suffering and the inescapable result of sin.

THE WORM

Some of the most harrowing of the Bible's language about hell comes when it speaks of a worm constantly gnawing at those who are condemned to spend eternity there.

In a passage that we noted earlier in this chapter, God says of these in hell that "Their worm will not die" (Isaiah 66:24). Nearly 800 years later, Jesus quoted these words when warning people that those sent to hell would find themselves in an appalling state where "Their worm does not die and the fire is not quenched" (Mark 9:48).

The idea of a worm gnawing away at a person's body forever is so revolting that some people have used it as an excuse to throw out the whole idea of hell and dismiss it as being nothing more than a bizarre fairy tale. That kind of reaction totally ignores the fact that when the Bible speaks of hell, the language used is often symbolic and not meant to be taken literally. If the fire and the worm are literal it would be impossible for any human being on earth to imagine or describe their horror; but what if they are symbolic? Would that make hell much less traumatic, and perhaps even bearable? Two straightforward facts provide the answer.

Firstly, as symbols are meant not to blur an issue but to make it clearer, God would hardly try to deceive us by using pictorial language, especially on an issue of such eternal importance. As Bruce Milne says, "No doubt some of the language used to describe hell is necessarily symbolic, just as the language describing heaven. However, the fact that we are thrown back on symbols does not mean that we can disregard or devalue them. They are God-given and while they cannot tell us everything, they will not mislead us."[22]

The second point to make here is that in common communication the thing being symbolized is always greater than the symbol. In the case of hell, this has to be so, because without symbols employing things we understand we would never be able to grasp anything of the nature of hell. By using symbols, God accommodates our ignorance. When telling us about heaven He speaks of it as "the city of pure gold" (Revelation 21:18) with "each gate made of a single pearl" (Revelation 21:21), but this does not mean that heaven has any kind of commercial value. The language is obviously symbolic and "combines to convey, as far as it is possible for the human mind to grasp and human language to express, the infinite and inexpressible beauty and perfection of heaven".[23] In the same way, even if we can prove that hell's "fire" and "worm" are metaphorical we shall not have removed one iota of their horror or terror.

THE COMPANY

We shall look at the meaning of the fire and the worm in the next chapter, but for the time being we need to add one further factor relating to hell's environment, and that is the identity of those who will be there. George Bernard Shaw once remarked that all the interesting people would be in hell, but that kind of comment does nothing to help us in establishing the facts. Hell's profile has been emerging throughout this chapter, but we can now be more specific as to its population.

Firstly, Jesus said that the eternal fire of hell was "prepared for the devil and his angels" (Matthew 25:41), while John added the names of "the beast and the false prophet" (Revelation 20:10)—so we know that all the demonic spirits in the universe will be there. On another occasion Jesus said that "everything that causes sin and all who do evil" will be thrown "into the fiery furnace" (Matthew 13:41-42). The first phrase points to those who have been a snare or a stumbling-block to others—drug-pusher, porn barons, prostitutes, and others are obvious modern examples—but in Revelation other unsavory groups are identified: "the cowardly, the unbelieving, the vile, the murderers, the sexually immoral, those who practice magic arts, the idolaters and all liars" (Revelation 21:8).

These will be among Shaw's "interesting people"; they hardly sound like pleasant company! Nor does hell offer sinners the appealing prospect of enjoying their chosen sins to the full. The pictures of hell are those of a rubbish dump, a prison, a pit, and a place of impenetrable darkness whose inmates will endure the uninterrupted pain inflicted by unquenchable fire and an undying worm.

Hell is the ultimate horror.

The Pains of Hell

If all the pains, sorrows, miseries and calamities that have been inflicted upon the sons of men . . . should meet together and center in one man they would not so much as amount to one of the least of the pains of hell."[1] Those words by Thomas Brooks remain as true today as when they were originally written, nearly 400 years ago. In the last chapter, we looked at what the Bible teaches about hell's environment, the factors that make hell what it is. In this chapter, we shall examine the Bible's teaching about what it will be like to be there. What does Scripture tell us about the "pains of hell"?

THE UNDYING WORM

We begin by looking at something we touched on when examining hell's "environment," but which properly belongs to this chapter. What did Jesus mean when he said of people condemned to hell that "Their worm does not die"? (Mark 9:48). The vital clue seems to be that whereas in the same sentence He said, "The fire is not quenched," He did not speak of "*the* worm," but of "*their* worm," as if this part of the suffering was internal rather than external. As one seventeenth-century writer put it, "Not only will the unbeliever be in hell, but hell will be in him too."[2] If this is the case, it suggests that the "worm" refers to the sinner's conscience.

Conscience exercises a powerful influence on the emotions, either positively or negatively. Even in the most traumatic of situations, a clear conscience can be the source of tremendous peace, strength, and resolve. When the apostles were released after being jailed and flogged for preaching, they went straight back on the streets to continue where they had left off, "rejoicing because they had been counted worthy of suffering disgrace for the Name" (Acts 5:41). Their consciences were clear, because God had given them specific instructions to preach and, as Peter told the local religious leaders, "We must obey God rather than men!" (Acts 5:29). Later, when defending himself against false accusers, Paul was able to claim, "I strive always to keep my conscience clear before God and man" (Acts 24:16).

When William Penn (1644-1718) was imprisoned in the Tower of London, he is reported to have said, "My prison shall be my grave before I will budge a jot, for I owe my conscience to no man. Right is right, even if everyone is against it; and wrong is wrong, even if everyone is for it." An English proverb says, "A quiet conscience sleeps in thunder"; Penn found that to be true.

A guilty conscience has the opposite effect. It nags and gnaws at the mind, unbalances the judgment, blurs the vision, and cripples initiative—and it hurts! In Shakespeare's *Richard III*, the king, nearly paralyzed with guilt, cried out,

My conscience hat a thousand several tongues.
And every tongue brings in a several tale,
And every tale condemns me for a villain

King Charles IX of France, whose reign during the mid-sixteenth century was marred by fierce persecution of the Huguenot Christians, is reported to have told his doctor, "For months I have been in a fever physically and spiritually. If only I had spared the innocent, the weak-minded and crippled, I might get some sleep. But my conscience torments me day and night." It was said of Richard III that, having murdered his two nephews in 1483 in order to usurp the English throne for himself, he was so tormented by his conscience that he often used to get up in the middle of the night and take up his sword to fight off the evil spirits he felt were tormenting him.

Yet, however severe the pangs of conscience on earth, they are infinitely greater in hell. There, the sinner's conscience will be more active and alert than when it was at its most sensitive on earth. In one of his letters, Paul warns Timothy about those who would abandon their profession of faith and become "hypocritical liars, whose consciences have been seared as with a hot iron" (1 Timothy 4:2). These people argued themselves into such a position that they could justify anything they did while condemning much the same kind of behavior in others. Like those Paul mentioned elsewhere, they "lost all sensitivity" (Ephesians 4:19); their cauterized consciences no longer troubled them.

Things will be very different in hell, where the wicked will have a capacity for suffering far beyond any they had on earth and where their consciences will be their worst tormentors. Nor will there be any way in which they can be stifled or silenced. As John Flavel wrote in the seventeenth century, "Conscience, which should have been the sinner's curb on earth, becomes the whip that must lash his soul in hell. Neither is there any faculty or power belonging to the soul of man so fit and able to do it as his own conscience. That which was the seat and center of all guilt, now becomes the seat and center of all torments."[4]

Conscience will make the sinner acutely aware that he deliberately, freely, and gladly chose the lifestyle that led him to hell, that he is there because of his willfulness and obstinacy. In addition, it will force him to admit the truth of every charge it brings, and the justice of every pain he suffers, so that, in Flavel's words, "In all this misery, there is not one drop of injury or wrong."[5] As if this were not horrifying enough, the castigation will be uninterrupted; the sinner will have "no rest day or night" (Revelation 14:11). As never before, he will discover the truth of God's words that "There is no peace . . . for the wicked" (Isaiah 48:22). What is more, the agony will never be over, the worm "does not die." In Anthony Hoekema's words, "The inner anguish and torment symbolized by the worm will never end."[6]

SHAME AND CONTEMPT

Closely linked to the truth that the conscience will endlessly gnaw at the sinner's soul is a remarkable statement by the prophet Daniel written about 600 years before Jesus gave His teaching, and in which he foretells the resurrection of the dead and the result of the final judgment: "Multitudes who sleep in the dust of the earth will awake; some to everlasting life, others to shame and everlasting contempt" (Daniel 12:2). What do Daniel's words tell us about sinners' emotions in hell? No instrument known to man can measure the pain caused by guilt; and no human mind can imagine the agony caused in hell by an accusing conscience which has total recall and is impossible to silence.

When he realized the enormity of his sin in committing adultery with Bathsheba and then arranging for her husband to be killed, David cried out to God, "I know my transgressions, and my sin is always before me" (Psalm 51:3). Those words will mean far more for sinners in hell. Every sinful word, thought and deed, all the pride, envy, jealousy, hatred, selfishness, dishonesty and impurity, every neglected opportunity to hear and respond to the gospel, every failure to help those in need, all these will be endlessly replayed, endlessly remembered, and be the cause of endless remorse.

Yet their greatest shame will come from knowing that they had failed in the one purpose for which they were created, which was to bring glory to their Creator by their obedience to his will. Their job description was to reflect the glory of God, to tell the truth about him by radiating his character in every part of their lives. The Bible's uncompromising verdict on their performance is that "All have sinned and fall short of the glory of God" (Romans 3:23). By their sinful, self-centered lives they told lies about God, slandered and libeled their Creator. In hell, they will realize to the full the meaning and the extent of their crime. Not least, they will be forced to admit that although God had given them "life and breath and everything else" (Acts 17:25) they had squandered his generosity by living for themselves. No wonder Daniel says that they will experience shame.

But he also speaks of "contempt," which translates the Hebrew word *deraon*. Its only other use in Scripture is where Isaiah says that those condemned to hell will be "loathsome to all mankind" (Isaiah 66:24). Sinners in hell will have company but no sympathy. Everyone there will be loathed by everyone else, which will add both to their distress and to their shame. The inhabitants of hell will be caught in a vicious vortex of accusation and guilt, recrimination, and regret, "shame and contempt."

JUST DESERTS

The two features we have already mentioned share something in common with all the other "pains of hell" which we shall look at in the remainder of this chapter: they are part of the punishment which God metes out to unrepentant sinners. The idea of punishment is not very popular in these days. In 1981, the Chairman of Britain's Police Federation admitted: "Long ago people in power stopped talking about the punishment of crime and began to talk of treatment, as if every young thug was sick and in need of a prescription from the chemist. Discipline has disappeared in our schools and the concept of parental responsibility went out with the Ark."[7]

In many countries capital punishment has been abolished, and more and more criminals are given "treatment" rather than punishment. Some "experts" suggest that child molesters should not be branded as criminals but be seen merely as people in need of help. This, so the argument runs, would encourage them to own up! In 1992, the Scottish Law Commission proposed legislation to outlaw virtually all corporal punishment of children by parents. Under the Commission's proposals, only a "mild parental smack" delivered with the open hand and causing pain or discomfort "for a very short time" would be allowed.[8]

When we turn to the Bible, a very different framework emerges. In Old Testament times, God warned, "I will punish the world for its evil, the wicked for their sins" (Isaiah 13:11). Later, He reinforced the warning by saying, "The days of punishment are coming, the days of reckoning are at hand" (Hosea 9:7). Jesus said of religious hypocrites, "Such men will be punished most severely" (Mark 12:40). On the Day of Judgment, those who are condemned "will go away to eternal punishment" (Matthew 25:46). Here on earth civic authority is seen as "God's servant, an agent of wrath to bring punishment on the wrongdoer" (Romans 13:4). Later in the New Testament we are told that the person who rejects the Son of God "deserves to be punished" (Hebrews 10:29). Peter speaks of God knowing how to "hold the unrighteous for the day of judgment, while continuing their punishment" (2 Peter 2:9), and Jude refers to those "who suffer the punishment of eternal fire" (Jude 7).

Punishment is a vein that runs throughout the Bible and through all the stages of God's dealings with the wicked. He punishes them in some measure during their earthly lives, in their disembodied intermediate state, and forever in hell. Hell is not a sudden outburst of punishment inflicted out of character as God suddenly "blows His top"; it is the inevitable conclusion of a process that He has pursued throughout human history. In His eternal punishment of the wicked, God is not aiming at their good but at His glory. The time for correction and discipline will be over. What matters then is that God's justice is satisfied, His majesty vindicated.

Modern arguments against the concept of punishment usually suggest that we are not totally or mainly responsible for our behavior. It is claimed that our characters are predetermined by our environment, our family background, our upbringing, our economic situation, our genetic make-up, or other factors over which we have no control. Wrongdoers are to be seen as patients, not sinners or criminals; wrong behavior is to be viewed as an illness, not sin; and the remedy needed is to be sought in terms of treatment, not punishment. The twentieth century has seen a massive shift to these ideas, yet they remain fragile and flawed, and totally unproven. What is more, they come into direct conflict with the Bible's teaching.

Nobody would deny that our behavior is influenced by certain background factors in our lives, but none of these things determines how we behave. We are responsible beings, not robots; people, not puppets. Made "in the image of God" (Genesis 1:27), all of us "have sinned and fall short of the glory of God" (Romans 3:23); and "we will all stand before God's judgment seat" (Romans 14:10). The Bible focuses our attention on God, not on man. Life is not about bringing happiness and comfort to humans, but about bringing glory to God. People are sinners by nature, by choice and by desire. Jesus located the source of sin not in circumstances or social background, but in the human heart: "For from within, out of men's hearts, come evil thoughts, sexual immorality, theft, murder, adultery, greed, malice, deceit, lewdness, envy, slander, arrogance and folly. All these evils come from inside . . ." (Mark 7:21-23). We face God as guilty sinners, not as helpless victims of our circumstances.

Even the "smallest" sin is rebellion against our Creator. Every time we sin we are shaking our puny fists in God's face and defying His right to rule our lives. As God is not only a God of love and mercy, but also of law, order, and justice, we should hardly be surprised to discover that He "does not leave the guilty unpunished" (Exodus 34:7), but ensures that unrepentant sinners get their just deserts. The principle is so clear that W. G. T. Shedd says, "If there were no hell in Scripture, we should be compelled to invent one."[9]

DEATH-WISH

This last point underlines one of hell's most tragic truths, which is that this dreadful destiny is the sinner's own choice. J. I. Packer says bluntly, "Nobody stands under the wrath of God save those who have chose to do so. The essence of God's action in wrath is to give men what they choose, in all its implications; nothing more, and equally nothing less."[10]

Another theologian makes the same point and says, "For those who take God seriously, human freedom means the capacity to make moral decisions which have radical and enduring consequences. Hell, then, is not a place created by God bent on getting even, but the alienation we choose for ourselves."[11]

Coming at it from a completely different angle (and certainly not trying to make a serious theological point) a character in the Woody Allen film *Crimes and Misdemeanors* says much the same thing: "We are, in fact, the sum total of our choices."[12]

At yet another level of thinking, C.S. Lewis wrote, "There are only two kinds of people in the end: those who say to God, 'Thy will be done' and those to whom God says, in the end, 'Thy will be done.' All that are in hell choose it."[13]

This alarming truth runs right through Scripture from beginning to end. In the Garden of Eden, Adam and Eve were given freewill, the ability to choose between right and wrong, obedience and disobedience. They made the wrong choice, and all of humanity has lived (and died) with the consequences. Generations later, when they were wandering in the desert, cut off from their geographical and spiritual moorings, God told the Israelites, "This day I call heaven and earth as witnesses against you that I have set before you life and death, blessings and curses. Now choose life. . . ." (Deuteronomy 30:19). Many made the wrong choice, and God "ended their days in futility and their years in terror" (Psalm 78:33).

Thousands of years later, Jesus gave this uncompromising assessment of the bulk of humanity: "This is the verdict: Light has come into the world, but men loved darkness instead of light because their deeds were evil" (John 3:19). Here is another example of people making a perverse and tragic choice. Later, lamenting over the city's rejection of the salvation He offered, Jesus cried, "O Jerusalem, Jerusalem, you who kill the prophets and stone those sent to you, how often I have longed to gather your children together, as a hen gathers her chicks under her wings, but you were not willing. Look, your house is left to you desolate" (Matthew 23:37-38).

Paul wrote about people who "did not think it worthwhile to retain the knowledge of God" (Romans 1:28)—in other words, who deliberately pushed God out of their thinking—and went on to warn them, "You are storing up wrath against yourself for the day of God's wrath, when his righteous judgment will be revealed" (Romans 2:5).

Exactly the same thing is happening today. There is no law which forces people to lie, steal, cheat, or fornicate. There are no regulations which compel people to be proud, envious, jealous, or selfish. Even more to the point, there are no sanctions against acknowledging that God has the prior claim on our lives, no man-made laws which make it impossible to worship God, thank Him for His goodness, pray for His help, or seek to live godly lives in obedience to His Word. These are all commands God has given us, but they are also options—and most people choose to opt out. They choose to live their own lives, set their own standards, "do their own thing"; as Jesus put it, they choose "darkness instead of light." What the Bible makes crystal clear is that they must live forever with the consequences of that choice.

One modern writer makes the point very well: "In a strange way, hell is the final confirmation of the significance and dignity of man. God must punish sin and exclude evil from his new universe. But he will not break man or remake him. He allows man to stand in his rebellion. He confirms his choice. That is hell's necessity and its horror."[14]

C. S. Lewis underlines the eternal consequences of that choice: "I willingly believe that the damned are, in one sense, successful, rebels to the end; that the doors of hell are locked on the inside.'[15]

We can now begin to look at what the Bible says about the nature of the punishment that goes on behind what Lewis calls "the doors of hell."

THE MINUS FACTORS

The punishment of the wicked in hell is described in the Bible in both negative and positive terms. The first negative aspect is banishment. In the previous chapter we saw that Jesus likened the kingdom of heaven to a feast, and said that those unfit to share in it will be "thrown outside" (Matthew 8:12). We saw the same picture in the parable about the improperly dressed guest at the wedding reception: the king's instructions were to "throw him outside" (Matthew 22:13). Jesus also said that when He condemns the wicked on the Day of Judgment, they will "go away to eternal punishment" (Matthew 25:46).

This hardly sounds like punishment to some. They would say, "I want nothing to do with God now, and will be perfectly happy for that arrangement to continue." They are like the people in the Old Testament who said to God, "Leave us alone! We have no desire to

know your ways" (Job 21:14). But this kind of talk betrays both arrogance and ignorance, because while the wicked may want nothing to
do with God while they live on earth, they should be grateful that God
still wants something to do with them. They are not living without
God; regardless of how they treat Him (or even of whether they
believe He exists). He still provides them with "life and breath and
everything else" (Acts 17:25). One of the psalmists put it like this:

"[God[makes grass grow for the cattle,
and plants for man to cultivate—
bringing forth food from the earth:
wine that gladdens the heart of man,
oil to make his face shine,
and bread that sustains his heart"
(Psalm 104:14-15).

Theologians call this "common grace." It is what Jesus had in
mind when He said that God "causes his sun to rise on the evil and
the good, and sends rain on the righteous and the unrighteous"
(Matthew 5:45). When an atheist shouts, "There is no God!", he can
do so only because God gives him air to breathe and strength to draw
it into his lungs. Sinners can ignore God and still get a great deal of
enjoyment out of life only because God supplies them with the natural resources, energy, intelligence, and senses to do so. Food, drink,
clothing, company, friendship, sport, music, art, laughter, happiness—all of these, and hundreds of other things that contribute to
man's well-being, are gracious gifts from a generous Creator. In this
life, nobody is forsaken by God, banished from all links with Him.
But in hell, all those life-giving and life-enhancing links are gone. In
hell, sinners will not benefit in any way from the love, goodness,
patience and mercy of God. They will receive from God nothing of
any value, nothing that is of any benefit to them, or that gives even a
moment's pleasure. They will be banished.

NO HELP; NO HOPE

Another negative element in the punishment of the wicked in hell will
be *separation*. As we have already seen, at the Day of Judgment Jesus
will tell them, "Depart from me, you who are cursed" (Matthew
25:41), whereas His invitation to the righteous is to enter into the full
enjoyment of their eternal heritance. In the words of the well-known

Bible expositor Matthew Henry, "Those who would not come to
Christ to inherit a blessing must depart from him under the burden of
a curse."[16] Sinners are separated from all the blessings that God graciously provides.

The Bible also says that hell involves another separation. Human
beings love company. There is something natural about friendship,
fellowship, and relationships. When Adam was the only human being
on earth, God said, "It is not good for the man to be alone. I will make
a helper suitable for him" (Genesis 2:18). Centuries later David
wrote, "God sets the lonely in families" (Psalm 68:6). The family unit
was God's idea, and all the blessings that flow through loving family
relationships are among His greatest gifts. No earthly ties are greater
than those involving husband, wife, father, mother, son, daughter,
brother, and sister. In hell, no relationship of any kind will exist; everyone there will be there alone.

There may be a hint of this in the Bible's statement that "Each of
us will give an account of himself to God" (Romans 14:12) and
another in the story of the rich man and Lazarus, in which the rich
man in Hades cries, "Father Abraham, have pity on me and send
Lazarus to dip the tip of his finger in water and cool my tongue,
because I am in agony in this fire" (Luke 16:24). All his concerns are
self-centered and point to a sense of isolation. In hell, there will be no
companionship, no love, no sympathy, no kindness, no pity, no help,
no comfort. In the final sentence of his book on the subject of eternal
punishment, W. G. T. Shedd says that the person who rejects God's
way of salvation "must through endless cycles grapple with the dread
problem of human guilt in his own person, and alone."[17] All of hell
is solitary confinement.

A third negative aspect of sinners' punishment in hell is that of
deprivation—there are things they will be without. Like all who have
died, they will be without all their earthly pleasures and possessions,
but whereas the righteous in heaven will enjoy "eternal pleasures at
[God's] right hand" (Psalm 16:11) and have "a treasure in heaven that
will not be exhausted" (Luke 12:33), the wicked will be destitute.
David speaks of the wicked as "men of this world whose reward is in
this life" (Psalm 17:14), inferring that they have no reward in the life
to come. There will be no good things in hell, and the hardest hit will
be those who had more than their share of good things on earth.
Many of the most ungodly people in history have also been among
the wealthiest, surrounded with the finest of everything and revelling

in their luxurious lifestyles. In hell, those things will all be history. Never again will they enjoy a good day, a luxurious home, a fine meal, a soft bed, or good company. In the words of the seventeenth-century preacher Ralph Venning, they will be "stripped naked and deprived of all the good things they have had in this life."[18]

Yet the greatest deprivation will be the loss of hope. On earth, all except the most senseless cling to some hope of forgiveness and heaven, even if it has no biblical basis. In a survey taken in the United States in 1990, seventy-eight percent of those interviewed said they believed there was a heaven, and the same percentage said they thought they had a good or excellent chance of getting there.[19] For the sinner, all such hope ends at death: "When a wicked man dies, his hope perishes; all he expected from his power comes to nothing" (Proverbs 11:7). The same terrible truth is put even more starkly later in the same book, when the writer gives the reason why God's people should never be envious of the position or possessions of the wicked:

"Do not fret because of evil men
or be envious of the wicked,
for the evil man has no future hope,
and the lamp of the wicked will be snuffed out"
(Proverbs 24:19-20).

In hell, the sinner's situation is quite literally hopeless. As one writer has put it, "Despair is the damp of hell, as joy is the serenity of heaven."[20]

TORMENT, AGONY, PRESSURE

Turning to the positive aspects of sinners' punishment after death, we discover that the Bible uses a variety of words. The first is "torment." In His story about the wealthy but ungodly man who died and went to Hades, Jesus said that "He was in torment" (Luke 16:23), and the man himself called Hades "this place of torment" (Luke 16:28). In a passage from John's vision of the world to come, we are told that the wicked will be "tormented with burning sulfur" and that "The smoke of their torment rises for ever and ever" (Revelation 14:10-11). Later, John says that "The devil . . . the beast and the false prophet . . . will be tormented day and night for ever and ever" (Revelation 20:10).

In one form or another the word "torment" occurs another fifteen times in the New Testament. Sometimes it refers to severe distress caused by sickness or disease, and at least once to being tortured, but without exception the word carries with it the meaning of severe, conscious suffering.[21] In the case of hell's torments, this suffering will last forever. Over 1,500 years ago John Chrysostom, Bishop of Constantinople, emphasized what this will mean: "The damned shall suffer an end without end, a death without death, a decay without decay . . . they shall have punishment without pit, misery without mercy, sorrow without succour, crying without comfort, torment without ease."[22]

A second biblical word for the suffering of the wicked in hell is "*agony*," which means pain, anguish, and distress.[23] In the Old Testament it is used of godless nations which come under God's judgment; they will "writhe in agony" (Zechariah 9:5) and "grieve bitterly' (Zechariah 12:10). Paul uses the word to express his feelings over the fact that many of his fellow Jews are in danger of eternal condemnation: "I have great sorrow and unceasing anguish in my heart" (Romans 9:2). The word is also used of the sufferings of the wicked after death. In Jesus' story, the rich man in Hades cries out, "I am in agony in this fire" (Luke 16:24). Whatever agonies we may experience here on earth, they are as nothing compared to those the wicked will endure beyond the grave, when the torments and agonies of hell will be felt in body, soul, mind, conscience, and will, and when all of their senses—sign, sound, smell, taste, and touch—will convey the agony to them.

Two other descriptions are used together when Paul has this to say about the fate of the wicked: "But for those who are self-seeking and who reject the truth and follow evil, there will be wrath and anger. There will be trouble and distress for every human being who does evil" (Romans 2:8-9). Paul seems to have put these two together because they have the same "feel" to them. One expert says that "trouble" includes the idea of pressure, oppression, and affliction,[24] while the main idea of "distress" is the anguish caused by being pressed or crushed into a confined space. It is used in the Old Testament when Moses warns his people of "the suffering that your enemy will inflict on you during the siege of all your cities" (Deuteronomy 28:55). Many people today are under pressure of one kind or another; poverty, unemployment, ill-health, overwork, and fractured relationships are some of the areas in which it can build up, to say nothing of the pain of mental pressure and the greater pain of chronic guilt. It is no exaggeration to say that we live in a world of pressure, nor to say that in the world to come the wicked will be under pressures which will make their worst experiences in this life pale into insignificance. The greatest pressure of all will be the inescapable sense of God's sovereign power bearing down on them.

NO LAUGHING MATTER

One of the most vivid descriptions of the eternal suffering of the wicked occurs in seven statements which we have already touched on in these two chapters about the environment and experience of hell. When those who reject Christ in spite of their privileges are shut out of God's kingdom "there will be weeping and gnashing of teeth" (Matthew 8:12); when people are condemned like the weeds pulled out of the field and the bad fish pulled out of the lake they will be thrown into "the fiery furnace, where there will be weeping and gnashing of teeth" (Matthew 13:42, 50); when the improperly dressed wedding guest is ejected "there will be weeping and gnashing of teeth" (Matthew 22:13); the wicked servant will be sent to share the fate of the hypocrites, "where there will be weeping and gnashing of teeth" (Matthew 24:51); the worthless slave will be thrown into the darkness, where "there will be weeping and gnashing of teeth" (Matthew 15:30); and when those who neglected their opportunity to trust in Christ see themselves shut out of the kingdom of God there will be "weeping there, and gnashing of teeth" (Luke 13:28).

This description of hell has encouraged some people to think it does not even exist and to mock the Bible's statements on hell as nothing more than religious fantasy. They even joke about this particular picture—"What about people with no teeth?" Answer: "Teeth will be provided." But stupidity is not an adequate response to Scripture, and we ought to take very serious notice of the fact that Jesus used the phrase "weeping and gnashing of teeth" more than any other in His descriptions of the sinner's experience in hell. Only a fool will treat casually what Jesus said so often.

What does the expression "weeping and gnashing of teeth" mean? "Weeping" is a very strong word, indicating much more than tears (which can sometimes be associated with laughter). The meaning of this particular word is "wailing, not merely with tears, but with every outward expression of grief."[25] The weeping of the wicked in hell will be triggered by all the factors which make hell so terrible—the environment, the company, the remorse, the torment and agony, the

shame and contempt and the never-ending sense of God's anger. The
tears of the wicked will be those of "inconsolable, never-ending
wretchedness, and utter, everlasting hopelessness."[26]

The phrase "gnashing of teeth" focuses on another emotion, as we
can discover by looking at its use elsewhere in Scripture. At one point
in his life, when he felt at the end of his tether, Job cried out, "God
assails me and tears me in his anger and gnashes his teeth at me" (Job
167:9). When Stephen was about to be stoned to death he accused his
opponents of betraying and murdering Jesus, the righteous Son of
God. Their response was predictable and passionate: "When they
heard this, they were furious and gnashed their teeth at him" (Acts
7:54). From these two examples we can see that "gnashing of teeth"
is a way of expressing anger. In hell, that anger will be more intense
than any this world has ever seen. The wicked will be angry at the
things which gave them pleasure on earth but now give them pain in
hell; angry at the sins that wrecked their lives; angry at themselves for
being who they are; angry at Satan and his helpers for producing the
temptations which led them into sin; and, even while compelled to
acknowledge His glory and goodness, angry at God for condemning
them to this dreadful fate.

No weeping on earth can compare to the weeping in hell and no
anger on earth can compare to the anger in hell. In the original Greek,
the Bible does not speak of "weeping and gnashing of teeth" but of
"the weeping and the gnashing of teeth"—and this is true in each one
of the seven statements we are studying. This makes the point in a
very powerful way. It is often said that we live in a vale of tears. One
poet wrote,

The world! it is a wilderness,
Where tears are hung on every tree.[27]

He was hardly guilty of too much poetic license. Think of all the
tears that must have been shed by sixty billion human beings over
thousands of years.

Wars alone have caused such an unimaginable amount of suffering, sorrow and tears. As I write these words, a memorial service is
being held to commemorate the seventy-fifth anniversary of the Battle
of Passchendaele, in Flanders, when 250,000 British soldiers were
killed in 100 days in the summer and autumn of 1917. Who can cal-
culate the grief that has been wrung out of human lives as a result of

that one battle? I remember standing at the magnificent Vietnam Veterans Memorial in Washington, DC—a black granite wall inscribed with the names of 57,939 American service personnel, with an average age of eighteen, who died in that disastrous conflict. Near to where I was standing, a man knelt quietly in front of one of the names. As tears welled up in his eyes, I wondered how many other tears had been shed over Vietnam in the previous thirty years, and how many as a result of all the other wars in human history.

And what of all the tears shed in concentration camps and torture chambers, or those caused by accident or injury, sickness and disease, violence and bloodshed? What of the tears caused by rumor and gossip, lies and libel, poverty and neglect, tension and depression? It is impossible to imagine all the agony involved, yet even if we could find a way of quantifying it, we should still fall infinitely short of "the weeping and gnashing of teeth." Ralph Venning wrote, "The punishment that sinners must undergo will be such a state of misery that all the miseries of this life are not to be compared with it . . . The gripings and grindings of all the diseases and torments that men can or do suffer in this life are like flea bites to it . . . Hell would be a kind of paradise if it were no worse than the worst of this world."[28]

As we saw in chapter 1, people often use the word "hell" when speaking about suffering experienced in this life. An organization called Shelter, concerned with providing housing for those in acute need, once ran a poster campaign with the slogan: "Homelessness is hell." The famous musician Yehudi Menuhin told a national newspaper, "I think we make our own heaven and hell."[29] The writer Malcolm Muggeridge once described Calcutta, with over a million people sleeping rough in its dirty streets, as "the nearest place to hell on earth."[30] In all of these cases, the people concerned are speaking of things that are genuinely horrific, but they can never begin to approximate to the biblical picture. It is never true to say that something "hurts like hell"; nothing hurts like hell.

As if this were not enough, all of the sinner's weeping will be to no avail because, as Thomas Brooks put it, "Could every damned sinner weep a whole ocean, yet all those oceans together would never extinguish one spark of eternal fire."[31]

When that intensity of anguish is added to a greater grief than has ever consumed any human being on earth, this single description by Jesus of what it will mean to be in hell should make any sensible person tremble at even the possibility that this might be his or her experience beyond the grave.

WHAT OF THE FIRE?

As we come toward the end of our study on the experience of the wicked in hell one major question needs to be answered. In chapter 9, we established that "fire" was by far the Bible's most frequent description of hell. But what does "fire" mean? Is it literal or symbolic? When Mount Etna erupted in April 1992 and threatened to engulf the Sicilian village of Zafferana, scientists estimated that the temperature of the lava core was over 1,000 degrees Celsius, hot enough to melt hardened steel in ten seconds. If this temperature can be found on earth, will hell be hotter? Or are we not to think in terms of temperature, but some other kind of intensity?

Writers like Dante obviously thought of hell-fire as being literal but Dante is hardly a reliable guide. There are places in Scripture where a literal meaning seems possible, but others where a symbolic meaning seems to be the only true one. The right approach must be to interpret the first in the light of the second and conclude that the fire of hell is not a material phenomenon that could, for example, drive a steam engine or generate electricity. Virtually every interpreter agrees that when Jesus spoke of hell's "worm" He was using a metaphor; it would be strange if in the same breath He should speak of "fire" and not be doing the same thing. Again, when the Bible speaks of "the wine of God's fury" (Revelation 14:10) it is surely not saying that God's anger is either liquid or alcoholic? Yet even if hell's "fire" is metaphoric, we have not begun to answer the real question: another question will help us to do so. We have seen that fire is the most pervasive element in hell; what then is the single greatest factor that makes hell to be hell? The answer is the presence of God.

The Bible teaches that God is everywhere. God made it clear that He is not localized or limited:

> "'Am I only a God nearby,'
> declares the Lord,
> 'and not a God far away?
> Can anyone hide in secret places
> so that I cannot see him?'
> declares the Lord.
> 'Do not I fill heaven and earth?'

declares the Lord"
(Jeremiah 23:23-24).

In one of his great prayers, King Solomon says, "The heavens, even the highest heaven, cannot contain you" (1 Kings 8:27). A statement by David is of particular significance:

"Where can I go from your Spirit?
Where can I flee from your presence?
If I go up to the heavens, you are there;
if I make my bed in the depths, you are there"
(Psalm 139:7-8).

The word "depths" here is Sheol which, as we saw in chapter 3, Old Testament writers used to mean several different things. David says it is opposite to "the heavens."

Other writers move us even closer. Job says, "Death is naked before God; Destruction lies uncovered" (Job 26:6). Here, the word "Death" is Sheol and "Destruction" is the same word as "Abyss" in Revelation. When Isaiah speaks of a "fire pit . . . deep and wide, with an abundance of fire and wood," he adds, "The breath of the Lord, like a stream of burning sulfur, sets it ablaze" (Isaiah 30:33). Isaiah's primary reference is to the judgment which was to fall on the godless King of Assyria, but there is more than a hint that this is also a picture of the punishment of all the ungodly. What Isaiah is saying is that God does not cause hell to ignite by remote control, but by the "breath" of His own holy presence.

Exactly as we should expect, these hints come into much clearer focus in the New Testament, and, in John's vision of the fate of the ungodly, we are told that they "will be tormented with burning sulfur in the presence of the holy angels and of the Lamb" (Revelation 14:10). As "the Lamb" is obviously the Lord Jesus Christ (He is given the name over thirty times in Revelation), John is telling us that the Son of God, the Judge of all mankind, is present when the ungodly are being punished. Preachers often warn people about the danger of "eternal separation" from God and describe hell in this way, but the Bible never uses the term. It would be more biblical to warn people about the danger for them of the eternal presence of God. In John Flavel's words, "The worst terrors of the prisoners in hell come from the presence of the Lamb."[32] In a sermon delivered in 1742, Jonathan Edwards said that for the unrighteous and the righteous eternity would be spent "in the immediate presence of God . . . God will be the hell of the one and the heaven of the other."[33]

TOGETHER AND APART

How does this fit in with what we know about the Day of Judgment, when Jesus will say to sinners, "Depart from me, you who are cursed, in the eternal fire" (Matthew 25:41)? What about the parables in which the improperly dressed wedding guest and the worthless servant are said to be thrown outside? And what of these words by Paul on the fate of the wicked: "They will be punished with everlasting destruction and shut out from the presence of the Lord and from the majesty of his power"? (2 Thessalonians 1:9). These statements seem to point to the fact that those condemned to spend eternity in hell will be separated from God, not that they will forever be in God's presence. How can elements or people be both separated and together at one and the same time?

The question is not as difficult to answer as it seems. As a Channel Islander, I can remember seeing bottles of rich Guernsey milk topped with golden cream, the dividing line between the two as clear as if they had been in separate containers rather than in the same bottle. It was their distinct properties that kept them apart. A better illustration would be oil and water, which can never mix, even when shaken together in the same container. There are no such liquids as watery oil or oily water. When the Iraquis blew up Kuwait's pipelines in 1991, millions of gallons of oil poured into the Persian Gulf, creating one of the greatest ecological disasters of modern times, but not one globule of oil mixed with a single drop of water. They were together, yet separated.

Yet the best illustration of all is in the area of human relationships, where we have all the evidence we need to come to the conclusion that absence and separation are no more synonymous than presence and union. There are times when a husband is forced to live apart from his wife for weeks or even months at a time, yet their relationship often remains as close as ever. Sometimes it even seems to deepen. My own ministry has sometimes taken me thousands of miles away from home, yet my wife and I have often proved the truth of Haynes Bayly's famous saying that "Absence makes the heart grow fonder."[34]

The opposite can also be true. Quite apart from the increasing number of marriages that now end in divorce, there are countless others that no longer have any meaning. I know a couple who have been married for over thirty years, but for the last twenty they have had no physical or spiritual relationship. Their home is full of bitterness and anger. At times, their arguments have flared into violence, leaving the wife black and blue. Even when things are relatively quiet, there is not a spark of love anywhere in that home. They hate each other. They live in each other's presence but could not be more separated were they thousands of miles apart.

We tend to think of separation in terms of distance; the Bible speaks of it in terms of relationship. In hell, the sinner will not be separated from God in the sense that he will not see Him or know of His existence; instead he will live forever in His awesome presence. It is perfectly legitimate to think about sinners in hell being separated from God, but it might be more helpful if we thought in terms of alienation. As there is no evidence in Scripture that God will have changed His mind about the sinner, nor that the sinner will have changed his mind about God, the conclusion seems to be that they will hate each other. The sinner will certainly have greater knowledge than he did on earth; there will be no atheists in hell, and all who denied the deity of Christ will have to acknowledge that "Jesus Christ is Lord, to the glory of God the Father" (Philippians 2:11). What is more, the sinner in hell will have a greater knowledge of himself. As one scholar has put it, "All creatures will share in God's abhorrence of sin and evil; the sinner will hate himself, he will appreciate the value of his life and see it as God does. Hell is nothing but full knowledge of the truth, remorse in agreement with God."[35]

Yet none of these things will change the basic situation; God and the unrepentant sinner will stand in eternal opposition to each other. God will hate the wicked with a perfect hatred, the outcome of His holiness, righteousness, and justice. The wicked will hate God with a sinful hatred, the result of his corruption, depravity, and vileness. There is no evidence that these attitudes will ever change.

RIGHTEOUS ANGER

It is possible to escape a sense of God's presence in this life but not in the life to come. The presence of God will be as real to the lost as to the saved. Trying to run away from God is utterly futile. No wonder the French existentialist Jean-Paul Sartre admitted, "The last thing I want is to be subject to the unremitting gaze of a holy God."[36]

What, then, is the link between "fire" and God's presence in hell? The answer lies in something the Bible says about God's character. The Old Testament statement that "The Lord your God is a consuming fire, a jealous God" (Deuteronomy 4:24) is confirmed by a New Testament writer, who says that "Our God is a consuming fire" (Hebrews 12:29). Nor do we have to speculate about what God's "fire" means. One Old Testament prophet says, "His wrath is poured out like fire" (Nahum 1:6) and another likens it to "a refiner's fire" (Malachi 3:2). In line with this, God warns the Israelites to turn from their sin, "or my wrath will break out and burn like fire because of the evil you have done—burn with no one to quench it" (Jeremiah 4:4). These scriptures all point us to the fearful conclusion that the fire of hell is the indescribably and unrestrained wrath of God unleashed against sinners in exactly the way their sinfulness deserves and God's holiness demands.

Not only will "the pure in heart . . . see God" (Matthew 5:8), the impure will also see Him. The pure in heart will see him as their Savior; the impure will see Him as their jailer. The pure in heart will see Him in all His beauty; the impure will see Him in all His fury—and never be able to close their eyes.

The idea of God as a God of wrath has never been popular. One writer has said that the main reason people object to it is because (without realizing it) they substitute Greek philosophy for biblical revelation.[37] In Greek philosophy anger was thought to be a sign of weakness and wickedness, and the gods were believed to be above such things, totally unaffected by what was going on in human society. Today there are people who think of anger as something irrational or evil and therefore something which could never be attributed to God.

Others reject the wrath of God because they believe it is an out-of-date idea limited to the Old Testament: "The Old Testament God is a God of anger; the New Testament God is a God of love." But nothing could be further from the truth! The Old Testament does speak about God's wrath (nearly 600 times, using some twenty different Hebrew words) but so does the New Testament—and the New Testament's teaching is more terrible. In the Old Testament, God's wrath against sin is largely limited to temporal punishment, but in the New Testament, the emphasis shifts very strongly toward eternal punishment. In other words, most of the Bible's teaching about hell comes from the New Testament and, as we have already seen, the strongest teaching of all comes from the lips of Jesus.

Another reason for rejecting the idea of God's wrath is that it is directed against sin and sinners, and even the most hardened have at least an occasional stab of conscience which warns them that they are vulnerable. In J. I. Packer's phrase, "No man is entirely without inklings of judgment to come."[38] The comfortable thing to do when thoughts of eternal judgment begin to niggle is to push them into the background and get on with enjoying life.

But all of this reasoning must give way to biblical revelation, which says more about God's anger than it does about His love. Packer even goes so far as to say that because it contains so much on the subject, "The Bible could be called the book of God's wrath."[39] Editing Scripture to suit our own ideas is neither sensible nor honest. As an article in *Punch* put it, "You can't just have the bits of God you like and leave out the stuff you're not so happy with."[40]

Scripture reveals at least four aspects of God's anger that are particularly relevant here.

Firstly, it is *personal*. God's anger is not what some people have seen as the inevitable outworking of the law of cause and effect in a moral universe. Instead, it is something personal and measured. This comes across in a powerful way in those places in Scripture where we read, for example, that God is "slow to anger" but "abounding in love" (Psalm 103:8) and that He "does not willingly bring affliction" (Lamentations 3:33). These statements speak of God's feelings, not of some clockwork concept that He dispassionately set in motion, so that all who disobey His laws are left to "step in their own juice" while God remains totally unaffected. The Bible has many examples of God holding back His judgments and pleading with sinners to change their ways and avoid His wrath. God's anger is not a piece of moral mechanism. "It is, rather, a personal quality, without which God would cease to be fully righteous and his love would degenerate into sentimentality."[41]

Secondly, God's anger is *pure*. It is never to be confused with human anger, which is often bad-tempered, irrational, bitter, or "over the top." God never "loses His cool." His anger is never flawed by any of man's fallen characteristics. It is completely righteous and consistent, "the controlled and permanent opposition of God's holy nature to all sin."[42]

Thirdly, God's anger is *powerful*: "Who knows the power of your anger? For your wrath is as great as the fear that is due to you" (Psalm

90:11). Like all of God's characteristics, His anger is utterly beyond our understanding, and it is terrifying in its intensity.

Fourthly, it is *permanent*; it has been operating throughout human history. The Bible speaks of it in both the present and future tenses. It says, "The wrath of God is being revealed from heaven against all the godlessness and wickedness of men" (Romans 1:18), but it also warns of "the coming wrath" (Matthew 3:7), when God's anger will no longer be tempered with mercy but poured out in all its terrifying fullness. In one of the most fearful statements in Scripture (though using a different metaphor), we are told that the wicked "will drink of the wine of God's fury, which has been poured full strength into the cup of his wrath" (Revelation 14:10). Every phrase here is full of meaning. On earth, sinners have only the merest taste of God's anger, in hell, they will be forced to "drink" it. On earth, God's anger comes in dribbles; in hell, it will be "poured." On earth, God's anger is diluted with mercy and patience—David says that "He does not treat us as our sins deserve or repay us according to our iniquities" (Psalm 103:10); in hell, all that will change, and God's anger will be poured out "full strength," in all its uninhibited fury, something infinitely greater than anything that any human being has ever experienced or could possible imagine.

PULLING IT ALL TOGETHER

In the early part of chapter 9, we established the principle that in trying to describe the environment of hell and the experience of being there, it was vital to keep strictly to Scripture. We can now see that there is no need to do otherwise, either by decorating the Bible with imagination or distorting it by exaggeration. The facts speak for themselves, and do so with stunning power.

According to the Word of God, hell is a real place. It is God's rubbish dump, where wasted and unwanted humanity is thrown. It is a dark pit, a prison without companionship or comfort of any kind. In hell, the wicked are gnawed by the work of an accusing conscience, ashamed and contemptible. They will be banished from all good and deprived of every blessing that could have been theirs. They will be in indescribable torments and agony, wailing in frenzied anger. And they will be exposed to the awesome fire of God's holy and uninhibited anger.

It is utterly impossible to imagine anything worse.

Too Bad to be True?

Nobody can think seriously about hell and remain emotionally and psychologically unaffected. The idea that after a few years of life on earth an untold number of human beings, many of whom would be thought of as decent, law-abiding citizens, will be thrown away as worthless and spend eternity in indescribable agony and exposed to God's relentless anger is overwhelming. Nor do we need pagan lies or poetic license to make us feel overwhelmed: the plain teaching of Scripture, which we have tried to represent in the last two chapters, is quite sufficient.

People's reactions to the paralyzing prospect of everlasting punishment are varied but predictable. Some put reason before revelation and dismiss the whole idea of hell because they reject the authority of Scripture. Sir Arthur Conan Doyle is a good example: "Hell, I may say . . . has long dropped out of the thoughts of every reasonable man."[1] As we looked at the authority of Scripture in chapter 2, there is no need to spend any further time demolishing that position.

Others take the Bible as a general starting-point, but mix its teaching with their own religious or philosophical ideas. This is the typical approach of false cults and others. Christian Science (which treats the teachings of its founder Mrs. Mary Baker Eddy as superior to the Scriptures she claimed to interpret) declares that there is no such place as hell but that those who fail to reach perfection after death will in some way be self-annihilated. The so-called Jehovah's Witnesses teach that "The grave and physical death are the only hell."[2] Seventh-Day Adventists replace hell with annihilation. Mormonism has no equivalent to the biblical doctrine of hell, though it teaches that all non-

Mormons will experience some form of temporary damnation. Theosophy, a baffling brew of religious ideas, says that hell is "only a figment of the theological imagination."[3] Others could be quoted, but all are disqualified by their refusal to submit to the total authority of Scripture.

There are also those who would claim to base their beliefs on Scripture, but set it aside whenever its teaching produces any kind of theological, psychological, or emotional block to their way of thinking. The doctrines of original sin and the wrath of God are two prime targets on their "hit list"; the doctrine of hell is another. Nor do they beat about the bush in expressing their feelings. One of them wrote, "If the doctrine of eternal punishment was clearly and unmistakably taught in every leaf of the Bible, and on every leaf of all the Bibles of all the world, I could not believe a word of it."[4] Nels Ferre says that the doctrine of eternal punishment is "subjustice and sublove," and that by believing it, "God's name is libeled beyond belief."[5] David Edwards, the liberal Provost of Southwark, comes at it from another angle: "I would rather be an atheist than believe in a God who accepts it as inevitable that hell (however conceived) is the inescapable destiny of many, or of any of his children, even when they are prepared to accept 'all the blame.'"[6]

In the 1960s, John Robinson, the Bishop of Woolwich, suggested that the idea of hell was dead and buried: "There are some who would like to bring back hell, as some want to bring back birching and hanging. They are usually the same types who wish to purge Britain of horror comics, sex and violence."[7] Elsewhere he wrote, "In a universe of love, there can be no heaven which tolerates a chamber of horrors, no hell for any which does not at the same time make it hell for God. He cannot endure that . . . and he will not."[8]

But any approach to Scripture which picks and chooses which parts to believe is not only unbiblical and dishonest; it also leaves us without any assurance that God is speaking in any part of Scripture. If we reject the Bible's teaching about hell, how can we trust what it says about the love of God, the offer of forgiveness, or the hope of heaven?

SOFTENING THE BLOW?

Then what if we do take the Bible seriously and believe it to be "the living and enduring word of God" (1 Peter 1:23)? Must we accept all the horrific implications of the biblical statements we have examined in the last two chapters at face value, or is there some way in which we can submit to what Scripture says about the existence and nature of hell and yet somehow intepret this in a way that will soften its impact? Is it possible to reduce hell to manageable proportions and still remain faithful to Scripture?

Many sensitive Christians have wrestled with questions like these, and it is interesting to notice how some have expressed their turmoil. C.S. Lewis wrote, "There is no doctrine which I would more willingly remove from Christianity than this, if it lay . . . in my power. I would pay any price to be able to say truthfully, 'All will be saved.'"[9] In one of his books, the evangelical writer and preacher John Stott says that he approached the subject "with a heavy heart," that the thought of people being lost forever was "almost unbearable," and that people who could speak glibly about the subject showed "a horrible sickness of mind or spirit."[10] The British writer Paul Helm writes, "Hell is a dreadful topic, which anyone with any sensitivity naturally shrinks from thinking about."[11] John Wenham, another contemporary author, says that to read everything Jesus said about hell "is to receive an awesome and indelible impression which remains with one for life."[12]

These are honest and understandable reactions. Man is a great survivor and a stubborn optimist. Faced with what the Bible has to say about hell, the human mind instinctively starts looking for possible alternatives. In the next three chapters we shall examine the main ideas that have been put forward and see whether there is any ray of hope that the horrors of hell can be avoided or reduced.

A GOD OF LOVE?

One of the most persistent attempts to defuse hell is to say that even if such a place exists, it does so only as a warning, and that when the Bible speaks of human beings suffering eternal torment there, its language is purely hypothetical. The commonest way of expressing this is by asking, "How can a God of love send anyone to hell?" John Hick, one time professor of theology at Birmingham University, put the case like this: "For a conscious creature to undergo physical and mental torture through unending time . . . is horrible and disturbing beyond words and thought of such torment being deliberately inflicted by divine decree is totally incompatible with the idea of God as infinite love."[13] Clark Pinnock is just as blunt and says that "Everlasting torment is intolerable from a moral point of view because it makes God into a bloodthirsty monster who maintains an everlasting Auschwitz for victims who he does not even allow to die."[14] Superficially, this sounds perfectly reasonable: God is a God of love; sending someone to hell is not a loving thing to do; therefore God could never do it. The argument seems plausible and is very popular. How do we answer it?

To call God "a God of love" is undoubtedly biblical. Both Old and New Testament authors speak of God's love hundreds of times and in some of the most beautiful language in literature. Nor is the love of God a fluctuating emotion, but "apart and parcel of the very nature of God himself."[15] John expresses this in one of the greatest statements in Scripture: "God is love" (1 John 4:8). However, although "God is love" is the truth, it is not the only truth. The construction of John's words in the original language shows that "God is love" is not the same as saying, "Love is God." Love is an attribute of God, an integral part of His very essence, but it is not a definition of God. There is much more to God than love, and it is dangerous to argue against the likelihood of anyone going to hell by singling out one of God's attributes and assuming that in deciding people's eternal destinies this is the only one that comes into play.

It is even wrong to say that love is God's dominant characteristic. The attribute of God that stands out more than any other in Scripture is not his love but his holiness. Alec Motyer has pointed out that God's name is called His "holy name" more often than all other descriptions taken together.[16] In the Hebrew language, emphasis is sometimes given to a quality by repeating the word used to define it, but there is only one place in Scripture where the formula is used to repeat the word twice. This is when the prophet Isaiah sees a vision of heaven in which angelic beings cry out, "Holy, holy, holy is the Lord Almighty; the whole earth is full of his glory" (Isaiah 6:3). The Bible reveals many other attributes of God, but it is important at this point to concentrate on His holiness because it presupposes His settled aversion to sin. Notice Isaiah's immediate reaction to his vision of God's holiness: "'Woe to me!' I cried. 'I am ruined! For I am a man of unclean lips, and I live among a people of unclean lips'" (Isaiah 6:5). Isaiah knew that a holy God could not tolerate sin in any way, shape, or form. Another prophet acknowledged this by crying out to

God, "Your eyes are too pure to look on evil; you cannot tolerate wrong" (Habakkuk 1:13).

The same truth came across when the Israelite leader Joshua addressed his people at a mass rally just before his death: "You are not able to serve the Lord. He is a holy God; he is a jealous God. He will not forgive your rebellion and your sins. If you forsake the Lord and serve foreign gods, he will turn and bring disaster on you . . ." (Joshua 24:19-20).

This is the consistent biblical position. In His perfect holiness, God is utterly intolerant of sin. Anything that falls short of His own perfection is an abomination to Him. In today's permissive society, when sin is trivialized to the point where almost any kind of behavior is swept under the carpet, this is strong language, but as one writer shrewdly comments, "All caricatures of God which ignore his intense hatred for sin reveal more about man than about God."[17] When we understand God's holy hatred of sin, perhaps the more relevant question is not "How can a God of love send anyone to hell?" but "How can a God of holiness allow anyone in heaven?"

How then do we reconcile the amazing love of God with His awesome holiness? Is God schizophrenic? Is He a Jekyll and Hyde, switching irrationally and moodily between two modes of behavior? Not at all; and questions like these show that God can never be grasped by feeble human logic. We must settle for the facts as we have them. God is both loving and holy, and He always acts in character. This means, in the first place, that "He can only love in ways that are suitable to the kind of person he is," and that "There is a moral strictness about the love of God."[18] It also means that He cannot tolerate sin. As the contemporary American scholar Larry Dixon puts it, "If his nature is allergic to sin, one of the things which God cannot do is to act contrary to his nature."[19] Yet a God of love still condemns people to eternal torment. How is this possible? One very popular solution is to say that "God hates sin but loves the sinner." This neatly lets sinners off the hook by allowing them to escape eternal punishment for their sins and avoids the need to think of God as having a split personality. It seems to be the perfect solution to the problem; but is it?

GOD'S HOLY HATRED

While writing this chapter, I have tracked down thirty-three places in the Bible where God's hatred is expressed. In twelve, He is said to have sinners' actions (such as robbery, idolatry, formal religion, dishonesty, and divorce), but in the other twenty-one He is said to hate the sinner.

For example, He warns His people about absorbing the lifestyles of the surrounding heathen nations: "You must not live according to the customs of the nations I am going to drive out before you. Because they did all these things I abhorred them" (Leviticus 20:23). The word translated "abhorred" has the meaning of loathing.[20]

One of the fullest expressions of the truth we are examining is where David writes,

> "You are not a God who takes pleasure in evil;
> with you the wicked cannot dwell.
> The arrogant cannot stand in your presence;
> you hate all who do wrong.
> You destroy those who tell lies;
> bloodthirsty and deceitful men
> the Lord abhors"
> (Psalm 5:4-6).

In this instance, the word translated "abhors" is exceptionally strong and has links with the noun "abomination."[21]

David also says, "The Lord examines the righteous, but the wicked and those who love violence his soul hates" (Psalm 11:5). That last phrase could hardly be more emphatic. God hates the sinner with every fiber of his being. So much for "God hates sin but loves the sinner!"

God certainly loves all people in the sense that He gives them all the benefits of common grace, regardless of whether they in turn love Him or hate Him. As Jesus said, "He causes his sun to rise on the evil and the good, and sends rain on the righteous and the unrighteous" (Matthew 5:45). But we dare not confuse this with the love that opens sinners' eyes to see their desperate spiritual condition, draws them to repentance and faith, and grants them the forgiveness of sins and eternal life. Sustaining love is not saving love. When God said, "I have loved you with an everlasting love; I have drawn you with loving-kindness" (Jeremiah 31:3), He was not addressing the whole of humanity. When John wrote, "How great is the love the Father has lavished on us, that we should be called children of God!" he was obviously not including everyone in the world, because in the next breath he says that "The world does not know us" (1 John 3:1).

When the "Jesus people" were making headlines in California and elsewhere in the 1970s, many of them wore large badges proclaiming, "Smile! God loves you!" But surely that kind of thing is misleading? It can give the impression that God is perfectly happy with the lifestyle of anyone who reads the slogan and that He gives His smiling approval to everything they are doing. Yet this is not the case. A friend of mine rightly said it would have been more accurate to have had badges saying, "Frown! You're under judgment." The Bible's verdict on the human race is blunt and uncompromising:

"All have turned aside,
they have together become corrupt;
there is no one who does good,
not even one"
(Psalm 14:3).

As God hates all sin and all sinners, as He is not only holy but just, and as the Bible warns us that He "will not leave the guilty unpunished" (Nahum 1:3), how can anyone blithely assume that "God is love" will see them safe? Those who imagine that they can live as they please because God is love, and are banking on God's love to guarantee that they will never go to hell, are making a terrible and tragic mistake.

It is easy to understand why many people reject the idea of God's holy justice and run for shelter under the umbrella of "God is love." An Australian doctor, John Hercus, once put it like this: "The truth is that men never really have any problem, never any real problem, in understanding the strong, awesome judgment of God. They may complain about it, but they have no difficulty at all in understanding the ruthless judgment that declares that black is black because only the purest white is white. True, we hear from ignorant pagans and even from highly-trained theologians the ignorant prattle from right, left and center, about 'All this hell-fire and brimstone talk isn't my idea of God. I think God is a God of love and I don't think he'd hurt a fly!' But it is easy to know why they talk like that; it's because they are terrified of the alternative!"[22]

Hercus is right, but fear, prejudice, and logic must give way to Scripture, which teaches that God, who is both loving and holy, does punish sin in hell. His holiness requires that He does. If He failed to demand holiness and to punish sin, He would cease to be God. This means, as Paul Helm puts it, that "Hell is a place of justice, where punishment is dispensed not in accordance with the warped and partial and ignorant procedures of human society, but immaculately, in accord with the standards of him who is supremely just."[23]

Two brief comments may help as we come to the end of this section. In his fine little book *How can a God of love send people to Hell?* John Benton makes the point that this is not the right question to ask, because it subtly distorts what the Bible teaches. The word "people" is neutral, and gives the impression that God faces a neutral situation and then makes an arbitrary decision to send some people to the excruciating agony of hell. But the starting position is not neutral. Man has rebelled against God's authority. He has become a sinner, and in doing so has aroused God's righteous anger. It is therefore wrong to use neutral terms because, as Benton says, "God does not send people to hell; he sends sinners to hell."[24]

The second comment is to underline God's consistency in everything He does. God is a God of love and demonstrates His love to mankind in countless ways; but He is also a God of holiness, which He expresses in His righteous anger against sin. However, while the Bible says, "God is love" it does not say, "God is hate" or "God is anger." Instead, it teaches that God responds in holy hatred and righteous anger only when people reject His amazing and undeserved love, and even then tempers His response with patience, mercy, and grace for as long as He determines.

I realize that these notes leave a host of other unanswered questions, but Scripture does not give us all the answers we would like to have. There comes a point at which we have to yield before God's sovereign wisdom and cry out with Paul, "Oh, the depth of the riches of the wisdom and knowledge of God! How unsearchable his judgments, and his paths beyond tracing out!" (Romans 11:33). Doing this may bruise some people's egos, but it will not affect their sanity! At this point we will settle for the fact that there is no protection from God's righteous wrath on the other side of the grave for those who reject His amazing love on this side of it. As one writer puts it, "There is no meaningful way to say that God loves the wicked after death."[25]

BASIS OF JUDGMENT

Another approach says that "If people will be condemned only for their rejection of the Savior, then they will have to be given an opportunity, some time, to accept or reject him."[26] In this case, the entire premise is wrong, because it totally misunderstands the theology of judgment. The unevangelized are condemned, not for failing to avail themselves of a Savior of whom they never heard, but for sin, for failing to live up to the light which God gave to them outside of Scripture. This point was made in chapter 8, when we considered the basis on which mankind will be judged, but it is equally relevant here.

Even if this were not the case, this approach has another disturbing element, which can be put in the form of a question. Why would these people "have to be given an opportunity"? Is this something they will have deserved, or something God has promised? Or is it no more than pious hope married to philosophical speculation? The silence of Scripture is significant.

The idea that unrepentant sinners will have to be given an opportunity to get right with God after death, far from underlining the grace of God, undermines everything the Bible says about it. As Larry Dixon rightly observes, "To suggest that God had to provide salvation or that it must extend to all is not only not justified biblically, but turns his grace into debt and his mercy into duty."[27] God owes the unevangelized nothing, nor is He bound by anything He has said in Scripture to give rebellious sinners any post-mortem opportunity to change their minds. When the American theologian Donald Bloesch says, "We do not preclude the possibility that some in hell may yet finally be translated into heaven,"[28] he can hardly be including the Bible's authors in the "we," because none of them provides a basis for any such possibility. In the parable of the rich man and Lazarus, the former was told that between Hades and Paradise "A great chasm has been fixed, so that those who want to go from here to you cannot, nor can anyone cross over from there to us" (Luke 16:26). On another occasion, Jesus illustrated the urgency of repentance while here on earth by saying that there would come a time when "The owner of the house gets up and closes the door" (Luke 13:25). This clearly shows that there are what Dixon calls "God-revealed limits to his grace."[29] The whole thrust of Scripture is in the same direction: human destiny is sealed and settled at death.

A LARGER HOPE?

From time to time, influential communicators have put forward the idea that sinners who fail to get right with God in this life will have a second chance in the next. Alfred Lord Tennyson, who was appointed

Poet Laureat in 1859, wrote a poem entitled "In Memoriam," which included the following lines:

> *I stretch lame hands of faith, and grope*
> *And gather dust and chaff, and call*
> *To what I feel is Lord of all,*
> *And faintly trust the larger hope.*[30]

His phrase "the larger hope" became a rallying-point for many people, but one only has to read the whole piece to see that it has no biblical basis. Tennyson speaks of a "larger hope". The Bible says that when the wicked man dies "his hope perishes" (Proverbs 11:7). When the wish of man comes into conflict with the Word of God, no sensible person ought to have difficulty in deciding which is right.

In 1877, F. W. Farrar preached a series of five sermons in Westminster Abbey in which he denounced several popular views of the fate of the wicked and rejected as "a hideous incubus of atrocious conceptions"[31] the teaching that they would suffer every-lasting punishment. He went on to declare, "I say unhesitatingly—I say—claiming the fullest right to speak with the authority of knowledge—that not one of the words 'damnation,' 'hell,' 'everlasting' ought to stand any longer in our English Bibles,"[32] and claimed that texts including these words were "alien to the broad, unifying principles of Scripture."[33] In one particular sermon, he said that the belief "that good shall fall at last . . . to all does indeed derive much support from many passages of Scripture"—none of which seemed to be at hand—and told his hearers that if there were any of them striving to "creep nearer to the light" then there was hope for them "even if death overtake you before the final victory is won."[34]

Because of his position in the church (he was Canon of Westminster), Farrar's series attracted a great deal of media attention, and the sermons were published a year later under the title *The Eternal Hope.* Yet his ideas owed more to sentimental feeling than to scriptural fact, even when he had remodeled them for another book, *Mercy and Judgement,* published in 1881, and they were conclusively answered by scholars of his day. One said that in Farrar's call for the "hell" words to be removed from Scripture, "There is neither textual truth, nor accurate scholarship, nor reverence for God's Word, nor the humility nor the sacred fear either of a true teacher or learner."[35] In the light of God's Word, this verdict is not an exaggeration.

Others have put forward the idea of a "larger hope" on the basis of seeing hell as a kind of "finishing school" where sinners finally graduate to heaven. Nels Ferre says, "Beyond earthly life lies the larger school where we are expected to mature according to new conditions."[36] Elsewhere, he suggests that God will "put on the screws tighter and tighter until we come to ourselves and are willing to consider the good which he has prepared for us."[37] These ideas are understandably attractive; what they lack is any kind of biblical basis.

PREACHING IN PRISON

Some who speak of a "larger hope" or a "second chance" lean on one particular statement in Scripture: "For Christ . . . died for sins once for all, the just for the unjust, in order that he might bring us to God, having been put to death in the flesh, but made alive in the spirit; in which also he went and made proclamation to the spirits now in prison, who once were disobedient, when the patience of God kept waiting in the days of Noah, during the construction of the ark, in which a few, that is, eight persons, were brought safely through the water" (1 Peter 3:18-20, NASB).

This has proved a highly controversial passage, but nobody should seriously question its place in Scripture. The British preacher David Pawson has suggested that Peter may have got his information direct from Jesus when they met on the first Easter Day, and Peter's curiosity led him to ask Jesus what He had been doing during the previous seventy-two hours.[38] Be that as it may, the passage is clearly recording fact, not fiction; but what does it mean?

One writer says that Jesus went into this "prison" as a Savior to those "who still stretched out to him the hand of faith" and adds that "The preaching of Christ begun in the realms of departed spirits is continued there . . . so that those who . . . on earth did not hear at all, or not in the right way, the good news of salvation through Jesus Christ, shall hear it there."[39] Others say it shows that "Death is the occasion when the unevangelized have an opportunity to make a decision about Jesus Christ."[40] The influential liberal theologian William Barclay had no doubt that the passage contains "a breath-taking glimpse of nothing less than the gospel of a second chance."[41]

If this line of thinking is right, there is clearly more than a glimmer of hope here for those who die unrepentant and unforgiven; but is it right? We can begin to find out by putting down one clear marker, the Bible's consistent thrust that the opportunity for salvation ends at death. As the Word of God never contradicts itself, this passage must never be interpreted in a way that will overturn that principle.

Coming to the text itself, the first thing to notice is that there is no suggestion that Jesus is continuing what we might call His "prison ministry." To say that He preached in the "prison" is very different from saying that He is still preaching, or that He will do so at some time in the future. The literal translation of the relevant phrase speaks of Christ "having been made alive in the spirit, in which also to the spirits in prison having gone he did preach."[42] Far from suggesting an ongoing ministry, the words "having gone" point to the prison preaching being over before His physical resurrection but when He was already "able to move freely in the spirit world as the victorious Man."[43]

Secondly, Peter tells us that Jesus preached "to the spirits now in prison." Some people jump to the conclusion that this must mean human spirits in Hades awaiting resurrection to judgment, but this almost certainly is not the case. Nowhere in Scripture is Peter's word for spirits—*pneumata*—used alone and unqualified to describe human spirits in Hades. Unless this passage is an exception to this rule, Jesus preached not to human sinners but to fallen angels. Their sins are specifically mentioned in Genesis 6, which majors on the story of Noah, and when Peter mentions Noah in his second letter, he refers to God punishing these sinning spirits by '"putting them into gloomy dungeons to be held for judgment" (2 Peter 2:4).

This second point seems to be confirmed by the fact that when telling us what Jesus did on His prison visit Peter does not use the distinctive Greek word for preaching the gospel (*evangelizo*, from which we get "evangelize") but *kerusso*, which is more general and means "to make a proclamation . . . without any reference to the contents."[44] This suggests that Jesus preached not to departed human spirits but to fallen angels and that, as far as they were concerned, what He preached was not good news but exactly the opposite. It was an official proclamation of His triumph over evil, a declaration that He had struck the decisive blow against all His enemies (them included) and was on His way to His triumphant coronation. However inadequate the analogy, it might help us to thing in terms of a champion athlete doing a lap of honor prior to receiving his trophy.

Then how can people come to William Barclay's conclusion that Peter's words give "a breath-taking glimpse of nothing less than the gospel of a second chance"? Only by putting their imagination in overdrive! While writing this book, I have been rereading *Pursuit*, Ludovic Kennedy's fascinating account of the sinking of the German battleship *Bismark* at a crucial stage of World War II. *Bismark* was the German navy's pride and joy: a sixth of a mile long and displacing 42,000 tons, there had never been a warship like her, and she posed a fearful menace to Allied shipping in the Atlantic and elsewhere. Her counterpart in the British Navy was HMS *Hood*, but when they met on May 24, 1941, the British ship was destroyed in just twenty-one minutes, with the loss of over 1,500 men. Now came a desperate attempt to find *Bismark* and avenge this terrible loss, but a combination of bad weather and other factors frustrated all their efforts. They were on the point of giving up when a flight of Swordfish aircraft picked up a warship on their recently acquired radar. They immediately dived into the attack, but none of their torpedoes hit. This was just as well, because the ship they attached was not the *Bismark* but HMS *Sheffield*, which all but three of the pilots failed to recognize! Commenting on this, Kennedy wrote, "That they hadn't recognized Sheffield earlier is a proof of the power of suggestion . . . Expecting to see Bismark, Bismark was what they saw."[45]

The analogy may not be perfect, but it has some of the same elements. Those who come to Scripture wanting to find a "second chance" are keen to pounce on the first indication that they have found it. Claiming to have done so in 1 Peter 3:18-20 is a classic case of seeing what they want to see, rather than seeing what is actually there. As J. I. Packer comments, "Some have based on this one text a hope that all humans who did not hear the gospel in this life, or who having heard it rejected it, will have it savingly preached to them in the life to come, but Peter's words do not provide the least warrant for the inference."[46]

THE VIEW FROM HEAVEN

One particularly emotive argument brought against the doctrine of the everlasting punishment of the wicked asks how it would be possible for believers to be happy in heaven if they knew of any human beings, especially members of their own families, who were suffering in hell. Nels Ferre says, "If eternal hell is real, love is eternally frustrated and heaven is a place of mourning and concern for the lost. Such joy and grief cannot go together . . . heaven can be heaven only when it has emptied hell, as surely as love is love and God is God."[47]

How do we respond to this? We could take several long chapters (or large volumes) to mull over a wagonload of philosophical and theological issues, but that might leave us no further ahead. Instead, as on every issue we are considering in this book, we need to settle for the scriptural facts. The first is that *the wicked will suffer in hell*, in all the ways we have discovered in previous chapters; the second is that *the righteous will be absolutely happy in heaven*. My use of the word "absolutely" is deliberate. Not only are we told that there will be endless praise and worship in God's presence but that "He will wipe every tear from their eyes" (Revelation 21:4). That statement could not be more specific. When the believer draws his last breath, he will have shed his last tear. C. H. Spurgeon used to say that the believer's resurrection body would not have any tear glands because they would not be necessary! Whatever we may think of Spurgeon's physiology here, his theology is flawless.

What then of the premise behind the problem? To glance at the other side of the picture for a moment, a warning Jesus gave to the wicked makes it clear that those in hell will know of the happiness of those in heaven: "There will be weeping there, and gnashing of teeth, when you see Abraham, Isaac and Jacob and all the prophets in the kingdom of God, but you yourselves thrown out" (Luke 13:28). Knowing that others are saved while they themselves are lost will exacerbate the anger and the agony of the wicked in hell.

As to believers in heaven, we need first to examine the premise: will they know anything about unbelievers in hell? Some have found a clue in the Old Testament, where God tells Isaiah of a time when believers will "look upon the dead bodies of those who rebelled against me; their worm will not die, nor will their fire be quenched, and they will be loathsome to all mankind" (Isaiah 66:24). Jesus would seem to have had this passage in mind when He spoke of hell as a place where "their worm does not die, and the fire is not quenched" (Mark 9:48), and in one modern writer's opinion, "Isaiah's words are surely meaningless if they do not teach that in heaven the redeemed will be able to see the damned in their torments."[48] He may be right, though there are students of Scripture who suggest that to apply Isaiah's words in this way may be going too far.

Another clue may be found at one point in John's vision of the future life. When Babylon is cast down to destruction, the command is given: "Rejoice over her, O heaven! Rejoice, saints and apostles and prophets! God has judged her for the way she treated you"

(Revelation 18:20). There might seem support here for the idea that the righteous will rejoice over the suffering of the wicked, but before jumping to that conclusion we need to bear two points in mind. The first is that the primary meaning of "Babylon" was the ruthless Roman Empire that had persecuted the early Christian church with savage brutality. The second is that those invited to rejoice are the victims of that particular persecution. Even if we feel there is a general principle there (and there are places in Scripture where Babylon represents all godless power) the most we could say would be that the feelings of the righteous at the overthrow of all opposition to God are such as we might experience at the collapse of an evil regime such as Nazism or Soviet Communism. As has been rightly said, "We have no right to assume that they reflect the way believers will react when they see individuals they have loved and cherished come under the condemnation of God."[49]

This brings us back to the question of how the joy of the righteous will be unaffected if they know of the agonies of the wicked. "If" may be the key word. Among the marvelous gospel promises God makes to His people are these:

> "I will be their God
> and they will be my people . . .
> I will forgive their wickedness
> and will remember their sins no more"
> (Jeremiah 31:34).

These promises will obviously find their eternal fulfillment in heaven, and it is significant that John's vision in Revelation echoes some of Jeremiah's words: "They will be [God's] people, and God himself will be with them and be their God" (Revelation 21:3). The second part of the promise recorded by Jeremiah tells us that the God whose memory is infallible will infallibly forget. If we can dare to use such language, God will have a mental block as far as the sins of His people are concerned.

What is more, so will they, or they could not be perfectly happy. In a parable Jesus told to illustrate the kingdom of heaven, the faithful servants are welcomed with the words: "Come and share your master's happiness" (Matthew 25:21, 23). There may well be more to this than meets the eye: the servants' joy was to be the same as their master's; it was his happiness they were invited to share. So in heaven the believer's joy will be God's joy. They will be totally identified with

God, knowing what He knows, loving what He loves, rejoicing as He rejoices—and forgetting what He forgets! None of the sins believers had committed, either before or after their conversion, will ever cross their minds. There will be no endless remorse, regrets, or sorrow. Believers in heaven will be "conformed to the likeness of [God's] Son" (Romans 8:29). They will rejoice in everything God is and in everything God does. As the nineteenth-century Scottish minister Robert Murray M'Cheyne put it, "The redeemed will have no mind but God's. They will have no joy but what the Lord has."⁵⁰

This much we know, but even this fails to clinch the point as to whether believers in heaven will be able to see sinners in hell, let alone whether they will be unmoved by what they see. Whatever the answers to those questions, we can be quite sure that the joy of the righteous in heaven will not be marred either by boasting (because they will be there entirely by the grace of God), nor by any adverse effect of knowing that the wicked are in hell (which is where they themselves would be but for that grace).

To return to the certainties we established at the beginning of this section, the wicked will suffer in hell, and the righteous will be absolutely happy in heaven. If this leaves us with unanswered questions, we have no option but to wait until we discover the answers in the world to come. To reject one or the other of the biblical certainties because we can find no way of fitting both into our logic is a mark not of intelligence but of unbelief.

THE PUNISHMENT AND THE CRIME

Another possible moderation of the horror of hell can be approached like this: as God is a God of justice, will some people's punishment be less than others? Are there degrees of punishment in God's judgment of sinners? Even with our own imperfect ideas of justice, this is certainly what we would expect. Not all crimes deserve the same punishment. Killing your neighbor's dog is not as serious as killing his wife, nor is illegal parking as serious as robbing a bank; a court that handed down identical penalties for all four crimes would be acting perversely. As God is "the righteous Judge" (2 Timothy 4:8) we should expect to find His punishment of sinners to be directly related to their sin—and we do.

When Jesus sent His twelve disciples on a preaching mission, He warned them that they would face great opposition and then added,

"If anyone will not welcome you or listen to your words, shake the dust off your feet when you leave that home or town. I tell you the truth, it will be more bearable for Sodom and Gomorrah on the day of judgment than for that town" (Matthew 10:14-15). Apart from making the point about degrees of punishment, Jesus also made it clear that rejection of the gospel is more serious than the sexual immorality which characterized Sodom and Gomorrah. Social morality will not lessen the impact of God's judgment.

Jesus said a similar thing when speaking of people who remained unrepentant even though living in towns where He had performed most of His miracles: "Woe to you, Korazin! Woe to you, Bethsaida! If the miracles that were performed in you had been performed in Tyre and Sidon, they would have repented long ago in sackcloth and ashes. But I tell you, it will be more bearable for Tyre and Sidon on the day of judgment than for you. And you, Capernaum, will you be lifted up to the skies? No, you will go down to the depths. If the miracles that were performed in you had been performed in Sodom, it would have remained to this day. But I tell you that it will be more tolerable for Sodom on the day of judgment than for you" (Matthew 11:21-24). Here again, there will be differences in the degrees of punishment inflicted on the day of judgment, and those who remain unrepentant after hearing the gospel and seeing the power of God at work will be dealt with more severely. Larry Dixon makes a significant point here: "Capernaum was Jesus' headquarters on the north shore of Galilee. Its townspeople could see and hear Jesus almost any time they wished. But they didn't bother."[51]

On another occasion Jesus told a parable about a manager put in charge of his master's servants, and then applied it to the stewardship of life: "That servant who knows his master's will and does not get ready or does not do what his master wants will be beaten with many blows. But the one who does not know and does things deserving punishment will be beaten with few blows. From everyone who has been given much, much will be demanded; and from the one who has been entrusted with much, much more will be asked" (Luke 12:47-48). Once again the lesson is clear: the greater our privileges, the greater our responsibilities—and the greater our guilt if we neglect them. The person who heard the gospel and rejected it will be more heavily punished than the person who never heard it. An unrepentant sinner brought up in a Christian home will be in a worse position than someone who never had that privilege. J.C. Ryle was right to warn that "The saddest road to hell is that which runs under the pulpit, past the Bible and through the midst of warnings and invitations."

Jesus also pointed to degrees of punishment when criticizing some of the religious leaders of His day: "Watch out for the teachers of the law. They like to walk around in flowing robes and be greeted in the market-places, and have the most important seats in the synagogues and the places of honor at banquets. They devour widows' houses and for a show make lengthy prayers. Such men will be punished most severely" (Mark 12:38-40). These men were guilty of hypocrisy, pride, greed, dishonesty, and extortion, all of which would add to the severity of their sentence on the Day of Judgment.

God's meticulous justice in measuring punishment to the wicked also comes across in John's vision of the judgment of "Babylon," a term used partially to symbolize "the world with all its seduction and charms":[52] "Pay her back even as she has paid . . . To the degree that she glorified herself and lived sensuously, to the same degree give her torment and mourning" (Revelation 18:6-7, NASB). Here is a clear example of the degree of punishment being in direct proportion to the sin that had been committed. There is no doubt that there will be degrees of punishment in hell, but we have only to pull some other facts together to see that this provides no comfort whatever.

Firstly, hell is a place of justice, where sinners will be punished in the light of God's perfect standards: "We can have an absolute confidence that God, the righteous judge, will take absolutely everything into account . . . Not one soul will be in hell who does not deserve to be; and no one's hell will be darker or deeper than is right."[53]

Secondly, although not everyone will suffer to the same degree, none will suffer to a small degree. God's justice will ensure that the punishment fits the crime, but everyone in hell will be a moral and spiritual criminal, and every sin they committed will be treated as a massive offense against the majesty and authority of their Creator. The intensity of the punishment will increase with the gravity of the offense, but there is no such thing as a small offense. There are no "little sins" because there is no little God to sin against. There will be no cool spots in hell, no shade from the heat of God's holy anger.

Thirdly, those hoping they might be able to get away with a lesser degree of punishment because of their own religious or moral efforts are making the terrible mistake of failing to realize that every day they live is adding to their punishment, not reducing it. As Jonathan Edwards put it, "The longer sinners live, the more wrath they accumulate."[54] This must be the case, because every day adds to the aggregate of sins they have committed. To quote Edwards again, "They may alter their business in some respects; they may sometimes be about one thing and sometimes another; but they never change from this work . . . This is the first thing they set themselves about when they awake in the morning, and the last thing they do at night."[55] Sinners in hell would give anything to turn the clock back and have committed even one sin less.

This may be what Jesus meant when He said that "If anyone causes one of these little ones who believe in me to sin, it would be better for him to be thrown into the sea with a large millstone tied around his neck" (Mark 9:42). To lead an impressionable young Christian astray, either by example or direct suggestion, is a very serious sin which will add greatly to the sinner's punishment. It would therefore have been better for the sinner to have drowned there and then, rather than to have committed that particular sin. If a sinner is to remain unconverted, the sooner he dies the better, otherwise every further sin he commits will make things that much worse for him in eternity. This is exactly the point Paul makes when he warns the sinner that "Because of your stubbornness and your unrepentant heart, you are storing up wrath against yourself for the day of God's wrath, when his righteous judgment will be revealed" (Romans 2:5).

These are terrifying words. Every day the sinner lives, every selfish penny he makes, every unholy pleasure he enjoys, every ungrateful breath he takes, are storing up God's anger against him. When God allows the sinner to prosper, He is not making things better for him, but worse. Newspapers recently carried the story of a man in his early forties who had just bought a house that cost 6,000,000 pounds earned from pornography. This might seem a sign of success, but unless that man gets right with God every penny of his filthy lucre will count against him on the Day of Judgment and plunge him deeper into hell. Millionaires are few, but the same principle applies to paupers and to everyone in between. Even to take breath refusing to recognize that it comes from God is to add to the sinner's punishment. All his godless enjoyment of possessions and pastimes, food, sport, music, art, friendship, and the rest will turn to ashes and increase the severity of his sentence. Even the time spent arguing the case for a lighter sentence, or trying to bring it about by better behavior, will produce exactly the opposite effect. Every moment sinners spend talk-

ing about greater or lesser degrees of punishment will guarantee that
their punishment will be greater, not less.

CHANGE FOR THE BETTER?

Another issue can be dealt with more briefly. Is there any possibility
that the sinner will be able to improve his circumstances in hell? Will
he be able to do anything to lessen the pain, relieve the pressure, move
to a better position or "take the heat off"? When preaching in an
open-sided building on a camp in Hang Nam, in central Thailand, I
was told that during the hot season a water sprinkler deployed on the
roof could sometimes lower the temperature by two degrees Celsius;
very little, but at least it provided some relief. Can anything be done
in hell that will produce a change for the better? There are at least five
reasons why the answer to that question must be in the negative.

Firstly, there is not a single word in the Bible which gives any hope
that the sinner's punishment in hell will ever be moderated in any way.

Secondly, those serving prison sentences are sometimes given
improved conditions or granted special privileges as a reward for
good behavior. These advantages are earned, but there is no good
behavior in hell, because the sinner's moral compass is locked into
position at the moment of his death. The Bible speaks of death as
being like a tree uprooted by a storm and says, "In the place where it
falls, there will it lie" (Ecclesiastes 11:3). Nobody's character changes
after death, whatever happens between then and the Day of
Judgment. In hell, the ungodly will have no inclination to be anything
else. The idea that there may be "remedial discipline and growth in
the unseen world" [56] owes everything to speculation and nothing to
revelation.

Thirdly, any moral change a person makes is the result of being
influenced or encouraged to make such a change, but as we saw in an
earlier chapter, there will be no such influences or encouragements in
hell, no promises or incentives to do anything that is right or good.
Nothing whatever in either his company or his own constitution will
be inclined in that direction.

Fourthly, hell is not a place of probation but punishment. It is
where sinners are sent not to learn a lesson but to pay a price. In our
culture, penalties such as imprisonment are thought of largely in terms
of their likely benefit to the criminal or to society. Punishment is seen
as a tool of social engineering, a device to bring good out of evil. The

Bible nowhere teaches that hell is meant to serve this kind of purpose. Instead, it says that hell is ordained by a just and holy God as the proper punishment for rebellion against His authority. Nowhere does it tell us that hell has any other purpose than to demonstrate the perfect justice of a holy God who "cannot tolerate wrong" (Habakkuk 1:13).

Fifthly, as hell is punishment due to the sinner "for the things done while in the body" (2 Corinthians 5:10)—that is to say, while living here on earth—nothing done after death can change the punishment. Whatever the intensity of the sinner's punishment in hell, it will be in accordance with the immaculate judgment of a God who knows the precise nature of every sin, all the circumstances in which it was committed, and exactly what punishment is deserved. Those condemned to spend eternity in hell will have no cause for complaint. Instead, they will identify with David's confession when he cried out to God,

> "Against you, you only, have I sinned
> and done what is evil in your sight,
> so that you are proved right when you speak
> and justified when you judge'
> (Psalm 51:4);

though they will not share David's longing for purity of heart. Their cry will be a desolating admission of guilt, unrelieved by any hope of forgiveness.

LONGFORD'S LAPSES

In this chapter we have looked at some of the ideas put forward in reaction to the Bible's terrifying teaching about the reality and horror of hell. One other reaction—much less ingenious and much more "comfortable"—is simply to turn a blind eye to those parts of Scripture which make the strongest statements on the subject. When the *Sunday Telegraph* asked the well-known social reformer Lord Longford for his views on hell, he replied, "Hell? I don't think that's compatible with a loving God. . . . I read the gospels every day. I have done so for forty years. But I'm a selective reader of the gospels. There's a gospel which mentions the eternal darkness; I don't read that one."[57] As the Gospel concerned is by Matthew, and is the only one which records the Sermon on the Mount, this is an unfortunate omission.

More to the point, a blinkered approach to Scripture (in effect, editing what God is saying) is neither wise nor honest. Nor is reading into Scripture something that is not there. At another point in the interview, Lord Longford, a staunch Roman Catholic, said, "Though I believe in the infinite mercy of God, I also believe very strongly in purgatory. . . . I can't imagine arriving in heaven straight away, so to speak."[58] Yet, as we saw in chapter 6, purgatory is a purely human invention and has not a shred of biblical evidence in its favor. Believing something which is absent from Scripture is no better than ignoring something that is present. Neither is the right approach. Scripture must be taken as it stands.

As far as the destiny of the wicked is concerned, it does not say that hell is "too bad to be true," but that it is both unimaginably bad and undeniably true.

"... Happily Ever After?"

W e must now consider two widely held theories which appear to soften the impact of biblical teaching on hell while claiming Scripture as their basis. The first is universalism, which is particularly popular in the liberal wing of the church; the second is annihilationism (sometimes called conditional immortality) which is currently enjoying a revival among evangelical Christians and which we will examine in chapters 13 and 14.

The *Concise Oxford Dictionary* defines a universalist as "one who holds . . . that all mankind will eventually be saved,"[1] but this hides the fact that there are two basic kinds of universalism. In its simplest form, it claims that everyone goes to heaven immediately after death, regardless of what they have believed or how they have behaved; regardless, even, of whether they were religious or irreligious. R.C. Sproul summarizes this position: "A prevailing notion is that all we have to do to enter the kingdom of God is to die. God is viewed as being so 'loving' that he really doesn't care too much if we don't keep his law. The law is there to guide us, but if we stumble and fall, our celestial grandfather will merely wink and say, 'Boys will be boys.'"[2]

When Barbara Cartland, author of 500 books and still turning out 26 novels a year at the age of eighty-nine, was interviewed for the *Sunday Telegraph*, she was asked whether she was afraid of dying. "Not a bid," she replied. "It will either be better than this life, or nothing at all, in which case there is no point in being frightened."[3] She was obviously backing both horses, universalism and annihilationism and, as far as the first was concerned, had no doubt that it would be "better than this life." In her opinion, judgment and punishment are out of the question.

The second illustration concerns the late Henry Longhurst, the well-known golf journalist and broadcaster. In July 1978, when he was confined to his home in England in the last stages of terminal cancer, his fellow commentator Peter Alliss telephoned him from Hawaii. Longhurst told him, "I'm very near the end now. I've never been a very religious man, but I know you and I will meet again, many years from now, in another place. The one good thing about me going first is that at least it will afford me the opportunity of finding the sponsor's hospitality room."[4] Here is universalism at its simplest. No religion is necessary; all one has to do is die, and rather than punishment for anybody there will be prize giving for everybody. This uncomplicated form of universalism is broadly based on three philosophies: God is so loving that there is no way in which He could inflict any punishment on one of His creatures after death, let alone send them to hell; sin is not serious enough to warrant anything more than the bumps and bruises we get here on earth; and if there is such a thing as final judgment, God will only have to point out the error of our ways, and we will instantly toe the line and be welcomed with open arms into Longhurst's "hospitality room."

It is a very attractive prospect but pure fantasy. In chapter 7, we saw that Scripture draws a clear dividing line between the righteous and the wicked, so that while there is no difference in the immediate fate of their bodies, the souls of the righteous are immediately taken to be "at home with the Lord" (2 Corinthians 5:8), while those of the wicked are sent to the "condemned cell" of Hades to await the final judgment. Then in chapter 8, we saw that on the Day of Judgment the righteous are welcomed, body and soul, into the glory of heaven, while the wicked are condemned, body and soul, to the horrors of hell. The idea that everybody immediately goes to heaven when they die must therefore be rejected out of hand. It is no more than wishful thinking.

ORIGEN AND OTHERS

The second form of universalism is what J.I. Packer criticized when he wrote, "For universalists, hell is never the ultimate state: It is, rather, a stage in the journey home."[5] One of the earliest church leaders to formalize this theory was the Egyptian theologian Origenes

Adamantius (c. 185-c. 254). Origen, as he has come to be known, was a man of great determination and personal discipline; he even castrated himself to avoid certain sexual temptations. He was a prolific writer, a famous preacher, and a persuasive teacher, but his theology was a hodgepodge of truth and error. It used to be said, "Where Origen was good, no one was better, where he was bad, no one was worse."[6]

Among his most controversial ideas were those relating to man's origin and destiny. With a great deal of Greek philosophy mixed into his thinking, he taught that God created a host of intellectual beings, almost all of whom he later rejected because of some unspecified sin. The least guilty became angels, the worst culprits devils, and the rest human beings. Our bodies are therefore a punishment for sin, but, by the exercise of free will, we can work our way back into God's favor. Our punishment and correction will continue after death, but eventually our purification will be complete, God will be satisfied, and we shall be restored to fellowship with Him. However, this restoration, or universalism, is not limited to human beings; every fallen angel, every evil spirit, and even the devil himself will eventually be reconciled to God.

These unorthodox views got Origen into serious trouble and his teaching was so decisively disowned by the church's ruling authorities that at the second Council of Constantinople, held in A.D. 553, he was listed among "ancient heretics,"[7] and for something like 1,500 years after Origen's death, universalism received little or no serious support. Surely these are pretty significant facts!

Toward the end of the eighteenth century, John Murray, an excommunicated Methodist preacher, left Ireland for America and began to spread the doctrine of universalism in New England, eventually being instrumental in founding the first Universalist Church. Although many other doctrines taught by Murray were biblically sound, his successors gradually abandoned these, and under the influence of men like Hosea Ballou (1771-1852), the Universalist Church threw out the doctrines of the Trinity, the deity of Christ, original sin, and the need for conversion. Within 100 years, the church had almost no doctrinal moorings and welcomed "all humane men"[8] into its membership. In 1961, it merged with the equally unbiblical Unitarians to form the Unitarian-Universalist Association.

In Europe, the German theologian Friedrich Schleiemacher (1768-1834), who denied the deity of Christ and the necessity of the Virgin

Birth, gave universalism a powerful boost by teaching that God had decreed the universal restoration of all souls. A century later, this impetus was given another shot in the arm by the Swiss theologian Karl Barth (1886-1968), who believed that, although the Bible's writers claimed to have written the Word of God, they could "never sustain that claim"[9] and that there were times when they were "actually guilty of error in their spoken and written word."[10] Barth taught that all humanity's destiny is fulfilled in Christ, and he reached the very brink of universalism by doubting that God could finally condemn anyone. He publicly denied that he was a universalist—even though he taught that "We are already in [God's] kingdom . . . we have our being and continuance here and nowhere else . . . we already belong to it"[11]—but his massive reputation made it easy for others to embrace the full-blown doctrine.

Barth's contemporary and fellow-countryman Emil Brunner (1889-1966), who wrote that "The Bible is full of errors, contradictions, erroneous opinions concerning all kinds of human, natural, historical situations,"[12] was another influential scholar who took a universalist line. He said that "The doctrine of forgiving grace . . . finds its crown in a proclamation of universal redemption."[13]

Nels Ferre, (1908-1971), put it more simply: "God has no permanent problem children";[14] in other words, after death, God will keep the pressure on until even the most rebellious sinner gives in and acknowledges God as his Father. Elsewhere Ferre wrote that "The final victory of final love is universal salvation" and that Christianity's message is "deceit except it end in a hallelujah chorus."[15]

The liberal British minister C.H. Dodd (1884-1973) taught that God would eventually forgive everyone and treat unbelievers as if they had believed.[16] Elsewhere, he wrote that "In the end no member of the human race is left outside the scope of salvation."[17]

The Scottish theologian William Barclay, another liberal, took the same line. He said that although God was both King and Judge, He was also Father—"indeed, Father more than anything else." From that base, Barclay argued that "No father could be happy while there were members of his family in agony. No father would count it a triumph to obliterate the disobedient members of his family. The only triumph a father can know is to have all his family back home."[18]

Broader arguments against universalism will be developed later in this chapter, but Barclay's case collapses even before we get to them, because he bases it on the assumption that God is the Father of all humanity, whereas Jesus told His enemies, "You belong to your father, the devil" (John 8:44). In terms of salvation, the idea of the universal fatherhood of God and brotherhood of man is nothing more than a convenient catch-phrase; the Bible makes it clear that the only way to become "sons of God" is "through faith in Christ Jesus" (Galatians 3:26).

Pope John Paul II has also made universalistic noises: "Man—every man without exception whatever—has been redeemed by Christ and . . . with man, with each man without any exception whatever, Christ is in a way united, even when man is unaware of it."[19] It is curious to find the pope appearing to endorse universalism, which stands on its head other Roman Catholic teaching about the fate of unrepentant sinners.

As these notes show, universalism has had a very bumpy history and attracted a mixed bag of friends. Yet it is not enough to denounce it as guilty by association. Universalism is not to be tested by Barth, Brunner, or Barclay but by the Bible. Where do universalists claim to find biblical support? The issue is obviously important, because if universalism is true, hell is virtually irrelevant. We must therefore examine universalism carefully in the light of Scripture.

WAS JESUS A UNIVERSALIST?

Universalists tend to look to the writings of Paul as proof of their position, though they also use statements by Jesus, Peter and John. In Jesus' case, they lean heavily on one particular sentence: "But I, when I am lifted up from the earth, will draw all men to myself" (John 12:32). There is no dispute about what being "lifted up from the earth" means, because the very next verse tells us that Jesus used the phrase to illustrate "the kind of death he was going to die." The crucifixion and resurrection of Jesus were to be the means of drawing sinners to salvation. The real issue is whether the words "all men" mean the whole of humanity.

Theoretically, they could mean that. When Paul told the Athenians that God "gives all men life and breath and everything else" (Acts 17:25) he clearly meant the whole of humanity; any other interpretation would be absurd. However, there are places in Scripture where the word "all" and phrases such as "the world" or "the whole world" do not refer to everybody. Two illustrations will be sufficient to prove the point and will help to explain other statements we shall examine in this section. When John the Baptist began his preaching ministry in the Judean desert, "Jerusalem was going out to him, and all Judea, and all the district around the Jordan" (Matthew 3:5, NASB). Are we meant to believe that every human being in the huge area of that district went out to the middle of the desert to listen to a preacher? Did Pontius Pilate the Roman governor go, along with all his officials? Did Caiaphas the high priest and all the religious establishment go? Did every shepherd and shopkeeper, every husband and housewife, every boy and girl, every newborn child go? Was an area of over 500 square miles totally evacuated? Common sense will answer the question.

The second illustration concerns a comment the Pharisees made when they were growing increasingly agitated at their failure to stop Jesus' popular following: "See, this is getting us nowhere. Look how the whole world has gone after him!" (John 12:19). Are we meant to take that literally? The answer comes a few verses later when we are told that in spite of the many miracles He was performing among the people living in that area, "They still would not believe in him" (John 12:37). The Bible tells us that Jesus was "despised and rejected by men" (Isaiah 53:3). When He died, He probably left no more than a few hundred genuine followers. Even today, although the Christian church is the largest religious grouping the world has ever known, it still constitutes a minority of the world's inhabitants. When the Pharisees said that "The whole world has gone after him," they were simply using a common idiom to express their alarm that Jesus' popular support was gathering momentum.

We can now return to the vital question: when Jesus said, "But I, when I am lifted up from the earth, will draw all men to myself," did He mean that all of humanity would be redeemed? The answer is as clear as daylight, because a few moments earlier He had said, "The man who loves his life will lose it, while the man who hates his life in this world will keep it for eternal life" (John 12:25), showing that there were two distinct and very different destinies. Later He warned that there would be those who would not be redeemed but would be condemned: "There is a judge for the one who rejects me and does not accept my words; that very word which I spoke will condemn him at the last day" (John 12:48). When Jesus spoke of "all men" being drawn to Him He meant people from every age, nation, culture, and background—a prophecy fulfilled to the letter in John's vision of heaven when the death of Jesus is said to have brought salvation to people "from every tribe and language and people and nation" (Revelation 5:9). The attempt to show Jesus as a universalist falls spectacularly at the first hurdle.

WAS PETER A UNIVERSALIST?

In Peter's case, universalists point both to his preaching and his writing. In his sermon after the healing of the cripple at the gate of the temple, he told his audience, "Repent, then, and turn to God, so that your sins may be wiped out, that times of refreshing may come from the Lord, and that he may send the Christ, who has been appointed for you—even Jesus. He must remain in heaven until the time comes for God to restore everything, as he promised long ago through his holy prophets" (Acts 3:19-21). Here, universalists latch on to the promise that God will "restore everything" as proof that all humanity will be saved (some universalists prefer to be called "restorationists") but the evidence is against them. Peter is clearly referring to the Second Coming of Christ, which he says will be delayed until the time comes for God to "restore everything." But when Jesus returns to the earth, it will not be to sweep all of mankind into the kingdom of heaven but to "judge the world with justice" (Acts 17:31), a moment when He will "separate the people one from another" (Matthew 25:32) and when some will be condemned to "eternal punishment" and others welcomed to "eternal life." That is hardly a basis for universalism!

The restoration of which Peter spoke was the fulfillment of Old Testament prophecy, the climax of which will be triggered off by the Second Coming of Christ. Peter tells us elsewhere that this restoration will include "a new heaven and a new earth, the home of righteousness" (2 Peter 3:13) but he does not give a glimmer of hope that all humanity will live there. If Peter believed that everyone would eventually be saved, why did he plead with his hearers to "Repent . . . and turn to God, so that your sins may be wiped out . . ."? Surely if they did not repent and turn to God, their sins would not be wiped out— and as unrepentant sinners can never enter heaven, it is absurd for universalists to claim Peter's support on the basis of what he said in Acts 3.

As to Peter's writing, the passage to which universalists turn is as follows: "The Lord is not slow in keeping his promise, as some understand slowness. He is patient with you, not wanting anyone to perish, but everyone to come to repentance" (2 Peter 3:9). Initially, this looks rather promising for the universalists' case, but the promise begins to disappear as soon as we notice that Peter is not writing for the benefit of the world at large, and making a promise to all humanity. His letter is specifically addressed "To those who through the righteousness of our God and Savior Jesus Christ have received a faith as precious as ours" (2 Peter 1:1).

These early Christians were being ridiculed by their pagan contemporaries for believing that Jesus would one day return to the earth and establish the kingdom of God in all its fullness. People were "scoffing and following their own sinful desires" and asking, "'Where is this 'coming' he promised?'" (2 Peter 3:4) and the Christians were hard put to explain the delay. Peter's response was to encourage the believers to "hang in there"! The Lord had not forgotten His promise but was patiently waiting until all of those Peter had described in an earlier letter as "God's elect . . . chosen according to the foreknowledge of God the Father" (1 Peter 1:1-2) had come to repentance. Peter is endorsing the fact that God has undertaken to save all those He "chose . . . in [Christ] before the creation of the world" (Ephesians 1:4) and assuring browbeaten believers that Jesus will not return until every one of God's people has come to repentance.

Peter says much the same thing a few sentences later, reminding his readers that "Our Lord's patience means salvation" (2 Peter 3:15). He did not mean that Jesus would delay His return until everyone comes to salvation—if He did that He would never return—but until all of God's chosen people are saved.

If Peter was a universalist, why did he warn people that when God "condemned the cities of Sodom and by burning them to ashes" he "made them an example of what is going to happen to the ungodly" (2 Peter 2:6)? Why did he say that arrogant blasphemers are "like brute beasts, creatures of instinct, born only to be caught and destroyed, and like beasts they too will perish" (2 Peter 2;12)? Why did he speak of "fire" that was "being kept for the day of judgement and destruction of ungodly men" (2 Peter 3:7)? If that is the language of a universalist, words are meaningless.

WAS JOHN A UNIVERSALIST?

In John's writings, there is one phrase in particular which universalists claim as their own: "My dear children, I write this to you so that you will not sin. But if anybody does sin, we have one who speaks to the Father in our defense—Jesus Christ, the Righteous One. He is the atoning sacrifice for our sins, and not only for ours but also for the sins of the whole world" (1 John 2:1-2). The words "atoning sacrifice" translate the Greek word *hilasmos*, which the Authorized Version renders "propitiation." To propitiate means to appease an offended person by meeting his demands for the removal of an offense and, as a result, to enable the offender to win back his favor. In His death, Jesus took the place of sinners and became a propitiation on their behalf, turning away God's wrath against them so that God can justly forgive them and bring them back into a living relationship with Himself. Put more simply, God can act favorably toward sinners who place Jesus took when He died on the cross.

Then, is Jesus the atoning sacrifice for every sinner in history, so that the penalty of all of their sin has been paid in full, and they will go scot free for all eternity? Far from it! In none of his writings on the subject did John ever use "world" in a statistical sense but rather to mean people of every kind and nation, in exactly the same way in which Jesus used the phrase "all men" in saying, "I will draw all men to myself." John is not saying that Jesus paid sin's penalty for every human being in history, but that in all the world's history, there is no other propitiation.

Was John a universalist? Not when he wrote, "Anyone who does not love remains in death" (1 John 3:14); not when he wrote that "No murderer has eternal life in him" (1 John 3:15); and certainly not when he wrote that "He who does not have the Son of God does not have life" (1 John 5:12). No honest person can say that these statements are those of a universalist.

NINE STEPS TO NOWHERE

Although they quote an occasional phrase from others, the star attraction for universalists is Paul. Is the evidence they find in his writings real or imagined? Paul's statements are so crucial to the universalists' case that we will look carefully at ten of those on which they lean most heavily.

The first is this: "Consequently, just as the result of one trespass was condemnation for all men, so also the result of one act of righteousness was justification that brings life for all men" (Romans 5:18).

This requires an extended comment, some of which will also apply to other statements Paul made.

Firstly, there is no doubt that the phrase "all men" in the first part of this statement means every human being in history (with the obvious exception of Jesus). When Adam sinned—Paul calls it "one trespass"—he did so as the representative head of all his successors, dragging all of humanity into condemnation with him. Adam's sin has placed humanity under judgment; we were "made sinners," as Paul says in the next sentence.

Secondly, the "one act of righteousness" which Paul mentions is clearly Christ's perfect life and substitutionary death on behalf of sinners.

Thirdly, the result of Christ's "act of righteousness" was to bring about "justification." Justification is God's declaration that a sinner is considered righteous in His sight because on his behalf Christ has not only obeyed God's law in every part but also paid its penalty in full. The sinner is therefore made right with God, not on the basis of his own merit or efforts, but on the basis of the life and death of Christ.

Now to the crucial issue: when Paul says that the justification provided by Christ "brings life for all men" does he mean the whole of humanity? The answer emerges from the previous verse: "For if, by the trespass of the one man, death reigned through that one man, how much more will those who receive God's abundant provision of grace and of the gift of righteousness reign in life through the one man, Jesus Christ" (Romans 5:17). The only ones who "reign in life" are "those who receive God's abundant provision of grace and of the gift of righteousness"; those who do not receive these things remain under the devastating reign of death.

Why then does Paul say that justification brings life for "all men"? The Jews of his day had a stubborn belief that in God's eyes they were superior to the Gentiles, in other words, to all non-Jews. To counter this, one of the points Paul hammers home again and again in the early part of Romans is that both Jews and Gentiles were in the same boat; they were guilty, lost, and helpless sinners needing the grace of God to bring them to repentance and faith, and without that grace, they would both be eternally doomed. Here is an example of the way he puts this: "To those who by persistence in doing good seek glory, honor and immortality, [God] will give eternal life. But for those who are self-seeking and who reject the truth and follow evil, there will be wrath and anger. There will be trouble and distress for every human being who does evil: first for the Jew, then for the Gentile; but glory, honor and peace for everyone who does good: first for the Jew, then for the Gentile. For God does not show favoritism" (Romans 2:7-11). It is against that background that Paul says justification "brings life for all men"; not to every human being, but to Jews and Gentiles alike. There is not a hint of universalism here.

THE TWO ADAMS

A second statement by Paul which is a favorite of the universalists is this: "For as in Adam all die, so in Christ all will be made alive" (1 Corinthians 15:22). Here, the explanation begins to take shape when we realize that the passage in which this statement occurs is about the final resurrection of Christians. Paul describes Christ as "the first-fruits of those who have fallen asleep" (1 Corinthians 15:20), establishing a clear distinction between the deaths of believers and unbelievers. Paul is showing that Adam and Christ were representatives of others—later in the chapter he actually calls Jesus "the last Adam" (1 Corinthians 14:45)—and says that what Adam and Christ each did had inevitable and radical effects on those they represented.

This reinforces what we say in Romans 5:18. Everyone in Adam (in other words, the whole of humanity) shares in the separation from God which Adam's sin produced, while everyone in Christ (all those for whom He died) will be "made alive." Just as surely as Christ rose from the dead and will never die again because "Death no longer has mastery over him" (Romans 6:9), so the person who is "in Christ" can rejoice in the assurance of sharing with Christ the glories of eternal life. For those who remain "in Adam" there is no such assurance. To say that *in Christ* all will be made alive is very different from saying that *all* will be made alive in Christ!

We return to Romans for a third key statement by Paul: "For God has bound all men over to disobedience so that he may have mercy on them all" (Romans 11:32). Here, the background is the same as for Romans 5:18, the tension created by the Jews' insistence that they were superior to the Gentiles. Paul insists that this is not so, but that "all men," Jews and Gentiles, are "bound over to disobedience." This is a rather confusing translation of a phrase which literally means that they were "locked up together." It is exactly the word one would use about imprisonment, and Paul is saying that because of their disobedience, God has put both Jews and Gentiles into the same "prison," where they are cut off from God and without spiritual life; but among "all," but Jews and Gentiles, there are those on whom God has mercy, bringing them out of their "prison" and into what Paul elsewhere calls "the glorious freedom of the children of God" (Romans 8:21).

"ALL MEN"

Fourthly, universalists appeal to Paul's statement that "The grace of God that brings salvation has appeared to all men" (Titus 2:11), but William Hendriksen's response is so good that it will be sufficient to quote him in full: "Does Titus 2:11 really teach that the saving grace of God has appeared to every member of the human race without any exception? Of course not! It matters little whether one interprets 'the appearance of the saving grace' as referring to the bestowal of salvation itself, or to the fact that the gospel of saving grace has been preached to every person on earth. In either case it is impossible to make 'all men' mean 'every individual on the globe without exception.'"[20]

A fifth verse claimed by the universalists can be just as firmly rejected. Writing to a fellow preacher, Paul says, "This is a trustworthy saying that deserves full acceptance (and for this we labor and strive), that we have put our hope in the living God, who is the Savior of all men, and especially of those who believe" (1 Timothy 4:9-10). The first and most obvious thing to say about this statement is that if it teaches universalism the phrase "and especially of those who believe" is nonsensical. It would mean that God saved believers and unbelievers alike, whereas the Bible teaches that "Without faith it is impossible to please God" (Hebrews 11:6) and that "The righteous will live by faith" (Romans 1:17).

Paul's meaning turns on the sense in which he is using the word "Savior." We normally think of it only in terms of salvation from sin, but a careful study of the way the word is used in Scripture, especially in the Old Testament, shows that it has a much wider connotation and includes all of God's gracious provision for His creatures. John Calvin makes the point in this way: "In this sense he is 'the Savior of all men,' not in regard to the spiritual salvation of their souls, but because he supports all his creatures . . . his goodness extends to the most wicked, who are estranged from him, and who do not deserve to have any intercourse with him, who ought to have been struck off from the number of the creatures of God and destroyed; and yet we see how

God extends his grace to them; for the life which he gives them is a testimony to his goodness."[21]

The Roman Emperor used to be called "the Savior of the world" because of the great benefits which Roman citizens enjoyed under his reign. Here, Paul is saying that all men, believers and unbelievers, are saved from countless dangers, difficulties and deprivations because of God's gracious sovereignty—but adds that God is in a special, spiritual, eternal way the Savior of those who put their trust in Him. There is no basis for universalism here.

A sixth statement by Paul which universalists employ was also written to Timothy: "This is good, and pleases God our Savior, who wants all men to be saved and to come to a knowledge of the truth. For there is one God and one mediator between God and men, the man Christ Jesus, who gave himself as a ransom for all men—the testimony given in its proper time" (1 Timothy 2:3-6). In this case, universalists seem to have two pieces of evidence for the price of one, but in fact the evidence is non-existent.

The second "all men" is obviously being used in the same way that Paul uses it elsewhere; it means people of every race, nation, and culture. As to the first use of the phrase, it is important to notice that Paul says God *wants* all men to be saved, not that He *determines* that they will be. This phrase occurs only three other times in the New Testament, and on each occasion it means to wish, not to will; to desire, not to determine. The difference is obvious. For example, it is God's desire that everyone should keep the Ten Commandments—but nobody does. There is a perfect illustration of God's desire that all be saved in something Jesus said about the city of Jerusalem when He gave one of His last messages there: "O Jerusalem, Jerusalem, you who kill the prophets and stone those sent to you, how often I have longed to gather your children together, as a hen gathers her chicks under her wings, but you were not willing" (Luke 13:34). Jesus was willing to save them, but they were not willing to be saved. In the same sense, Paul's words that God wants all men to be saved point, "not to God's purpose to save all men, but to his benevolent desire toward the human race, as shown in his provision of a Redeemer and offer of salvation."[22]

RECONCILIATION AND CONFESSION

Elsewhere Paul writes that the gospel message is the news "that God was reconciling the world to himself in Christ, not counting men's sins against them" (2 Corinthians 5:19). That certainly has a universalistic ring about it, but this is silenced as soon as we realize that "the world" has the same meaning as "all men," a phrase we examined earlier. What Paul means here is that in the death of Christ, God punished human sin and satisfied His own righteous judgment, because Christ took upon Himself the sin, guilt, and condemnation of those on whose behalf He died, people of every age, race, and condition. It is because God has made such all-embracing provision for salvation that those who are saved are urged by Paul to make an urgent appeal to others: "Be reconciled to God" (2 Corinthians 5:20). If everyone is inevitably reconciled, the appeal would be pointless.

The next statement made by Paul and claimed by universalists runs as follows: "For God was pleased to have all his fullness dwell in [Christ], and through him to reconcile to himself all things, whether things on earth or things in heaven, by making peace through his blood, shed on the cross" (Colossians 1:19-20). The idea that this points to the salvation of every human being is more than blunted by noticing that human beings are not even mentioned! They are not excluded, but Paul is painting a much broader picture. Just as the whole created order was put out of joint by the entrance of sin—Paul speaks elsewhere of creation "groaning as in the pains of childbirth" (Romans 8:22)—so Christ, in dealing with sin by means of His death on the cross, has in principle repaired all the damage it caused, so that eventually "The creation itself will be liberated from its bondage to decay" (Romans 8:21). When this happens, all created beings, human and spiritual, whether saved or lost, will be in total submission to Christ.

The ninth and last of Paul's statements we will consider comes at the end of a passage in Philippians in which he writes about Jesus voluntarily laying aside His eternal glory in heaven, coming to earth as a man, and dying on the cross in the place of sinners. Paul then goes on:

> "Therefore God exalted him to the highest place
> and gave him the name that is above every name,
> that at the name of Jesus every knee should bow,
> in heaven and on earth and under the earth,
> and every tongue confess that Jesus Christ is Lord,
> to the glory of God the Father"
> (Philippians 2:9-11).

This last phrase is partly a quotation from the Old Testament, where God tells the Israelites, "Before me every knee will bow; by me every tongue will swear" (Isaiah 45:23). This makes Paul's words a powerful piece of evidence for the deity of Christ; but does Paul teach universalism here? Not at all! What he is saying is that the day is coming when Jesus will be acknowledged as Lord by "the whole body of created intelligent beings in all the departments of the universe."[23]

This does not mean that all of them will be saved. The word "confess" occurs eleven times in the New Testament and not once does it imply the salvation of the person making the confession. In every case the word means "to agree" or "to acknowledge." The day is coming when every creature in the universe will acknowledge that Jesus is Lord (in other words, that He is God). The angels and all other heavenly creatures, and every human being who knows Him as Savior, will do so with indescribable joy. Satan, the evil spirits, and all unrepentant sinners will do so with bitterness and anger. There is an anticipation of this elsewhere in the New Testament when an evil spirit cried out to Jesus, "I know who you are—the Holy One of God" (Mark 1:24) and when demons shouted at Him, "You are the Son of God!" (Luke 4:41). What Paul is telling us here is that in eternity those who went through life refusing to submit to the lordship of Christ will be compelled by the blinding light of truth to acknowledge that He is everything the Bible claims Him to be. There may be a case for saying that the most agonized cries of those doomed to spend eternity in hell will be the words: "Jesus is Lord." The words will come with great conviction and certainty—but they will come too late.

Was Paul a universalist? Not one of the ten statements we have examined even hints that he was. As he also wrote that "The wages of sin is death" (Romans 6:23); that the person "who sows to please his sinful nature, from that nature will reap destruction" (Galatians 6:8); that there are people on whom "the wrath of God is coming" (Colossians 3:6); and that unrepentant sinners will be "punished with eternal destruction and shut out from the presence of the Lord and from the majesty of his power" (2 Thessalonians 1:9) the answer to the question is hardly in doubt.

GUILTY IS GUILTY

Universalism originated in the Garden of Eden when Satan brushed aside God's warning and assured Eve, "You will not sure die"

(Genesis 3:4). It has remained popular ever since, and its appeal is understandable; not only are man's occasional moral lapses over looked, but even the most outrageous behavior is conveniently flushed away. If ever there was a doctrine to encourage moral license, self-centered living, and the irrelevance of conscience, universalism is it; no wonder people are so reluctant to abandon the idea. Even among those who take a more serious view of life, universalism has theoretical appeal. As the nineteenth-century American theologian Robert Dabney put it, "It is presumed that there is not a right-minded man in any church who would not hail with delight the assurance that every creature of God will be finally happy and holy, provided only it could be given with certainty, and in a way consistent with the honor of God."[24] The proviso is the problem!

After centuries of trying to attach itself to Scripture, universalism still comes unglued at every point. It has a blinkered view of God, seeing Him only as a God of love, and ignoring His holiness, justice, and righteous anger. It has a warped view of sin, seeing it as something which might at most warrant a post-mortem slap on the wrist, but certainly nothing approaching the Bible's description of hell. It has an inflated view of man, seeing him as being able to save himself, or at least to make a significant contribution to his salvation, if not in this world then in the next. And it has a distorted view of hell, seeing it either as terrifying but empty, or as a kind of moral "finishing school," where sinners are fine-tuned for heaven. This totally ignores the fact that hell is not a place of preparation for anything, but a place of eternal punishment. The idea that the pains of hell amount to nothing more than a learning process which eventually results in reformation has obvious attractions, yet it disintegrates when faced with the simple fact that hell's punishment must continue for as long as the reason for it continues, and as the primary reason is the sinner's guilt, and guilt, by definition, is never-ending, the punishment it incurs can never come to an end. Neither the passing of time, nor the amount of punishment suffered by the guilty, can ever convert guilt into innocence.

At a human level, a judge adjusts the length of a law-breaker's sentence in accordance with certain criteria, but this takes no account of any spiritual issues, let alone God's honor. But all sin is infinite because it is an offense against an infinite God, and as such it incurs infinite guilt. W.G.T. Shedd put it like this: "The continuous nature of guilt necessitates the endlessness of retribution . . . The whole infinite guilt of . . . sin against God lies upon the sinner at each and every instant of time ... The transgressor at any and every point in his end-less existence is infinitely guilty, and yet cannot cancel his guilt by what he endures at a particular point."[25]

The universalist's position is also fatally flawed in that it makes its primary concern man's welfare rather than God's glory. The most important air of universalism is to ensure that man is satisfied with the end result. But how can this ever be achieved when sinners in hell are infinitely guilty? The only way for the situation to be remedied would be for the sin to be pardoned, and in order for it to be par-doned, there must be repentance. However, the ability to repent is not something that man has by nature; nor is it something he develops while on earth (even though surrounded by many motives) or acquires at death and takes with him to hell. One writer says that those in hell "are not in a penitential mood; they continue in their senseless rebel-lion."[26] What is more, as repentance is a gift of God's sovereign, sav-ing grace, how can a sinner ever repent in hell when all God's grace, common and saving, has been permanently withdrawn, and the wicked are specifically described by Jesus as "you who are cursed" (Matthew 25:41)? As someone once put it, God's love for the sinner "stops short at the gates of hell."[27]

RIDDLES FOR THE RELUCTANT

The aim of getting unrestrained and rebellious sinners from hell to heaven is one which universalism will never be able to achieve. In addition to those we have examined in this chapter, it poses a whole host of other problems. To illustrate how untenable the universalists' position is, here are ten questions for those reluctant to abandon the idea, all of them related to statements Jesus made.

1. During one of His frequent confrontations with the Pharisees, Jesus told them, "I am going away, and you will look for me, and you will die in your sin. Where I go, you cannot come" (John 8:21). Why did He damn them in this way if He knew perfectly well that eventu-ally, along with all the rest of humanity, they would be with Him in heaven?

2. At one point, the Pharisees accused Jesus of using satanic power to perform miracles. Jesus easily exposed their stupidity by explain-ing that Satan would hardly cooperate in the destruction of his own kingdom, then added this devastating verdict: "And so I tell you, every sin and blasphemy will be forgiven men, but the blasphemy

against the Spirit will not be forgiven. Anyone who speaks a word against the Son of Man will be forgiven, but anyone who speaks against the Holy Spirit will not be forgiven, either in this age or in the age to come" (Matthew 12:31-32).

The phrase "every sin and blasphemy" means "all kinds of sin and blasphemy." Even "a word against the Son of Man" is included in the scope of God's gracious forgiveness; many of Christ's critics have subsequently been converted. The one exception Jesus made was "blasphemy against the Spirit." This is not an isolated act, but "an attitude of defiant and deliberate rejection of light."[28] It is an unrepentant refusal to accept the truth of the gospel revealed in Scripture by the Holy Spirit, and Jesus said that this sin would not be forgiven "either in this age or in the age to come." If universalism is true, will there be those in heaven with unforgiven sin?

3. In the course of a final meal with His disciples, when Jesus revealed that Judas Iscariot was about to betray Him to the religious authorities, He added, "But woe to that man who betrays the Son of Man! It would be better for him if he had not been born" (Matthew 26:24). If Judas is to be in the kingdom of heaven along with the rest of humanity, and will rejoice forever in God's glorious presence, how could Jesus say that never having been born would be even better for him?

4. In the story of the rich sinner who died and went to Hades and the poor believer who died and went to Paradise, Jesus said that between the two places "a great chasm has been fixed" and that it would be impossible for anyone to move from one place to the other. Why did He not add that the chasm would one day be "unfixed" and that everyone not already there would cross over into heaven?

5. When someone asked Him, "Lord, are only a few people going to be saved?" Jesus replied, "Make every effort to enter through the narrow door, because many, I tell you, will try to enter and will not be able to" (Luke 13:23-24). Why did He say such a thing if eventually there will be nobody left outside?

6. Toward the end of the Sermon on the Mount, Jesus used a similar metaphor: "Enter through the narrow gate. For wide is the gate and broad is the road that leads to destruction, and many enter through it. But small is the gate and narrow the road that leads to life, and only a few find it" (Matthew 7:13-14). If everyone will eventually find "the road that leads to life," why did Jesus make such a misleading statement?

7. Speaking of His death on the cross to pay the penalty for the sins of believers, Jesus said, "I am the good shepherd. The good shepherd lays down his life for the sheep" (John 10:11). If His death secures the salvation of everyone, why did He not say, "The good shepherd lays down his life for the sheep and for the goats," that is to say, for the believers and unbelievers?

8. After the parable of the wedding feast, Jesus added this post-script: "For many are invited, but few are chosen" (Matthew 22:14). Why exclude so many from the wedding feast of heaven if He knew that nobody would be excluded?

9. When Jesus warned that unrepentant sinners would "go away to eternal punishment" (Matthew 25:46) was He showing Himself to be ignorant (not knowing that their punishment would not be eternal) or unethical (frightening people to repent of their sin and trust Him as their Savior when He knew that they would be saved regardless of their response)?

10. When Jesus promised the penitent criminal being crucified alongside Him, "I tell you the truth, today you will be with me in paradise" (Luke 23:43) why did He not extend the promise to the unrepentant criminal hanging next to Him?

These are not the only biblical knots the universalist has to untie, but they are sufficient to show that the task is impossible. Whichever way universalism is presented, it makes no biblical sense. As A.A. Hodge put it, "There is not the slightest trace in Scripture of such an ultimate restoration, either in the design of it, or in the means of it, or the results of it. On the contrary . . . the Scriptures positively affirm the precise reverse to be true."[29] All the ways to hell are one-way streets. The idea that those who go there will eventually be released and join the rest of humanity in heaven has not a shred of biblical evidence to support it.

Children are sometimes told fictional adventure stories with the delightful ending: "And they all lived happily ever after." We call that kind of story a fairy tale.

Universalism is exactly that.

The Last Loophole

In June 1964 Nelson Mandela, the South African anti-apartheid campaigner, was sentenced to life imprisonment for attempting to overthrow the government. For the first fifteen years his punishment included hard labor, breaking boulders in a limestone quarry on Robben Island, a penal colony offshore from Cape Town. Later, his conditions were improved, though he was still imprisoned in one jail or another. But at 2:15 P.M. on Sunday, February 11, 1990, he was released from Victor Voerster Prison Farm, near Cape Town, in a massive media event seen on television by millions of people all around the world. Including the time he spent under arrest awaiting trial, Mandela had been imprisoned for nearly 10,000 days; he was in his late forties when he was arrested, in his early seventies when he was released.

In *TIME Magazine*, he spoke of "long, lonely, wasted years"[1] yet he also said that he never gave up hope because he knew that from the first day there were those who were bringing pressure to bear on the authorities to have him released. Eventually, the South African government felt that the time had come when Mandela should be freed. He had been sentenced to life imprisonment, but although he had been detained for nearly twenty-seven years, "life" in his case did not mean life, and on that Sunday in February 1990 Prisoner 446/64 was free.

Mandela's case is not a perfect illustration of the issue we are now going to examine, but it helps to introduce it. For the last two chapters we have been trying to find an alternative to the Bible's apparently bleak insistence that the wicked will spend eternity suffering the unrelieved pains of hell. We looked at the argument that a God of love could never send anyone to hell but discovered that God is also a God of justice and holiness who could never admit an unrepentant sinner to heaven. We considered the Bible's teaching that there are degrees of punishment in hell but found that while not everyone will suffer to the same degree, none will suffer to a small degree. In Robert Morey's words, "All sinners in hell will be perfectly miserable but not equally miserable."[2] We looked at the possibility of the prisoner being moved to a less painful place in hell but found no scriptural support for this.

Then, in chapter 12, we examined in some detail one of the two major hopes people have that hell may be less horrific than appears on the surface of Scripture. This is the theory that those in hell will eventually be released and taken to heaven, either as a reward for their improved behavior or because God would not allow any of His creatures to endure endless punishment. Yet this glimmer of hope turned out to be nothing but a mirage which dissolved as soon as we approached it with the Bible in our hands. We now turn our attention to the second of these major hopes, which, as far as I know, is the only remaining serious alternative to the doctrine of conscious, endless punishment put forward by those claiming to have the Bible as their basis—the last loophole.

DEFINITIONS AND DIFFERENCES

The terms commonly used to describe this are "annihilationism" and "conditional immortality." They are sometimes used as if they were identical, but this is misleading, as there are four forms of annihilationism, not all of which are tied in to conditional immortality.

The first says that everyone is extinguished at death, but this idea was dismissed in chapter 5 where we saw that it made no claim to be biblical but was driven by godless philosophies such as atheism (there is no God), materialism (only physical matter exists), existentialism (everything is meaningless), and secular humanism (life leads to nothing).

Another form of annihilationism says that all the wicked, but only the wicked, are extinguished at death; but this contradicts the Bible's statement that "Man is destined to die once, and after that to face judgment" (Hebrews 9:27). There is no mileage whatever in the idea that the wicked are annihilated the moment they die.

The third brand of annihilationism accepts that both the righteous and the wicked are raised from death on the Day of Judgment, but says that when the wicked "go away to eternal punishment" (Matthew 25:46) it means that they are annihilated on the spot. In Paul Helm's words, this would mean that "'Hell' is simply another name for non-existence."[3] This notion appeals to many people, but it runs aground on a single sentence from Scripture: Jesus spoke of sinners being "thrown outside, into the darkness, where there will be weeping and gnashing of teeth" (Matthew 8:12). How can anyone weep or gnash their teeth (however we interpret those words) if they no longer exist? "Hell = non-existence" is an equation that makes no biblical sense.

The final kind of annihilationism correctly teaches that at the Day of Judgment the righteous are welcomed into heaven and the wicked are sent away into hell, but then goes on to say that eventually, as a result of what they endure there, they disintegrate into nothingness. In other words (and here is our "last loophole") the pains of hell will come to an end and those who have suffered them will finally be extinguished and pass into non-existence.

So much for annihilationism. Conditional immortality, on the other hand, says that man is naturally mortal, but that God will grant him immortality if he turns from sin and puts his trust in Christ. Conditional immortality therefore opens the door to all except the first of the four annihilationism theories. Conditionalists rightly reject the idea that everyone is annihilated at death, but they are not agreed as to when this annihilation of the wicked takes place. Some say it happens at death, others that it is the immediate execution of the death sentence passed on the Day of Judgment, and others (perhaps most) that the wicked are extinguished after an unspecified period of punishment in hell.

ARNOBIUS AND AFTER

As with universalism, it will be helpful to take a quick look at the history of annihilationism and conditional immortality. The first name usually associated with these is that of Arnobius of Sicca, who lived in the early part of the fourth century. Arnobius was a teacher of rhetoric in Numidia, in North Africa, and professed conversion rather late in life. When his local bishop hesitated over admitting a former enemy, Arnobius wrote a treatise entitled *Adversus Nationes (Against the Heathen)* to show that his conversion was genuine. From a literary standpoint, his presentation has been assessed as "badly constructed" and "full of contradictions."[4] More significantly, a respected historian has pointed out that the whole work contains only one quotation from Scripture.[5] The most important point about it in the context of our present study is that Arnobius denied the immortality of the human soul and claimed that it "depends solely on God for the gift of eternal duration."[6] Those who do not receive this gift, he said, "go to the fire of Gehenna, and will ultimately be consumed or annihilated."[7]

This theory of "conditionalism" was condemned as heresy at the Second Council of Constantinople in 553, and nearly a thousand years later the Lateran Council of 1513 confirmed that the church's verdict remained unchanged. The theory reappeared toward the end of the sixteenth century, largely through the teaching of Fausto Sozzini, whose humanistic ideas led him to deny the deity of Christ and original sin and to teach that salvation was something man achieved by his own efforts. Sozzini taught that the soul died with the body "except for the selective resurrection of those who persevered in obeying Jesus' commandments."[8] Those who followed the teachings of Fausto Sozzini and his uncle, Lelio Sozzini, became known as Socinians and were the forerunners of the modern Unitarians.

Other than these, prominent teachers of conditionalism have been very thin on the ground. Donald Macleod, Professor of Systematic Theology at the Free Church of Scotland College, Edinburgh, says bluntly, "It was never accepted as part of Christian orthodoxy. Church Fathers, reformers and Puritans all believed in eternal punishment."[9]

Today, conditionalist ideas are promoted by a number of religious cults. The so-called Jehovah's Witnesses, who deny the Trinity, the deity of Christ, the personality of the Holy Spirit, and several other major biblical doctrines also reject the immortality of the soul and have a rather complicated idea of the fate of mankind. They teach that only Christ and His 144,000 "body members" (Jehovah's Witnesses, of course) have been born again and that this "anointed class" will rule over the earth. People who missed out on the "kingdom preaching" which Jehovah's Witnesses present will be given a chance to hear it during some future era. Those who respond favorably will inherit an earthly paradise; those who fail will be annihilated.

Christadelphians, who also reject the immortality of the soul, give conditionalism a different twist. They teach that after the general resurrection Jesus will return to live permanently in Jerusalem; all true believers (that is, all Christadelphians) will be granted immortality and live forever on a renewed earth (heaven does not exist) while all non-Christadelphians will be annihilated.

Seventh-Day Adventists, who accept a great deal of orthodox biblical teaching but who have struggled over the crucial issue of the basis for man's salvation, have a similar scenario to Christadelphians, with believers living forever on a renewed earth, governed by Jesus from Jerusalem, while unbelievers are annihilated.

This is a pretty unimpressive pedigree, yet in recent years annihilationism has been attracting growing interest and support. Several prominent writers have questioned the doctrine of conscious, eternal punishment, but it is interesting to note that many of the best-known spokesmen have seemed at times to be somewhat less than totally convinced of their position.

John Wenham's book *The Goodness of God*, first published in 1974, is often quoted as being in favor of conditionalism, but if one reads it carefully, it seems less than dogmatic. Wenham actually spells out five strong cautions to those tempted to abandon traditional beliefs of hell. He also says that while holding to the doctrine of eternal punishment would make it more difficult to defend some of Christ's teaching, it would make it easier to accept "the hard facts of Scripture and Providence," and he eventually admits that his book "provides no basis for decision on so grave and complex an issue."[10]

John Stott is the best-known contemporary Christian spokesman said to be in favor of conditional immortality, largely on the basis of a chapter in *Essentials*, which he co-authored with David Edwards and was first published in 1988. The book is in the form of a dialogue between Edwards (a liberal) and Stott (an evangelical), and at one point Edwards challenges Stott to come clean on whether or not he believes in the everlasting suffering of the wicked. With characteristic honesty, Stott openly admits that he does not, and gives his reasons, but he then adds, "I do not dogmatize about the position to which I have come. I hold it tentatively."[11]

Stephen Travis is another evangelical quoted as a strong annihilationist. In *I believe in the Second Coming of Jesus*, first published in 1982, he says that the twentieth century has seen a growing number of evangelical writers and preachers supporting the idea of annihilation as against eternal punishment. He adds that, if pressed, he would go along with them, but he also makes a telling admission: "In my view the New Testament does not express itself clearly for one or the other of these options."[12]

Anybody who writes on the subject of hell would be foolish to give the impression that he "knows it all," but as Donald Macleod has suggested, there may be another reason why writers like those I have mentioned have carefully added reservations to their statements on the subject: "They know that the biblical case for eternal punishment is a strong one. They also know that history is against them . . . It is hardly surprising that men with a keen sense of history feel acute embarrassment when they find themselves departing from what has been held 'always, by everybody, everywhere.'"[13]

ARGUMENTS AND ANSWERS

That being the case, what are annihilationists saying, and how should we respond? Although massive volumes have been written on the subject (the Seventh-Day Adventist author LeRoy Edwin Froom's work, first published in 1976, ran to 2,476 pages) we shall have to confine ourselves to noting some of the major arguments put forward in favor of conditional immortality and annihilationism and indicating some of the biblical answers that can be made.

The obvious place to begin is with the issue of human mortality or immortality, on which two particular tests of Scripture are used. The first is Paul's description of God as "the blessed and only Ruler, the King of kings and Lord of lords, who alone is immortal" (1 Timothy 6:15-16). If only God is immortal, the argument runs, then all beings, man included, must be mortal. This seems perfectly logical and reasonable, but it misses the crucial point that Paul is speaking of God's essential immortality, as distinct from what we might call "endowed immortality." The Bible says that God is God "from everlasting to everlasting" (Psalm 90:2); He has neither beginning nor end, and is therefore essentially different from all of His creation.

The Bible speaks of all three members of the Godhead in this way: Paul refers to "the King eternal, immortal, invisible, the only God" (1 Timothy 1:17), while elsewhere in the New Testament we are told of "the eternal Spirit" (Hebrews 9:14) and that "Jesus Christ is the same yesterday and today for ever" (Hebrews 13:8). In this absolute or essential sense, it is true that God alone has immortality. Perhaps the best parallel to Paul's statement that God alone is immortal comes earlier in the New Testament, where Jesus said that "The Father has life in himself" (John 5:26). "Life" is not something that God has acquired at any time or that was granted to Him in any way; it is something that is essentially and independently His—but this can hardly mean that He cannot grant life to any of His creatures. This leads to the annihilationists' argument that the Bible nowhere states that God has done this and that as a result we can conclude that the human soul is mortal, but this approach is not nearly as impressive as it seems.

In the first place, while it is certainly true that the Bible nowhere uses the phrase "Man's soul is immortal," neither does it make any statement which formally establishes that the Godhead is a trinity. This fact is used by the Jehovah's Witnesses to deny the deity of Christ. But the absence of a formal statement does not mean that the doctrine is not true. The same can be said about immortality.

In the second place, there are a number of statements in Scripture which point very strongly in the direction of human immortality. Unlike any other creature, man is made "in the image of God" (Genesis 1:27); he is "made in God's likeness" (James 3:9). This is what makes man superior to other earthly creatures. This is why the life of a human being is more important than the life of a limpet, and his death more significant than the death of a dog. The very fact that humanity was created in such a way as to be able to enjoy a living relationship with an immortal God is at least a hint that he was created in the same "dimension." It is because he was created in this "dimension" that man has what someone has called a "God-shaped blank" in his life, something that can be filled only by the one whose being is eternal and immortal.

The Bible's statement that "God has . . . set eternity in the hearts of men" (Ecclesiastes 3:11) is another pointer in the same direction. So is the same writer's declaration that a person's death "The dust returns to the ground it came from, and the spirit returns to God who gave it" (Ecclesiastes 12:7). As far as the nature of man is concerned, the whole thrust of Scripture, from creation in the image of God, which we looked at in chapter 4, to his life after death, which we considered in chapter 5, is in the same direction. John Calvin summed it up by saying, "There can be no question that man consists of a body and a soul; meaning by soul, an immortal though created essence."[14]

Commenting on the fact that there is no formal statement in Scripture of the immortality of the soul, W.G.T. Shedd says that "This doctrine, like that of the divine existence, is nowhere formally demon-

strated, because it is everywhere assumed,"[15] and adds that a great
deal of the Old Testament would be "nonsense" if the human soul
was not immortal. He illustrates this by saying that "Every spiritual
desire and aspiration has in it the element of infinity and endlessness."[16] As an example, he cites David crying, "As the deer pants for
streams of water, so my soul pants for you, O God" (Psalm 42:1) and
comments, "The human soul can never 'pant' for a spiritual communion with God that is just for seventy years and then ceases for
ever."[17]

Man's innate sense of immortality is not something that can be
easily dislodged. One nineteenth-century scholar went so far as to suggest that the doctrine of man's immortality "seems to be graven on
man's heart as indelibly as the doctrine of God's existence."[18] C.S.
Lewis put it in his own inimitable way when he said, "We know that
we are not made of mortal stuff."[19]

Another Bible text claimed by annihilationists is the one in which
Paul says that "Our Savior, Christ Jesus . . . has destroyed death and
brought life and immortality to light through the gospel" (2 Timothy
1:10). This shows, so it is argued, that "immortality" is something
promised only to believers, leaving unbelievers as merely mortal and
therefore exposed to extinction at or after death. Yet there is another
explanation, one much more in tune with the Bible's teaching as a
whole. When the New Testament speaks of "immortality" it means
much more than endless existence or even, for the believer, bodiless
existence in heaven. The idea of immortality as nothing more than
endless existence was a pagan philosophy popularized by Plato and
others, but as the British scholar Ernest Kevan rightly commented, the
New Testament's teaching "leaves the philosophical concept of
'immortality' far behind and is infinitely greater than mere survival."[20] Pagan philosophers taught that at death the soul was permanently released from the evil prison of the body; the Bible teaches
that man's salvation will come to completion not in some kind of
ghostly existence but will include "the redemption of our bodies."(Romans 3:23).

When the New Testament uses the word "immortality" it means
much more than the survival of the soul. There are times when, in
effect, it means virtually the same as "eternal life" (sometimes abbre-
viated to "life"), so that when Paul says that Christ "has brought life
and immortality to light through the gospel" he is emphasizing one
great truth rather than referring to two totally different and unrelated

concepts. This is not to say that the opposite of immortality is extinction. This mistake is often made by those who teach that death means termination but, as we saw in chapter 4, this is a totally unbiblical idea. According to Scripture, death never means termination but separation. The opposite of immortality (if we use the word in the sense I have suggested, that is, as eternal life bestowed on the Christian believer) is not extinction but eternal death and, as a modern writer has accurately observed, "Both life and death are modes of existence."[21]

The American theologian Louis Berkhof agrees: "Eternal life is indeed the gift of God in Jesus Christ, a gift which the wicked do not receive, but this does not mean that they will not continue to exist."[22] When the Bible uses the words "life" and "eternal life" in this way, it means existence in a right relationship with God. The opposite, "death," is existence outside of that relationship.

In this connection, it is important to notice that in the New Testament the word "mortal" is used only of the body; for example, Paul urges his fellow Christians, "Therefore do not let sin reign in your mortal body" (Romans 6:12). Here and elsewhere, the Bible is saying that the human body will be reconstructed and reunited to the soul, so that the whole person appears before God on the Day of Judgment and goes on from there to his or her eternal destiny. This is why Louis Berkhof can say that the immortality of the soul "is in perfect harmony with what the Bible teaches about man."[23]

One more point can be made on the issue of immortality. If it can be shown from Scripture that man has one of only two destinies, that the righteous will enjoy endless bliss in heaven and that the wicked will endure endless punishment in hell, then the doctrine of man's immortality (using the word in its widest sense) will be established regardless of the presence or absence of any direct biblical statement on the subject. The closing chapters of this book will address this point, and we can begin by examining eight of the ways in which annihilationism is presented.

SENSE AND NONSENSE

One general argument can be set aside very quickly. In a dialogue with another theologian, Clark Pinnock writes, "It just does not make sense to say that a God of love will torture people for ever for sins done in the context of a finite life. . . . It makes no sense to suppose that, alongside the new creation, tucked away in some corner of it, there exists a lake of fire with souls burning ceaselessly in it."[24] The weakness of this argument is that the truth of a doctrine is made to rest not on what Scripture says but on what fits into the confines of human logic: if what Scripture says "makes sense," we may accept it; if not, we must look for some other explanation. It is puzzling to know how any honest theologian, let alone an evangelical, could come to that kind of conclusion. After all, that God should allow evil to enter into his perfect creation "makes no sense"; does that mean we must deny the presence of evil? Christ's love "makes no sense"— the Bible says that it "surpasses knowledge" (Ephesians 3:19); does this mean that it is not to be taken seriously? The Bible also says that the peace of God "transcends all understanding" (Philippians 4:7); does this mean that there is no such thing?

Job's friend Zophar had a much more biblical (and therefore sensible) approach when he asked,

"Can you fathom the mysteries of God?
Can you probe the limits of the Almighty?
They are higher than the heavens—what can you do?
They are deeper than the depths of the grave—what can
you know?"
(Job 11:7-8).

If we are honest, must we not say that there are times when even the Bible's record of God's dealings with His people "makes no sense"? Does this mean that we must find some explanation that will fit in with our own earth-bound ideas of love, or justice, or fairness? To do that would be tantamount to making God in our own image. Insisting that Scripture must be shaped until it fits into our own limited logic is to display rank unbelief and produce theological nonsense. As Alec Motyer says in another context, "A sinner's imagination is no gauge to the reaction of a holy God, and we need to beware of imprisoning the Almighty within the meager grasp of our fallen nature."[25]

STATISTICS AND SUPPOSITIONS

As to the Bible's teaching on the eternal state of the wicked, conditionalists deny that there is any evidence to support the doctrine of everlasting punishment and claim that there is a mass of evidence to endorse annihilation. Froom's work is a classic example of this, but as soon as one examines it closely his statistics become much less impressive. For example, he lists seventy biblical words or phrases which he claims "must mean annihilation,"[26] but as they include verbs such as "to tear," "to break" and "to scatter," and metaphors such as broken vessels, chaff carried away by the wind and ashes trodden underfoot, one can understand why the American writer John Gerstner comes to the conclusion that "Froom was better at gathering superficial statistics than penetrating analysis."[27] Froom's fellow Adventist and conditionalist Edward Fudge, whose 500-page *The Fire that Consumes* is a model of courtesy and fairness, is forced to admit that of Froom's seventy examples several "seem less than applicable to the subject, and a few appear to be completely out of place."[28]

John Wenham is another conditionalist with a penchant for statistics. We have already noted his cautious approach in *The Goodness of God*, but at the Fourth Edinburgh Conference on Christian Dogmatics, held in August 1991, his caution was abandoned: "I have thought about the subject for more than fifty years and for more than fifty years I have believed the Bible to teach the ultimate destruction of the lost, but I have hesitated to declare myself in print . . . Now I feel that the time has come when I must declare my mind honestly. I believe that endless torment is a hideous and unscriptural doctrine which has been a terrible burden on the mind of the church for many centuries and a terrible blot on her presentation of the gospel. I should indeed be happy if, before I die, I could help in sweeping it away."[29]

In the course of a major paper presentation at the conference, Wenham said he had found 264 New Testament references to the fate of the lost and claimed that "In all but one of the 264 references there is not a word about unending torment and very many of them in their natural sense clearly refer to destruction."[30] If his conclusions are right, the case against everlasting punishment and in favor of annihilation might seem to be as good as settled—but is he right?

At least three things can be said in reply to his claims. The first is that his case will stand up only if we can find a suitable explanation for the Bible's teaching about unquenchable fire, an undying worm, and eternal punishment and (as we shall see in the next chapter) squeeze out of certain key words used to describe the duration of the punishment of the wicked a meaning they never have when used in any other connection.

Secondly, it would be neither necessary nor appropriate for New

Testament speakers and writers to mention "unending torment" whenever they were referring to the fate of the lost, any more than it would be right for a preacher to deal with every single aspect of the gospel in every sermon. This principle applies particularly to the parables, which were usually intended to teach one particular lesson.

Thirdly, even if it were the case that the everlasting punishment of the wicked was stated in only one place in Scripture, that would be sufficient to establish its truth. God is not obliged to repeat Himself before he is to be taken seriously. Superficially, Wenham's case might appear to be very strong; closer examination shows it to be otherwise.

GOD UNDER THREAT?

Some argue for annihilationism out of a concern to uphold the biblical truth of God's full and final triumph over all the forces of evil in the universe. How, it is asked, can the time ever come when God will be "all in all" (1 Corinthians 15:28) if there is a "black hole" of godlessness remaining somewhere in the universe? John Stott suggests that "The eternal existence of the impenitent in hell would be hard to reconcile with the promises of God's final victory over evil."[31]

Philip Edgecumbe Hughes is another modern theologian who has written along the same lines: "The everlasting existence side by side . . . of heaven and hell would seem to be incompatible with the purpose and effect of the redemption achieved by Christ's coming . . . The renewal of creation demands the elimination of sin and suffering and death."[32]

One way of solving this dilemma would be by saying that everybody will eventually be saved, but that makes a mockery of everything Jesus said about the opposite and eternal destinies of the righteous and the wicked. If universalism is ruled out, it would seem to some to leave annihilationism as the only way in which the unqualified reign of God can be given its full meaning, and this is where John Stott leans: "It would be easier to hold together the awful reality of hell and the universal reign of God if hell means destruction and the impenitent are no more."[33]

Yet why should the promise of God's final victory over evil be inconsistent with the everlasting punishment of the wicked if this is what God has ordained? As we saw in an earlier part of this book, God will be glorified as greatly in hell as He will be in heaven; He will reign as completely in one place as in the other. He is sovereign in wrath as well as in grace. Paul Helm makes a good point when he says that hell "is not a demonic colony which has gained unilateral independence from God. Because there is full recognition of God's justice, God's character is vindicated."[34] There is therefore a sense in which hell is good news. It not only shows that in the final analysis God can never compromise with sin, but it puts an end to the possibility of sin ever again breaking out and ruining His creation.

It is significant that in Scripture the only definition of sin is where we are told that "Sin is lawlessness" (1 John 3:4). In hell, this irrational, unpredictable rebellion will be turned in upon itself and permanently excluded from the rest of God's universe. Nothing will more vividly demonstrate God's awesome power and justice than the fact that unrepentant sinners will be unable to escape the consequences of their impenitence or to bring either ease or end to the punishment that their wickedness properly deserves. God glorifies Himself in their eternal damnation.

The idea that the everlasting existence of sinners compromises the sovereignty of God also fails to take into account a point well made by Larry Dixon: "The Bible speaks of God being vindicated at the end of time, but there is more than one way for the Victor to display his triumph over his enemies than by putting them out of existence. He can give them life at hard labor; or, in connection with the holy God of the Bible, he can consign them to eternal (second) death."[35]

As a postscript to this section, one might add that the endless existence of a moral "black hole" is not the greatest unsolved problem with regard to sin. After all, if in His perfect holiness God can allow evil now, He can certainly do so in eternity. A much greater problem is the very existence of sin at all as such an absurd and irrational curse on the universe. Why did God allow it in the first place when He knew what indescribable horror would result and when He had the option of preventing it? This is the fundamental question with regard to sin, and in the absence of any biblical revelation we have no option but to bow before it in humble silence.

ABILITY AND INTENTION

Sometimes the argument for annihilation is on the basis of supposition, without claiming any biblical basis. Roger Forster, a contemporary British preacher, provides an example of this: "Why shouldn't God, who first made the creature, be able to unmake it? If God could extinguish the pain of those who are unwilling to be saved, wouldn't that be a more merciful thing for a loving God to do?"[36]

The first thing wrong with this approach is that it elevates God's love above all of His other attributes and characteristics, and eliminates all mention of His holiness, His justice, and His righteous anger. The same kind of line was taken by John Robinson, who argued that "[God] has no purpose but the purpose of love and no nature but the nature of love."[37] This may sound impressive, but as J.I. Packer rightly says, "It is not possible to argue that a God who is love cannot also be a God who condemns and punishes the disobedient."[38]

Secondly, if God's love is the only thing that counts, and being merciful to the nth degree is the inevitable outworking of that love, surely the end result would be not annihilation but universalism? It would seem to be more merciful for God to save people than to obliterate them.

The third flaw in Roger Forster's comment is that it virtually equates God's power with His performance, His ability with His intention. Nobody questions the fact that a God with the power to create has the power to uncreate—but to say that because He is able to do something we can bank on the fact that He will do it is pushing things too far. For example, God undoubtedly has the power to heal every sickness, disease, and disability in every human being on the face of the earth, instantaneously and without any medical means; but it is obvious that He has chosen not to do this. The most that the "Why shouldn't God . . . unmake?" suggestion can do is to say that in the absence of any other factor such a thing could be done; but as their are other factors—and many of them—the suggestion makes no profitable contribution to the discussion. Another contemporary writer has put it perfectly: "To reduce our body and soul to non-existence would, no doubt, be very easy for God to do, but we fail to see the slightest evidence in the Scriptures that this is what God will do in the case of any member of the human race."[39]

ENOUGH IS ENOUGH?

Another speculative approach can be put like this: "Surely there comes a point at which no more conscious punishment should be inflicted on the wicked, and they may then be annihilated?" But why should that be the case? If the wicked are punished by the pains of hell (even if the degree of their punishment is graded to fit the extent of their sin) and are then annihilated, one can only assume that the reason for their annihilation would be that they will have paid in full the penalty their sins deserve. But if this was so, surely a God of justice would then welcome them into heaven, rather than consign them to non-existence? The idea that sinners pay their dues and are then "rewarded" with annihilation is not merely improbably, it is immoral—and it is God who is being charged with immorality. In one of His parables, Jesus taught that the person sent into hell's prison would not get out until he had paid "the last penny" (Matthew 5:26), the inescapable inference being that the last penny can never be paid.

Another insuperable problem with this particular theory is that it contradicts the central message of the Bible, which is that in the death of Christ God has provided the only atonement for human sin.

CRIME AND PUNISHMENT

The next argument can also be put in the form of a question: "Even at a human level, it is one of the principles of justice that the punishment should fit the crime. How can it be right for God to punish twenty, or sixty, or eighty years of sin with suffering that never ends?" This seems to be a perfectly reasonable thing to ask, but there are some very telling points that can be made in response.

In the first place, the amount of time spent in wrongdoing is often irrelevant in determining the sentence. As I write these words, police in London are looking for thugs who attacked a forty-five-year-old man in broad daylight, almost severed his arm with a billhook, pummeled him with a baseball bat, and sprayed hydrochloric acid in his face. The assault was all over in less than a minute; would sixty seconds in jail be an appropriate sentence? As William Hendricksen says, "It is not necessarily the duration of the crime that fixes the duration of the punishment . . . . What is decisive is the nature of the crime."[40]

Secondly, God alone has the ability to determine the true nature of sin and of the punishment that would be appropriate. Even at an earthly level, the criminal who insisted on manipulating the law to suit his own case would be given pretty short shrift. In the case of God's law, the idea of even trying to do so is absurd. Does anyone seriously claim to know how enormous an evil sin is in God's eyes? As John Wenham freely admits "No sinner is competent to judge the heinousness of sin."[41]

The point has been well made by a contemporary theologian:

"The desire to find an escape clause for ourselves or for others is a natural enough reaction, but it simply does not come to terms with the authority of the Bible or with the justice and finality of the judgments of God. The Bible makes it plain enough that human concepts of justice and equity, distorted as they are by the sinfulness of fallen human nature, are deceptive and unreliable, and in any case are not binding upon God, who tells us explicitly, 'For my thoughts are not your thoughts, neither are your ways my ways" (Isaiah 55:8).[42]

Thirdly, as God is infinitely worthy of man's love, obedience, and honor, man's obligation to give to him "the glory due to his name" (Psalm 29:2) is infinitely great. By the same token, his failure to do so is an infinite evil. And as infinite evil demands infinite punishment, the infinite sufferings of hell exactly fit the crime of which the wicked are guilty and are ultimate example of God's perfect justice.[43]

Fourthly, the argument about the punishment needing to fit the crime ignores the issues of the sinner's continuing attitude. There is certainly no such thing as repentance in hell; if there were, the end result would lean toward universalism. But as Paul Helm rightly says, "When judgment is pronounced there is no opportunity for repentance."[44] Yet, the absence of repentance is in itself a sin deserving punishment; and as that sin will continue forever, it is difficult to see how everlasting punishment would fail to fit the crime. John Gerstner clinches the point: "Since punishment itself never produces repentance, justice requires it to go on for ever."[45]

Fifthly, the character of God is at stake here. God's punishment of sinners is not something done in a fit of temper which might blow over after a while. Instead, it is the outcome of His perfect justice and unchanging hatred of evil. That being the case, there will never be a time when God will "cool off" and take a more lenient view of the sinner's stubborn rebellion. The Roman historian Suetonius tells of a long-term prisoner of Tiberius Caesar who pleaded with the emperor to put an end to his misery by having him put to death, but the emperor replied, "Stay, sir, you and I are not friends yet."[46] So it will be in hell. However desperately the sinner might cry to God to be annihilated and put out of his misery, God's righteous nature and the sinner's evil nature will mean that the reply will always be, "We are not friends yet." The illustration is not perfect, and is not intended to reduce God to the level of a pagan Roman emperor, yet the general principle involved safeguards God's holy and unchangeable character.

Sixthly, the argument that something done finitely can never have an infinite result proves too much, because it rules out heaven for the righteous as well as hell for the wicked. Jesus said, "Whoever believes in the Son has eternal life, but whoever rejects the Son will not see life, for God's wrath remains on him" (John 3:36). I appreciate that heaven is a gift of grace while hell is "earned," yet it would seem that the only way in which to make Jesus' words mean that the sinner's punishment in hell will come to an end is to say that the believer's joy in heaven will also do so, and I am not aware of any serious Bible student who has ever suggested that.

As if these six points were not conclusive, the argument they answer begs an obvious question. If it would be wrong of God to punish finite sin with everlasting punishment, how can it be right for Him to punish it by annihilation, which by definition is itself everlasting? If (as some allege) endless punishment is "sadistic," surely the same would apply to limited punishment? Would indescribably (but pointless) torture followed by annihilation be any kinder?

PUNISHMENT OR PUNISHING?

Another argument presented by annihilationists is to say that when the Bible speaks of "eternal punishment," what lasts forever is the punishment, not the pain. As one supporter of this idea put it, "The lost will not be passing through a process of pain for ever but will be punished once and for all with eternal results."[47] In other words, when the Bible speaks of eternal punishment rather than eternal punishing it means that only the effects of the punishment are everlasting, not the punishment itself.

If we can get over the fact that the distinction between "punishment" and "punishing" seem unnatural, and even clumsy, this sounds like a very promising approach, but it soon runs into a number of serious problems. If annihilation is the punishment, what is the purpose of the suffering? If the horrors of hell are a meaningless prelude to extinction, surely God is seen as the supreme sadist?

Another fatal flaw in the argument is this: How can annihilation possibly mean punishment when the person being punished no longer exists? As W.G.T. Shedd says, "In order to be punished, the person must be conscious of a certain pain, must feel that he deserves it, and know that it is inflicted because he does."[48]

Another writer makes the point like this: "Once we have said the word 'punishment' we have also said, at least by implication, the word 'conscious'. . . . A punishment that is not felt is not a punishment. Someone cannot be punished eternally unless that someone is there to receive the punishment. One can exist and not be punished, but one cannot be punished and not exist."[49]

The argument that what lasts forever is the punishment, not the pain, disintegrates when it comes up against clear biblical statements which we have already considered. The wicked will endure "shame and everlasting contempt" (Daniel 12:2). "The smoke of their torment rises for ever and ever" and they will have "no rest day or night" (Revelation 14:11). They will be "tormented day and night for ever and ever" (Revelation 20:10). How can these statements possibly mean that the pain will end and only the effects continue? Commenting on the last of them, the American writer Luther Poellot says, "This is God's final answer to those who say there is no infinitely fearful, painful and eternal hell."[50]

THE SECOND DEATH

Another argument sometimes used by annihilationists is that in the book of Revelation there is mention of a "second death." Could this be the loophole that allows for the wicked to be judged, sentenced, condemned, and punished but finally eliminated? Clark Pinnock takes this line and suggests that God raises the wicked from the dead not to punish them forever, but "to condemn them to extinction, which is the second death."[51] So does John Wenham: "For those who have rejected the love of God there will be after the last judgment just retribution varying in severity according to individual desert but (in my view) the sufferings will end speedily and mercifully in the second death."[52]

Even if we leave out Wenham's pure invention that it will happen "speedily," extinction seems an attractive proposition, but when we turn to Scripture there is conclusive evidence against the idea. This can be seen in the four places in Revelation where "the second death" is mentioned.

In the early part of the book there is an assurance that the faithful believer "will not be hurt at all by the second death" (Revelation 2:11).

The second reference is also a promise: "Blessed and holy are those who have part in the first resurrection. The second death has no power over them. . . ." (Revelation 20:6).

Later, after describing the Day of Judgment, John says, "Then death and Hades were thrown into the lake of fire. The lake of fire is the second death. If anyone's name was not found written in the book of life, he was thrown into the lake of fire" (Revelation 20:14-15).

Finally, we are told, "But the cowardly, the unbelieving, the vile, the murderers, the sexually immoral, those who practice magic arts, the idolaters and all liars—their place will be in the fiery lake of burning sulfur. This is the second death" (Revelation 21:8).

The claim that "the second death" means annihilation can be answered in five ways. Firstly, as we saw in chapter 5, the biblical meaning of death is not annihilation but separation. There is not a single case in the first sixty-five books of the Bible where the equation "death = annihilation" will stand up, and there are scores of instances where insisting on such an equation proves ridiculous. Jesus once told a prospective follower to "let the dead bury their own dead" (Matthew 8:22); did He really mean that the non-existent should bury the non-existent? Paul wrote that a widow living in pleasure "is dead even while she lives" (1 Timothy 5:6); did He really mean that she was annihilated and alive at one and the same time? James wrote that "The body without the spirit is dead" (James 2:26); did He really mean that at the moment of death the corpse vanishes into nothingness? It would throw the whole of Scripture into chaos if in the sixty-sixth and final book the word "death" was suddenly given a new and radically different meaning.

Secondly, if "death" means annihilation in these verses in Revelation, how can there possibly be such a thing as "the second annihilation"? And if the first annihilation (whatever that may mean) did not prove final, why should the second one (or any others that might follow) do so? This almost smacks of reincarnation, which is certainly not what the annihilationist has in mind.

Thirdly, two of the Revelation references to "the second death" specifically identify it with "the lake of fire" or "the fiery lake of burning sulfur" which, as we saw in chapter 10, is the Bible's metaphor for the awesome, holy, avenging presence of God. The "second death" is not a sequel to the terrible trauma of bearing the full fury of God's righteous anger; it is that terrible trauma, something by which the wicked "will be tormented day and night for ever and ever" (Revelation 20:10).

Fourthly, in the first reference there is an assurance that believers "will not be hurt at all by the second death." This shows that the "second death" hurts, whereas annihilation would not only not hurt, it would put an end to hurts of every kind. What would be the sense in John promising believers that they would not suffer the pains produced by annihilation?

Fifthly, if "the second death" is the ultimate punishment for sin, making it mean annihilation collapses before the fact that when Jesus bore the full penalty for sin in His death on the cross, He was not annihilated. The point has been made earlier in this book, but it has equal relevance here.

For these five reasons I agree with Roger Nicole when he writes, "The second death does not mean that the soul or personality lapses into non-being, but rather that it is ultimately and finally deprived of that presence of God and fellowship with him which is the chief end of man and the essential condition of worthwhile existence."[53]

SMOKE SIGNALS

Another approach relates to the Bible's teaching on the fire of hell, and in particular the statement that as far as the wicked are concerned, "The smoke of their torment rises for ever and ever" (Revelation 14:10). Roger Forster puts forward this idea: "Smoke lingers long after something has been burned, the smell continues in our nostrils as a reminder of what has been. But the smoke is all that remains. The fire has gone out long ago—the point is that nothing remains."[54] John Stott also supports this idea (we will touch on his comments in the next chapter), but it is not an original theory, nor does it gain anything from being an old one. After my home had been broken into for the third time, with fairly serious loss of property, I decided to install an intruder alarm system. I got quotations from several companies and eventually chose one which was not only competitive in price but offered the added incentive of a free smoke alarm. But what good will this be if smoke indicates that a fire has "gone out long ago" (having presumably reduced my home to a pile of ashes)? Those who take Roger Forster's line have apparently given no thought to four obvious points which can be made.

Firstly, smoke is not necessarily a sign that the fire has gone out. It may mean exactly the opposite. To make "The smoke of their torment rises for ever and ever" mean "the smoke caused by the fire which no longer exists but which, when it did exist, was the cause of their purely temporary torment" shows a fair amount of ingenuity, but hardly qualifies as legitimate interpretation.

Secondly, if the smoke is rising because the fire "has gone out long ago," why is it said to rise "for ever and ever"? After a fire goes out, the time comes when the last wisps of smoke also die away, so that neither fire not smoke remains. No juggling of the Bible's words can produce that result there.

Thirdly, how can we square Roger Forster's assurance that the time will come when "The fire has gone out long ago" with Jesus' statement that "The fire is not quenched" (Mark 9:48)? There does seem to be a discrepancy here! The American theologian Clark Pinnock is another annihilationist who says that the fire is only temporary: "The fire will be quenched only when the job is finished, not before."[55] Putting Pinnock's "will be quenched" alongside Jesus' "is not quenched" and making them mean the same thing surely presents something of a problem?

Fourthly, it is important to notice that John speaks not of "the smoke of *the* torment" but of "the smoke of *their* torment." We came across the same kind of phrase in chapter 10 when we noticed Jesus quoting the prophet Isaiah in saying that "Their worm does not die" (Mark 9:48). The use of the personal pronoun links the torment so closely to the person being tormented that it is difficult to see why John would have used it if he meant "the smoke of the fire that once tormented them." There can surely be no reasonable doubt that "the smoke of their torment' rising "for ever and ever" means that the wicked are being tormented forever and ever. Anthony Hoekema says bluntly, "Though we must not think of literal smoke here, the expression is meaningless if it is not intended to picture a punishment that will never end."[56]

THE FIRE AND THE FUEL

A slightly different approach sees hell's fire continuing to burn, but says that while "The fire is not quenched" and "Their worm does not die" there is no reference to those who are being punished. In other words, it is argued that while the "fire" and the "worm" continue forever, those they are burning and gnawing will at some point have been extinguished. John Stott puts the case like this: "The main function of fire is not to cause pain, but to secure destruction, as all the world's incinerators bear witness."[57] This sounds fairly convicting, but it ignores the rather obvious point that the "main function" (that is, the purpose) of fire is by no means always the same and is determined by the person who lights it. Fire is used for many different purposes, such as lighting, heating, cooking, warning of danger, burning off unwanted material, and even providing a romantic atmosphere! Deciding that the purpose of hell's "fire" must be the extinction of the wicked has no foundation in nature or Scripture.

Others add the argument that as fire always consumes whatever is put into it, it would be impossible for anyone to endure the fire of hell forever; but there are two things that can be said in reply. The first is that if we think in terms of literal fire (which is how the point is being made), it is not true to say that fire always consumes. On the contrary, nothing that is burnt by fire is extinguished in the sense of becoming non-existent; it is simply changed into another form of existence, such as vapor, gas, or dust.

Secondly, there are two instances in Scripture where there was burning without consuming. At a crucial point in God's dealings with Moses, "The angel of the Lord appeared to him in a blazing fire from the midst of a bush; and he looked, and behold, the bush was burning with fire, yet the bush was not consumed" (Exodus 3:2, NASB). Many years later, when three of God's faithful servants, Shadrach, Meshach, and Abednego, infuriated King Nebuchadnezzar of Babylon by refusing to worship a golden idol, he had them thrown into a blazing furnace which had been heated "seven times hotter than usual" (Daniel 3:19). The heat was so intense that it killed several of the soldiers who threw the men into the flames, yet some time later Shadrach, Meshach, and Abednego walked out of the furnace, and everybody could see that "The fire had not harmed their bodies, nor was a hair of their heads singed; their robes were not scorched, and there was no smell of fire on them" (Daniel 3:27). These two instances alone should be enough to warn us against trying to force the teaching of the Word of God into the tiny limits of our own logic.

As to the main argument, we have to see it in the light of the Bible's teaching that the present order of things, including the earthly cycle of birth, life, and death, will one day pass away. When this happens, why would the fire and the worms continue if there were no further people to punish and therefore (to be crudely literal) there was no further fuel for the fire and no further food for the worm? However it may tear at our emotions, it seems much more natural to assume that the unquenched fire and the undying worm point to the continuation of the punishment they are inflicting and of those on whom the punishment is being inflicted.

It is not difficult to find reasons why the idea of annihilation should be so attractive. One of the most obvious has a strong emotional impetus. The thought of untold numbers of people suffering endless agony pounds at our feelings like a relentless sledgehammer. John Stott says, "Emotionally I find the concept intolerable and do not understand how people can live with it without either cauterizing their emotions or cracking under the strain."[58] I can understand that. More than one of my close relatives has died in the last five years without any pretense of Christian faith. I have family members now living who give every appearance of being "without hope and without God in the world" (Ephesians 2:12) and unless God graciously brings them to Himself, they will remain like that in the world to come. Nothing causes me more anguish than this; nothing has caused me to shed more tears.

At a remoter level, but with a vastly greater numerical impact, similar emotions sometimes grip me when I see large crowds of people. I remember being in Thailand watching thousands of people teeming through the streets of Bangkok at 6:30 in the morning and thinking with stunning horror that perhaps most of these, within a few years, would be beyond any opportunity of salvation and doomed to spend eternity suffering the pains of hell.

Yet however strong these natural emotions may be, they must never be allowed to determine our doctrine or dilute the teaching of God's Word. I heard recently of a seminary professor who refused to teach everlasting punishment of the wicked because he had a son who was living a godless life, and he could not bear the thought of someone he loved so dearly spending eternity under God's unrelenting judgment. One can understand the professor's trauma, but how can it be right to filter Scripture through the grid of one's own emotions? As John Stott rightly agrees, "Our emotions are a fluctuating, unreliable guide to truth and must not be exalted to the place of supreme authority in determining it."[59] That supreme authority is the Word of God, and our only legitimate response is to submit without reservation to everything it says.

Anthony Hoekema makes the point well: "If we take the testimony of Scripture seriously, and if we base our doctrines on its teaching—as indeed we should—we are compelled to believe in the eternal punishment of the lost. To be sure, we shrink from this teaching with all that is within us and do not dare to try to visualize how this eternal punishment might be experienced by someone we know. But the Bible teaches it, and therefore we must accept it.'[60]

As far as the doctrine of hell is concerned, we are now in a position to examine the exact words the Bible uses in regard to its effect and duration. Is there anything in these descriptions that will support the idea of a "last loophole"?

The Decisive Words

This book is being written with the conviction that the Bible is exactly what it claims to be, "the living and enduring word of God" (1 Peter 1:23) and, as one historic Confession of Faith puts it, "the only sufficient, certain and infallible rule of all saving knowledge, faith and obedience."[1] Not only is the Bible the Word of God, it consists of the *words* of God. Hundreds of times in Scripture the writers claim to be recording exactly what God said, and at one point we are told, "All Scripture is God-breathed" (2 Timothy 3:16).

Although they represented different ages, cultures, backgrounds, and lifestyles, each of the Bible's human authors was used by the divine Author to say what He wanted to say: "Men spoke from God as they were carried along by the Holy Spirit" (2 Peter 1:21). In his excellent book *Nothing But the Truth*, my friend Brian Edwards puts it like this: "The Holy Spirit moved men to write. He allowed them to use their own style, culture, gifts, and character, to use the results of their own study and research, to write of their own experiences, and to express what was in their mind. At the same time, the Holy Spirit did not allow sin to influence their writings; he overruled in the expression of thought and in the choice of words. Thus they recorded accurately all that God wanted them to say and exactly how he wanted them to say it, in their own character, style, and language."[2]

As an illustration of this, there is one place where a massively important doctrine hinges on whether one particular Old Testament word is in the singular or plural.[3] Those who suggest that the Bible is flawed because its authors were "men of their time" or unduly influenced by Greek philosophy or pagan culture have totally missed this point. The Bible is not the Word of God in some vague or general sense, but, in their original form, the exact words God intends us to hear.

WHAT HAPPENED TO THE DONKEYS?

We need to remember this as we now examine the exact words God used in Scripture to describe hell's effects and duration, and particularly as we continue to explore the possibility that annihilation is the "last loophole" which will bring the pains of hell to an end. One of the annihilationists' strongest arguments is to say that when speaking of the ultimate fate of sinners, the Bible sometimes uses words which must mean extinction. If this is so, the case for annihilation is proved—but is it? Turning firstly to the Old Testament, we will examine five of the main words that are alleged to be decisive.

In one of the clearest and most concise statements about the fate of unbelievers we are told that "The way of the wicked will perish" (Psalms 1:6; 37:20). Elsewhere in the Psalms the writer says that "The foolish and the senseless alike perish" (Psalm 49:10), while David, calling upon God to vindicate his righteousness, cries out, "May the wicked perish before God" (Psalm 68:2). In all these cases the Hebrew word translated "perish" is *abhad*; but does it mean annihilation? We can certainly agree that if this is what the writers had in mind *abhad* is one of the words they could have chosen, but it is a big step from allowing that a word might be used to express a certain meaning to proving that it does express it in a certain place. Important questions need to be asked here. Are the writers speaking only of temporal judgment (very common in the Old Testament)? And if they are speaking of final judgment, do they mean the reduction of the soul to nonexistence?

The first question must be answered from the context, which will immediately reduce the number of cases in which the use of *abhad* in the Old Testament refers to final judgment, as there are those where it certainly refers to physical death.

The second question gives an opportunity to respond to the annihilationists' claim that *abhad* must mean extinction. When the prophet Jeremiah was mourning over the devastation which Judah's sin had brought upon itself, he asked, "Why does the land perish and burn up like a wilderness?" (Jeremiah 9:12, NKJV). Later, he prophesied that when its enemies swept in, Moab would face desperate times: "The valley also shall perish, and the plan shall be destroyed" (Jeremiah 48:8, NKJV). Sometimes, *abhad* is translated differently: for example, "Now the donkeys belonging to Saul's father Kish were lost" (1 Samuel 9:3). But can *abhad* possibly mean annihilation in any of these three cases? Was Jeremiah talking of "black holes" appearing all over the country? Did Kish's donkeys evaporate? Isaiah provides even stronger evidence. At a time of religious persecution, he grieved at what was happening to some of his country's godliest people: "The righteous perish, and no one ponders in his heart" (Isaiah 57:1). If "to perish" means "to be annihilated," and this is the fate of the wicked, why does Isaiah say that the same thing was happening to the righteous? It is perfectly obvious that in this case the word "perish" means "are being killed"; it cannot possibly mean annihilation.

Another Old Testament example is the Hebrew word *karat*, which David uses when he says that "Evil men will be cut off" (Psalm 37:9). This is said to mean that they will be annihilated, but it is impossible to sustain this argument. Many times in the Old Testament religious law decreed that an offender should be "cut off from his people" (Leviticus 7:20-21, 25, 27; 17:3) and one only has to examine these statements in context to see that they mean excommunication, not annihilation. When the Philistines came across the body of King Saul after a fierce battle on Mount Gilboa, they "cut off his head and stripped off his armor" (1 Samuel 31:9). Does this mean that they annihilated him from the neck upwards? Even more telling is a messianic prophecy by Daniel which says that "the Anointed One will be cut off" (Daniel 9:26). Jesus was certainly criticized, persecuted, tortured, and crucified, but nobody seriously suggests that he was annihilated.

Annihilationists also claim that the Hebrew word *shamad* supports their case. David uses this word when he says, "The Lord watches over all who love him, but all the wicked he will destroy" (Psalm 145:20). Yet again, the claim that this must mean annihilation never gets off the ground. When Pharoah's servants were pleading with him to release the Hebrew slaves before the land was hit by another catastrophe (God had already sent seven devastating plagues) they asked him, "Do you not realize that Egypt is destroyed?" (Exodus 10:7, NASB). Years later, when Moses was reminding God's people how God had enabled them to overcome their enemies, he singled out the defeats of Sihon and Og, the kings of the Amorites, who had been "destroyed along with their land" (Deuteronomy 31:4). When a woman disguised herself as a widow and spun King David a yarn about one of her sons killing his only brother, she told him that she was now in trouble because the whole family was determined to lay hands on the murderer and "destroy the heir also" (2 Samuel 14:7, NASB). It only takes a moment's thought to see that in none of these cases can *shamad* possibly mean annihilation.

A further Old Testament example is the word *kalah*, which one of the psalmists uses in calling upon God to let his enemies be "ashamed and consumed" (Psalm 71:13, NASB). Was he asking for them to be annihilated? The rest of the verse answers the question, because he also asks that they be "covered with reproach and dishonor," a phrase which clearly indicates some kind of visible, temporal punishment. Other Old Testament evidence backs this up. If *kalah* means annihilation, then the Gibeonites were non-existent when they told David that Saul was "the man who consumed us" (2 Samuel 21:5, NASB), and David himself was non-existent when he was smarting under God's discipline and cried out, "I am consumed by the blow of your hand" (Psalm 39:10, NKJV). How can this make any sense?

Another word claimed by annihilationists is *tamam*, which David uses when he calls upon God to let unrepentant sinners be "consumed from the earth" (Psalm 104:35, NASB), but again the attempt to insist that this must mean extinction is ruled out by the word's use elsewhere. The Bible says that during an economic slump "The money of the people of Egypt and Canaan was gone" (Genesis 47:15); how can this possibly mean that it was non-existent? When Moses was reminding God's people of their nation's history, he spoke of a period during which an "entire generation of fighting men had perished from the camp" (Deuteronomy 2:14). To suggest that he meant they had been annihilated is surely going too far!

Other significant Hebrew words include *ephes* ("nothing"), *ayin* ("to be nothing; not to exist"), and *saphah* ("to come to an end"), but I have not been able to find a single instance in which any of them is used in such a way as to support the annihilationists' claims. The attempt to use Old Testament word meanings to show that the wicked will be annihilated is a comprehensive failure.

KORAH AND COMPANY

Turning to the New Testament we find the same pattern, with the annihilationists setting great store by words which cannot possibly support their claim. Here are four examples.

One of the most crucial words is the Greek verb *apollumi*, which occurs eighty-five times and is often used about the final fate of the wicked. Jesus warned certain people that "Unless you repent, you too will all perish" (Luke 13:5); and Paul wrote of those who would "perish apart from the law" (Romans 2:12). Sometimes the word is translated differently: Jesus said that God was able to "destroy both soul and body in hell," (Matthew 10:28) and James wrote of God as "the one who is able to save and destroy" (James 4:12).

The related noun (*apoleia*) is used in the same way: Jesus spoke of "the road that leads to destruction" (Matthew 7:13); Paul wrote of those whose "destiny is destruction" (Philippians 3:19), and Peter prophesied about "the day of judgment and destruction of ungodly men" (2 Peter 3:7).

These statements may seem to suggest annihilation, but damaging cracks appear as soon as we notice that *apollumi* can have a number of very different meanings. When Jesus was growing in popularity the Pharisees had an urgent meeting to discuss "how they might destroy him" (Matthew 12:14, NASB); but it would be ridiculous to suggest that they had annihilation in mind. The word *apollumi* is used over twenty times in the sense of "to die" or "to be killed." Sometimes a related word is more naturally translated "lost." Jesus said that He came into the world "to seek and to save what was lost" (Luke 19:10); but if "lost" means extinct, surely His coming was utterly pointless? When Jesus sent His apostles out on a preaching mission He told them that at that stage they were to ignore the Gentiles and Samaritans and go to "the lost sheep of Israel" (Matthew 10:6); but how could they have been sent to people who were non-existent? In one of His parables He told of a shepherd searching for a "lost sheep" (Luke 15:4), and followed this with a similar story which ended with a woman rejoicing over finding "my lost coin" (Luke 15:9). How can annihilation be meant in either of these cases?

Jesus followed these two parables with the famous story of the prodigal son, which provides two illustrations to prove that apollumi cannot mean "to be annihilated." When he realized what a fool he had been, the son remembered that while his father's servants had more than enough to eat, "I perish with hunger" (Luke 15:17, NKJV), and the story eventually comes to a climax with his father rejoicing that the boy "was lost and is found" (Luke 15:32). How could either word possibly mean annihilation? Another translation of the noun *apoleia* raises the same unanswerable question: when a woman honored Jesus by anointing him with a jar of expensive perfume, some of the disciples indignantly asked, "Why this waste?" (Matthew 26:8).

Another New Testament illustration proves particularly damaging for annihilationists. In the course of his brief letter, Jude warns about the dangers of rebelling against God's appointed leaders, and says that those who do so "have been destroyed in Korah's rebellion" (Jude 11). (This is an unusual, but not unique, way of expressing the certainty of something that is yet to happen by using a past tense, but the important thing is not this interesting use of Greek grammar, but what "destroyed" means.) Korah was a notorious trouble-maker who rebelled against Moses. Things eventually got to such a pitch that Moses faced Korah and his fellow rebels head on, accusing them of treating God with contempt. In a dramatic moment of divine judgment, the confrontation came to a devastating conclusion for Korah and the other mutineers when the ground opened up under their feet, and they were hurled to their deaths, the Bible adding that "They and all that belonged to them went down alive to Sheol" (Numbers 16:33, NASB). As it is this going down alive into Sheol that Jude described as being destroyed, it cannot mean annihilation.

As if this were not clear enough, the Korah incident gives us two pieces of evidence for the price of one, because the Old Testament adds that by being buried in this way Korah and his cohorts "perished and were gone from the community" (Numbers 16:33), the word "perished" being the Hebrew *abhad* which we looked at earlier. The obvious meaning is not that Korah and the others were annihilated, but that they disappeared out of sight.

THE PLANET AND THE PEOPLE

These illustrations make it clear that it is impossible to insist that *apollumi* and *apoleia* must mean annihilation, but there are others just as conclusive. In reminding his readers of the time when God punished men's wickedness by sending a catastrophic flood on the earth, Peter says that "The world of that time was deluged and destroyed" (2 Peter 3:6). Where is there a shred of evidence in Scripture to suggest that God annihilated our planet and created another one to replace it? When Jesus used God's punishment of the people of Sodom and Gomorrah as an example of the suddenness of His Second Coming, He said that "Fire and sulfur rained down from heaven and destroyed them all" (Luke 17:29). As He said elsewhere that the people of

Sodom and Gomorrah would appear "on the day of judgment" (Matthew 10:15), it is clear that when they were "destroyed" they were not annihilated.

To insist that *apollumi* and *apoleia* must refer to annihilation is absurd, as they never do so when applied to things other than human destiny. There is not a single occasion in the New Testament when *apollumi* refers to anybody or anything passing out of existence. Trying to make it mean so when it is used in connection with the destiny of the wicked is therefore pointless. The word simply does not bear that meaning. W. E. Vine says that the idea behind these words is "not extinction but ruin; loss, not of being, but of wellbeing,"[4] and J.I. Packer confirms that *"Apollumi* is the regular Greek word for the wrecking and ruining of something, so making it useless for its intended purpose."[5] Even more significantly, Thayer's *Greek-English Lexicon of the New Testament* defines *apollumi* as "to be delivered up to eternal misery."[6] This is a particularly damaging blow to annihilationism, as Thayer himself was a Unitarian and did not believe in eternal punishment.

Another word employed by annihilationists is the noun *olethros*, but it proves equally unhelpful to their cause. Paul uses the word in saying that the return of Jesus to the earth will be catastrophic for sinners because "Destruction will come on them suddenly" (1 Thessalonians 5:3). Then, in a second letter to the same believers, he says that at Christ's coming the ungodly will be "punished with everlasting destruction" (2 Thessalonians 1:9). These phrases sound pretty decisive, but in fact the Bible gives *olethros* a meaning very different from annihilation. Paul says that a "get rich quick" mentality plunges men "into ruin and destruction" (1 Timothy 6:9). The meaning of "ruin and destruction" begins to emerge in Paul's very next words, when he makes his well-known (and often misquoted) statement that "The love of money is a root of all kinds of evil" and adds that some people who have fallen for this philosophy "have wandered from the faith and pierced themselves with many griefs" (1 Timothy 6:10).

Paul has no need to elaborate; I know of several professing Christians, once contented with their fairly meager lot and living happy and effective lives, who suddenly made significant financial progress, became "upwardly mobile" and developed a passion for possessions. Now they live in larger houses, move in higher social circles, and seem to have all the material means they need—but their spiritual lives have shriveled. In not a few cases, their material successes has paved the way for boredom, dishonesty, immorality, depression, or divorce; but whatever their "griefs," annihilation is not one of them!

This all adds up to powerful evidence that in biblical language "to destroy" does not mean to annihilate, but even without this scriptural support our common use of "destroy" should lead us to the same conclusion. Driving in southern France some years ago, I came across the scene of a terrible accident. One of the cars involved had been sliced in two; one half of it lay on the left-hand edge of the road and the other on the right. As a means of transportation, it was utterly destroyed. It could never again serve the purpose for which it had been made. It was wrecked, ruined. In the expressive American phrase, it was "totaled"; but it was not annihilated.

In May 1992, race riots tore through some parts of Los Angeles, and in one news bulletin after another we were told that the whole area had been "destroyed." The damage was certainly horrific; hundreds of buildings were gutted, millions of dollars worth of damage was done, and many people were killed. South central Los Angeles lay in smoldering ruins; but it was not annihilated.

The words we have examined so far all have to do with the effects of hell, and none has provided the loophole which annihilationism claims to provide. What about those which refer to hell's duration? Do these provide the evidence annihilationism needs?

THE TWO AGES

As far as our present study is concerned, the crucial New Testament words are those translated "everlasting," "eternal," "forever" and "forevermore," because all four are used by the Bible in describing hell. Similar or related words are used many times in the Old Testament, but examining them would only belabor the same point. The first two words are adjectives and the last two adverbs, and the key to unlocking their meaning lies in the Greek noun *aion* from which each one of them is taken. The word *aion* means "an age," as does our English word "aeon." In the Bible, there are said to be two "ages," one finite and limited in time and the other infinite and beyond the boundaries of time, and there are several places which make the distinction crystal clear by referring to both in the same sentence.

When warning people about the danger of rejecting the Holy Spirit's witness to the truth, Jesus said, "Anyone who speaks against the Holy Spirit will not be forgiven, either in this age or in the age to come" (Matthew 12:32)—in other words, either in time or in eternity. He also spoke of faithful believers receiving rewards for their faithfulness "in this present age . . . and in the age to come" (Mark 10:30; Luke 18:30). Paul wrote that Christ was exalted to a place "far above all rule and authority, power and dominion, and every title that can be given, not only in the present age but also in the one to come" (Ephesians 1:21).

These references show a clear distinction between the two "ages," but we can go one step further by looking at a passage which uses the word "eternal." Writing to the Christians in Corinth, Paul encouraged them to persevere in face of the persecution they were facing: "For our light and momentary troubles are achieving for us an eternal glory that far outweighs them all. So we fix our eyes not on what is seen, but on what is unseen. For what is seen is temporary, but what is unseen is eternal. Now we know that if the earthly tent we live in is destroyed, we have a building from God, an eternal house in heaven, not built by human hands" (2 Corinthians 4:17-5:1). Here the adjective "eternal" (*aionios*) is used to describe three things; "glory," "what is unseen" and the believer's "house in heaven"; and these are said to be indirect contrast to "momentary troubles," "what is seen" and the believer's "earthly tent" (that is, his body). We are nearly getting ahead of ourselves here, but it is obvious that Paul is promising that the believers will enjoy the "eternal" things in the future as a glorious contrast to the limitations and pressures of the present. But he does more. He uses the words "momentary," "temporary," and "destroyed" to emphasize that the things they describe will come to an end; and when writing of the blessings the believer will enjoy in the future he replaces all three words with the one word "eternal." It seems as clear as daylight that by doing so he means to say that these blessings will never end.

We must now backtrack a little and establish a principle that will guide us through the remainder of this chapter: whenever we come across the adjectives "everlasting" and "eternal," we must get their meaning from the nouns they describe, and whenever we come across the adverbs "forever" and "forevermore" we must get their meaning from the verbs they qualify. This means, for example, that "everlasting" need not always mean something that lasts forever; nor need "forever" always mean never-ending. However, it is virtually impossible to find any of our four key word used in a context which gives them a meaning which is purely or mainly finite or temporary. Instead, of the more than 100 times they occur, almost all of them relate not to time but to eternity.

The first batch of examples all refer to God or to individual members of the Godhead. Paul writes of "the eternal God" (Romans 16:26) and of "the King eternal . . ." (1 Timothy 1:17). Elsewhere we are told that Jesus Christ is "the same yesterday and today and for ever' (Hebrews 13:8), and that He accomplished His work of salvation "through the eternal Spirit" (Hebrews 9:14).

Exactly as we might expect in a book which majors on future events, Revelation uses these words repeatedly: three times God is said to be the one "who lives for ever and ever" (Revelation 4:9, 10; 10:6); we are told that "He will reign for ever and ever" (Revelation 11:15); and we are given a glimpse of every creature in the universe acknowledging that "praise and honor and glory and power" are due to Him "for ever and ever!" (Revelation 5:13).

Other writers pick up these same themes. Paul says that God "is to be praised for ever" (2 Corinthians 11:31) and Jude ascribes to God "glory, majesty, power and authority, through Jesus Christ our Lord, before all ages, now and for evermore! Amen" (Jude 25). This last statement gives an added dimension, telling us that in God's case eternity looks back as well as forwards; these things were true of Him "before all ages," as well as continuing to be true "forevermore."

Taking all of these statements together, there is no way in which they can mean that Good took control of the universe at some time in the past, nor that He runs the risk of being ousted like an unpopular government at some time in the future. The plain, straightforward meaning of our key words in every one of these cases is that "There is no end to his being or rule."[7] To say that God is "eternal" may imply more than that He is everlasting; it cannot mean anything less.

THE AGES OF MAN

We can now turn to the largest batch of statements in which our four key words are used over sixty times to describe the future experience of the righteous. Jesus said that they will be welcomed into "eternal dwellings" (Luke 16:9). Paul added that they will obtain "the salvation that is in Christ Jesus, with eternal glory" (2 Timothy 2:10). John wrote that in heaven "They will reign for ever and ever" (Revelation 22:5) and that the person who does the will of God "lives for ever" (1 John 2:17).

As in the cases relating to God Himself, these expressions have been described as "the strongest words . . . to declare the whole of an age or period, and the entire duration of the subject to which they are applied".[8] I know of no serious Bible student who suggests that heaven's "eternal dwellings" provide nothing more than temporary accommodation, with the tenants liable to be moved on, or who believes that their "eternal glory" might fade away. Writing of the New Testament's references to what he calls "the divine and blessed realities of the other world," René Pache says, "In all these cases, it is beyond all doubt a question of duration without end."[9]

We have now considered all but ten of the cases in which our four key words are used in the New Testament. One of these, where Jude refers to fallen angels who are "bound with everlasting chains for judgment on the great Day" (Jude 6) can be passed by here as it refers to the period (but significantly the entire period) leading up to the Day of Judgment. That leaves us with nine, all of which we have touched on earlier in this book, but as they refer to the condition of the wicked after the Day of Judgment they provide vital evidence as to whether or not annihilation is that last loophole which will put an end to the pains of hell. Here are seven of them:

Jesus spoke of the danger of being "thrown into eternal fire" (Matthew 18:8).

Paul said that all who were not right with God would be "punished with everlasting destruction" (2 Thessalonians 1:9).

Jude warned of those who will "suffer the punishment of eternal fire" (Jude 7).

Jude also wrote of those "for whom blackest darkness has been reserved for ever" (Jude 13).

John had a vision of sinners "tormented with burning sulphur" in which "the smoke of their torment rises for ever and ever" (Revelation 14:11).

Later, he wrote of sinful and condemned humanity, "The smoke from her goes up for ever and ever" (Revelation 19:3).

Finally, John said that the devil, his agents and all who had been deceived by them "will be tormented day and night for ever and ever" (Revelation 20:10).

In every other instance when the four key words are used in a future sense they include the meaning of endlessness (though "eternal" sometimes includes a sense of quality as well as quantity); that being so, is it right to decide that in these seven cases they have a totally different meaning? Nobody who professes to accept the teaching of Scripture doubts that God is everlasting or that the joys of the righteous in heaven are everlasting. Then surely it must follow that unless there is clear evidence to the contrary this everlastingness must apply to the fire, the smoke, the torments, and the darkness experienced in hell? As Robert Dabney put it, the duration of hell is "parallel with the eternity of God."[10]

As long ago as 1744, and referring in particular to the words of Jesus, one scholar wrote, "It is hard to say how any doctrine can be taught more plainly . . . how could he have done it in plainer words or in a more emphatical manner?"[11] Over two hundred years later, William Hendricksen came to a similar conclusion: "The passages are so numerous that one actually stands aghast that in spite of all this there are people today who affirm that they accept Scripture and who, nevertheless, reject the idea of never-ending torment."[12]

DAY AND NIGHT

The seven verses we have just quoted, and the two we shall look at shortly, are those which give annihilationists their greatest problems. This can be seen from the way they handle the fifth of them, which in its fuller context reads, "He will be tormented with burning sulfur in the presence of the holy angels and of the Lamb. And the smoke of their torment rises for ever and ever. There is no rest day or night for those who worship the beast and his image, or for anyone who receives the mark of his name" (Revelation 14:10-11). John Stott says that the torment mentioned here "seems to refer to the moment of judgment, not to the eternal state," and adds, "It is not the burning itself but its 'smoke' (symbol of the completed burning) which will be 'for ever and ever.'"[13] Significantly, however, he makes no comment on the next sentence, which says that those tormented will have "no rest day or night"—a phrase which hardly sounds like "the moment of judgment" and is even more difficult to equate with extinction.

Edward Fudge, on the other hand, does tackle the phrase about having "no rest day or night," and comes to the curious conclusion that although the wicked "are not guaranteed rest during the day" and "There is no certain hope that relief will come at night," this "does not say within itself that the suffering lasts all day and all night."[14] This does sound suspiciously like special pleading, to say the least! Fudge seems to need this device because he sets his interpretation of all the punishment passages within a rigid framework which says that after the Day of Judgment the wicked are firstly sent to hell, secondly endure conscious punishment and finally are extinguished. This packages the process very neatly, but as one scholar has pointed out, "Not a single New Testament passage teaches exactly this sequence; instead, some texts speak of personal exclusion, some of punishment and the others of destruction, and these images need to be understood as giving us hints at the same eschatological reality . . . A fully biblical theology of hell must do justice to all three images: punishment, destruction and exclusion."[15]

CATCH—22

The other verses we have listed in this section prove no easier for annihilationists. To give just one further example, Paul's reference to "eternal destruction" produces a catch-22 situation. "Destruction" cannot mean "annihilation" because Paul could hardly speak of "everlasting annihilation" unless reincarnation was an alternative; and "everlasting" cannot mean "temporary" or it would open the door to universalism. Commenting on the phrase about the wicked being "tormented day and night for ever and ever," one modern writer makes this telling statement: "Annihilationists have simply dismissed it as 'difficult' (only because it doesn't fit in with their opinion) or 'symbolic' (without a word about what they think it symbolizes). Could there be a plainer statement? 'Tormented' can only mean conscious suffering; 'day and night' can only mean without respite; and 'for ever and ever' (literally, 'to the ages of the ages,' the strongest Greek expression to convey 'everlastingness') can only mean inconceivably endless."[16]

When the British preacher H. E. Guillebaud died in 1941, he left behind a manuscript that was published in 1965 under the title *The Righteous Judge* and regarded as a significant contribution to the annihilationist cause. But when Guillebaud came to this particular statement in Revelation, he made a damaging admission which ruined his whole thesis: "It must be admitted that the New Testament usage is against interpreting 'unto the ages of ages' as meaning anything short of endless eternity."[17]

Other attempts to change the obvious meaning of these and other phrases are equally flawed. For instance, the idea that the eternal punishment of hell is eternal only in its effects would seem to suggest that by the same token it is only the results of being in heaven that will be eternal, and not the conscious enjoyment of being there—the righteous themselves presumably being annihilated. Can anyone seriously believe that? If eternal punishment is not endured forever, eternal life is not enjoyed forever; what biblical basis is there for such an idea?

J. I. Packer adds: "The insistence [of Scripture] that the fire, punishment and destruction are eternal . . . would be pointless and inappropriate if all that is envisaged is momentary extinction; just as it would be pointless and inappropriate to dwell on 'unending' pain resulting from an immediately fatal bullet wound. Either these words indicate the endlessness of torment, or they are superfluous and misleading."[18]

CLEAR OR CONFUSING?

That brings us to the final two uses of our key words. Jesus said that at the Day of Judgment He would tell the wicked, "Depart from me, you who are cursed, into the eternal fire prepared for the devil and his angels," and that the moment would then come when "They will go away to eternal punishment, but the righteous to eternal life" (Matthew 25:41, 46). If the other references we have examined are difficult for the annihilationist, these are surely impossible! Why would Jesus use the same word to describe the "punishment" of the wicked and the "life" of the righteous if He meant that one would come to an end and the other would be endless?

Over 1,500 years ago Augustine wrote, "To say that life eternal shall be endless [but that] punishment eternal shall come to an end is the height of absurdity."[19] As one contemporary writer puts it in commenting on the second of the statements Jesus made, "Anyone with only a school boy's Greek can verify that the same adjective is used in both parts of the verse. If the 'life' to come for believers is everlasting, so must the 'punishment' of sinners be. But if scholars must tell us that Christ used the word *aionion* (eternal, everlasting) in two wholly different and mutually contradictory senses, then we may as well lay the Bible aside as an insoluble enigma."[20]

What was the natural, obvious, apparent meaning of what Jesus said? He was not talking to theologians, or professors in linguistics, but to ordinary people drawn largely from working-class backgrounds and with no formal theological training. Was He trying to make things clear, or was He being carelessly confusing? If He had wanted to tell them that both destinies were everlasting He could not have done so more clearly; if He had wanted to tell them that the two destinies were entirely different in duration, He could hardly have chosen a worse way of expressing it.

J.C. Ryle's comment on this verse makes the point perfectly: "It is clearly revealed in Scripture: the eternity of God, and heaven and hell, all stand on the same foundation. As surely as God is eternal, so surely is heaven an endless day without night, and hell an endless night without day."[21] The same kind of thing could be said about other statements Jesus made on the subject. If He had meant to say that the pains of hell would be temporary, why did He not speak of a dying worm instead of an undying one, and of a fire that would eventually be quenched instead of one that would not?

The technical evidence alone is sufficient to rule out annihilationism as the "last loophole," something emphasized by one theologian after another.

Writing about some of the words we have been studying, the American theologian A.H. Strong says, "If, when used to describe the future punishment of the wicked, they do not declare the endlessness of that punishment, there are no words in the Greek language which could express that meaning."[22]

A.A. Hodge makes the same point: "The ceaseless, hopeless, conscious suffering of those who die impenitent, both during the intermediate state before the resurrection and in the final state after the resurrection and judgment, is asserted over and over again in every form, in the most definite language, and with the greatest emphasis possible."[23] Elsewhere he adds, "There is nothing in the Scriptures which, even by the most remote implication, suggests that the sufferings of the lost shall ever end."[24]

Loraine Boettner writes, "If these expressions do not teach that the punishment of the wicked continue eternally, it is difficult to see how it could be taught in human language."[25]

Alec Motyer points out that "The notion of 'eternity,' in so far as it is revealed to us by the New Testament use of the word, excluded the idea of termination,"[26] while J. I. Packer says that "An endless hell can no more be removed from the New Testament than an endless heaven can be."[27]

In the light of such powerful evidence, it is hardly surprising that in 1880 E. B. Pusey, a well-known Professor of Hebrew at Oxford University, became so exasperated at people's repeated attempts to deny the endless punishment of the wicked that he suggested they "would do well to consider whether there is any way in which Almighty God could have expressed it which they would have accepted as meaning it"![28]

Another argument against annihilationism can be drawn from the fact that the Bible uses mixed metaphors to describe the fate of the wicked. For example, it speaks of hell both in terms of "blackest darkness" (Jude 13) and "eternal fire" (Matthew 25:41), leading some critics to say that as fire gives light both descriptions cannot be true. This misses the point we discussed in a previous chapter that these descriptions are symbolic, and not to be taken literally, and that each one (and each of the other symbols used) is intended to convey a different aspect of hell's horror.

Even more to the point we are discussing here, the very fact that the Bible uses symbols at all is impressive evidence against the annihilation of the wicked, because it is impossible to imagine any symbol which suggests non-existence. As Robert Morey rightly observes, "If annihilation were true, then there would be no need for the terrifying mental images of figurative speech used in the Bible to describe hell."[29]

When facing his executioners, Polycarp, the second-century Bishop of Smyrna said, "You threaten me with fire that burns for one hour and then cools, not knowing the judgments to come, nor the perpetual torment of eternal fire to the ungodly."[30] For nearly 2,000 years, Polycarp's convictions about hell have been shared almost unanimously by those who have carefully studied the Word of God and sought to submit without reservation to its authority. This is what we should expect, because as one major theological work puts it, "No one approaching the New Testament without preconceived opinions could get any other impression from the language on this subject than that the punishments of the wicked in hell are to be everlasting."[31]

Yet people do have preconceived notions. I have before me a letter from Holland on this very subject which includes the phrases: "To me it would make a lot more sense," "It seems to me . . . ," "I don't see . . . ," and "That isn't a loving God to me." It is not difficult to know why someone would write like that. The subject of hell is horrible. The idea of being judged by a holy God is frightening. The thought of countless human beings consciously exposed to the undiluted fury of God's wrath drains our emotions, dislocates our logic and defies our imagination—and nothing crushes us with greater force than the fact that hell is endless, because endlessness is beyond our ability to grasp.

Any illustration we try to use turns out to be useless. The highest mountain in Great Britain is Ben Nevis, which rises 4,400 feet above sea level. Imagine an eagle swooping across the top of it and dislodging a grain of soil. One hundred years later, another eagle does the same thing, and a century later the same thing happens again. If this were to happen regularly at the same rate, how many years would it take for Ben Nevis to be reduced to sea level? A computer print-out which stretched all around the equator would not be long enough to contain the figure—yet even the length of time is as nothing compared to the experience of the wicked in hell. In one of his most powerful sermons on the subject, Jonathan Edwards said, "The damned in hell will have two infinites perpetually to amaze them and swallow them up: one is an infinite God, whose wrath they will bear, and in whom they will behold their perfect and irreconcilable enemy. The other is the infinite duration of their torment."[32]

In hell, there is no such thing as an hour, a day, a week, a month, or a year. A character in a Tom Stoppard play asks, "Eternity is a terrible thought. I mean, where's it going to end?"[33]

It never will.

The Roads to Hell

If you are interested in going to Hell, just follow the signs along the main road and you're sure to get there . . . Should you wish to send a postcard from Hell, you'll find the Post Office in town happy to oblige." During a preaching visit to the West Indies I came across these words in a booklet published by the Cayman Islands Tourist Department. The "Hell" concerned is a tiny settlement at the northern end of Grand Cayman and gets its name from the rugged, surreal coral rock found in that area. This jokey approach is matched by the slogans on T-shirts, postcards and other souvenirs sold there. "I've been to Hell and survived," and "I went to Hell and my camcorder melted," were two of the milder ones I noticed. Needless to say, it is a popular place with tourists. Nearly everyone who visits Grand Cayman wants to go to Hell.

As far as the real hell is concerned, it is impossible to imaging anyone wanting to go there—and difficult to find anyone who thinks he is in danger of doing so. In the middle of the eighteenth century, Jonathan Edwards wrote, "Every natural man that hears of hell flatters himself that he shall escape it."[1] Were Edwards to return today, he would come to the same conclusion. British soldiers in World War I used to sing:

> *O death, where is thy sting-a-ling-a-ling,*
> *O grave thy victory?*
> *The bells of hell go ting-a-ling-a-ling*
> *For you but not for me.*

A poll published in Des Moines, Iowa in 1977 showed that only five percent of those interviewed believed they were going to hell; sixty-five percent thought they would go to heaven and thirty percent were not sure or had no opinion.[2] One year later, a sampling in Minnesota revealed that just four percent felt they were on their way to hell.[3] In 1988, a *Newsweek* survey suggested that seventy-six percent of Americans thought they had a "good or excellent" chance of going to heaven, while only six percent felt they were probably on their way to hell.[4] In 1991, a Gallup poll taken for *US News & World Report* produced almost identical results—seventy percent for heaven and four percent for hell.[5] The percentages are significantly consistent: most people think that if hell exists it is "for you but not for me."

ANYONE FOR HELL?

Who, then, will go to hell? Two of the polls produced some interesting information. Although virtually all those interviewed thought they were safe, thirty-one percent of the Iowans and twenty percent of the Minnesotans said they were sure they knew people who were not, which seems to mean that they had certain ideas about the kind of person who would qualify for hell.

Finding candidates from history would not be too difficult. Some would choose the Roman Emperor Diocletian, who in the early part of the fourth century amused himself by having countless Christians tortured, burned alive, and torn apart by wild animals. Others would opt for the thirteenth-century tyrant Genghis Khan, whose slaughterous campaigns created a bloodbath that stretched from China to Poland. From the twentieth century, many would think of Adolf Hitler, the German dictator who triggered off World War II and who was responsible for the extermination of millions of Jews. Some would condemn Joseph Stalin, Nikita Krushchev, and other leaders of Soviet Communism for their ruthless oppression of entire nations in Eastern Europe, wholesale executions, and notorious Gulag prison camps.

Many would no doubt include serial killers, rapists, child molesters, and drug pushers. In April 1992, Andrei Chikatilo, described by friends as "kindly, retiring and respected"[6] confessed to a Russian court that he had murdered fifty-three boys, girls, and young women, disemboweled them and eaten parts of their remains: few would doubt his fate. Sometimes, people have been very passionate in their convictions. When the Communist dictator Nicolae Ceausescu of Romania and his cohorts were overthrown, one young woman interviewed on television shouted, "The bastards will go to hell."[7] When the allied forces' first bombs fell on Baghdad during the Gulf War in 1991, Iraqui President Saddam Hussein screamed, "The criminals will rot in hell."[8]

An Australian poll conducted in 1988 asked people to give their reasons as to why a person would go to hell. One in five nominated murder, and about the same number "being bad" or "committing sins." Other offenses named were rape (eight percent), "not believing in God" (six percent), and child abuse (five percent). Adultery, sexual deviance, and "not repenting for sins" received only one percent of the votes. Elsewhere in the magazine feature which reported on the poll, others took more sidelong views. One young student nominated Prime Minister Bob Hawke, "because he came here and tried to be nice to us so our parents would vote for him," while cartoonist Gary Larson showed three doors leading into hell, marked "Terrorists," "Homicidal Maniacs," and "People who drive too slow in the fast lane."[9]

Religious and cultural trends have sometimes changed perspectives in relation to hell. John Bunyan, reflecting some of the seventeenth-century thinking of his day, listed the following as being doomed: "hunters, dancers, those who paint their faces, those that follow plays and sports, singing drunkards, and those who fail to attend church because they are afraid of wind and rain or are reluctant to leave their friends."[10] Interviewed for *US News & World Report* in 1991, the Chairman of Theology at the Roman Catholic University of Notre Dame in the United States remembered the time when "We were told hell was a real possibility for all of us. If you ate a hot dog on Friday and got hit by a truck before you went to confession, you'd suffer the same punishment as if you were a murderer."[11]

The pendulum has now swung so far in the opposite direction that even among those who believe that hell exists, the possibility of anyone going there is being questioned. A professor of theology at the Roman Catholic Fordham University in New York speculated, "Hell is there and ready to receive anyone who meets the condition for falling into it, but it's quite possible that no one will really go there."[12] From another denominational tradition, an Anglican writer dismisses discussion on whether hell means everlasting punishment or annihilation as "a waste of time" and concludes that "We cannot predict how many will go to hell: it may be many, a few, or none."[13]

Hell is also depopulated by attitudes toward the dead and the dying. On their deathbeds, the most unpleasant of people can attract unusual compassion and compliments, and even the worst of rogues is not likely to be condemned at his funeral. I remember attending a service for a man who made no pretension of faith, yet the minister assured us, "He is now at peace." Tributes paid to the departed are sometimes laughably "over the top." A monument in Ripon Cathedral is dedicated "To the memory of William Weddell, Esq., of Newby, in whom every virtue that ennobles the human mind was united with every elegance that adorns it, this monument, a faint emblem of his refined taste, is dedicated by his widow." Mrs. Weddell seems to have been fairly clear about his destiny!

Others, whose lifestyles would not have suggested it, are confidently said to have gone to heaven. At the memorial service for Republican Party chairman Lee Atwater, held in Washington D.C. in April 1991, Secretary of State James Baker said, "It may be hard to imagine Atwater, a self-confessed bad boy, with the angels. But I'm convinced that's just where he is. And the angels are simply going to have to adjust."[14] Baker also noted that Atwater had died on Good Friday, "the perfect moment to show up at the Pearly Gates to improve his odds."[15]

BACK TO THE BIBLE

These illustrations are all very interesting but, as we established much earlier in this book, we are not at the mercy of speculation when it comes to fundamental doctrinal issues. God is more reliable than Gallup! And on the question of who will go to hell, He has given us a great deal of detailed information. Paul wrote that those who looked at creation and failed to worship God were "without excuse" (Romans 1:20). The same applies to anyone who reads the Bible and then says he knows nothing about the roads that lead to hell.

The first thing we find when we look at Scripture is that it turns human opinion firmly on its head. Most people assume that if hell exists it is reserved for the scum of society and that almost everybody will escape it. Jesus said exactly the opposite. Toward the end of the Sermon on the Mount He urged His hearers, "Enter through the narrow gate. For wide is the gate and broad is the road that leads to destruction, and many enter through it. But small is the gate and narrow the road that leads to life, and only a few find it" (Matthew 7:13-14). If He had never said another word on the subject, that one statement should be sufficient to get our attention, because taken at its face value it seems to mean that the great majority of humanity will go to hell and only a minority to heaven.

But Jesus did say more. On another occasion He told his followers, "Do not be afraid, little flock, for your Father has been pleased to give you the kingdom" (Luke 12:32), which seems to imply that Christians will always be in a minority. At the end of one parable He said, "For many are invited, but few are chosen" (Matthew 22:14). Should that not set off alarm bells in our minds? Is Jesus not telling us that the average person's chances of going to heaven are considerably less than fifty percent and that well over half of humanity will go to hell? If that is so, nobody can afford to be complacent about the issue.

There are biblical scholars who question this. Some think that Christ will not return to the earth until Christianity is so dominant that the numbers who die impenitent will be greatly reduced. Others, on the basis of a passage in Revelation 20, look for a "golden age" of 1,000 years during which all previous eras of unbelief will be overturned. Some suggest that God will save those who would have believed if the gospel had been preached to them. In a book entitled *Christian Beliefs*, the British writer I. Howard Marshall said, "There are grounds for holding that men whose way of life is such that they would have accepted Christ if they had heard of him will be saved at the last day."[16]

Whatever may be said for these ideas—and Marshall's "grounds" amount to nothing more than speculation—they all seem to contradict what Jesus said about "only a few" being saved, whereas all the evidence we see around us would seem to endorse it. In thirty years of ministry all around the world, I have never visited a country, a state, a town, or a neighborhood where this was not the case.

Others maintain that all children dying in infancy will automatically go to heaven, and one respected scholar has even suggested that this would account for over fifty percent of the human race so far.[17] The eternal destiny of children who have died is a highly emotive issue, and there are no glib answers, but we can rest assured that it has not caught God by surprise: "Will not the judge of all the earth do right?" (Genesis 18:25). Nevertheless, to use this as an argument to inflate the population of heaven is an inadequate response. As Arthur Custance asks, "Can it really be termed a victory for the Lord when the soldiers in this warfare are saved only by being removed from ever encountering the enemy while they are still too young to have arrived at the battlefront?"[18]

A WARNING TO THE WEALTHY

The second general thing we discover in Scripture will come as a shock to many, and that is that the well-to-do are in much grater danger of going to hell than those who are lower down the social order. When a wealthy young man asked Jesus what he needed to do to receive eternal life, he was told to sell his possessions and give the proceeds to the poor. Unable to face the challenge, the man "went away sad, because he had great wealth." Turning to His disciples, Jesus said, "I tell you the truth, it is hard for a rich man to enter the kingdom of heaven. Again I tell you, it is easier for a camel to go through the eye of a needle than for a rich man to enter the kingdom of God" (Matthew 19:22-24).

There are two comments to be made here. Wealth can often be used as a lever to gain things denied to poorer people, but as one of the Old Testament writers put it, "Wealth is worthless in the day of wrath" (Proverbs 11:4). As "The earth is the Lord's, and everything in it" (Psalm 24:1), trying to buy one's way into heaven is a ludicrous proposition.

The second thing is that material possessions can distract a person from spiritual issues. This is why Jesus spoke about "the deceitfulness of wealth" (Matthew 13:22). It is difficult to convince wealthy people living in huge houses and enjoying luxurious lifestyles that they need something much more important and enduring than their material possessions. Gold not only glitters, it sometimes dazzles, blinding people to the brevity of life, the certainty of judgment, the awful reality of eternity, and the simple truth that "We brought nothing into the world, and we can take nothing out of it" (1 Timothy 6:7). As someone has rightly said, "It is not the fact that a man has riches which keeps him from the kingdom of heaven, but the fact that riches have him."[19]

Elsewhere in the New Testament there is an illustration of how this worked out in practice. Writing to church members in Corinth, Paul reminded them of their social status when they were converted:

"Not many of you were wise by human standards; not many were influential; not many were of noble birth. But God chose the foolish things of the world to shame the wise; God chose the weak things of the world to shame the strong. He chose the lowly things of this world and the despised things—and the things that are not—to nullify the things that are" (1 Corinthians 1:26). This suggests that even at that early stage of the church's history, earthly possessions and positions could be a hindrance to laying hold of eternal life—and could therefore pave the way to hell.

THE KINGDOM OF HEAVEN

Having established two general principles, we are now able to look directly at who the Bible says will be condemned. John Flavel listed twelve paths to hell: children denied biblical teaching by their parents, ignorance about Christ, worldliness, sinful habits, the lure of sensual pleasure, the cares of this world, groundless presumption, formal religion, profanity and debauchery, prejudice against Christianity, hypocrisy, and reliance upon respectability.[20] His arguments are powerful and penetrating and, as we shall see, they are a faithful reflection of the Bible's teaching, which is given in three ways. Firstly, it says who will go to heaven (and therefore infers that all others will go to hell); secondly it indicates who will *not* go to heaven (and therefore must go to hell); and thirdly it specifically identifies those who will go to hell.

As to the first of these, Jesus supplies some of the key information which is backed up elsewhere in the New Testament. In the Sermon on the Mount, He laid down several vital principles that have become known as the Beatitudes, the first of which reads, "Blessed are the poor in spirit, for theirs is the kingdom of heaven" (Matthew 5:3). There are two Greek words translated "poor" in our English New Testament: the first means "to have very little," the second "to have nothing." This is the second. To be "poor in spirit" is to be convinced of one's own spiritual poverty, to realize that one is spiritually penniless, bankrupt before a holy God. This is another way of saying that any vestige of trust in one's own ability to get right with God guarantees being shut out of heaven and condemned to hell.

Jesus illustrated this in a story about a Pharisee and a tax collector who went to pray at the temple in Jerusalem. The Pharisee stood and thanked God that he was so much better than his fellow men, but the tax collector hung his head in shame and cried out, "God, have mercy on me, a sinner." Jesus then turned to His hearers, identified as those who were "confident of their own righteousness," and said, "I tell you that this man, rather than the other, went home justified before God. For everyone who exalts himself will be humbled, and he who humbles himself will be exalted" (Luke 18:9, 13-14). Only the truly humble will go to heaven; all others will be condemned.

A few moments later, Jesus laid down another important principle that relates to our study: "Blessed are the pure in heart, for they will see God" (Matthew 5:8). To "see God" has several shades of meaning for believers while they are still here on earth, but the ultimate experience will come in heaven, when "They will see his face, and his name will be on their foreheads" (Revelation 22:4). The only people who will experience this are the "pure in heart," those who are sincerely seeking to follow the Bible's command: "Love the Lord your God with all your heart and with all your soul and with all your mind and with all your strength" (Mark 12:30). Those who are committed to such a lifestyle will never "see God" in heaven, but will be exposed to His wrath in hell.

NO ENTRY

Next we come to several statements Jesus made to identify those who would not go to heaven (and so, by implication, would go to hell). In conversation with a religious leader called Nicodemus, he said, "I tell you the truth, no one can see the kingdom of God unless he is born again" (John 3:3). Being "born again" is more than having religious convictions, or trying to meet certain moral standards. It is to experience a spiritual miracle which God alone can perform, and which results in a total reorientation of one's life. Without it, the way to heaven is barred. As Jesus told Nicodemus, "Flesh gives birth to flesh, but the Spirit gives birth to spirit" (John 3:6). Spiritual life (that is to say, eternal life) is not something we have by nature, nor can we cultivate it in any way: "There is no evolution from flesh to spirit."[21] Without a miracle of God's grace, heaven is shut and hell is certain.

Later in the Sermon on the Mount, Jesus underlined the need for genuine spirituality: "For I tell you that unless your righteousness surpasses that of the Pharisees and the teachers of the law, you will certainly not enter the kingdom of heaven" (Matthew 5:20). The Pharisees were religious experts who spent a great deal of time studying and teaching the Old Testament, but for the most part their religion was self-satisfied, hypocritical and external. As Martyn Lloyd-Jones put it, "The trouble with the Pharisees was that they were interested in details rather than principles, that they were interested in actions rather than in motives, and that they were interested in doing rather than in being."[22] In other words, their so-called "righteousness" was nothing but a sanctimonious sham. Anyone who thinks that God can be palmed off with that sort of thing will be in for a tragic shock on the Day of Judgment, because "Without holiness no one will see the Lord" (Hebrews 12:14).

On another occasion, Jesus called a little child to Him and said, "I tell you the truth, unless you change and become like little children, you will never enter the kingdom of heaven" (Matthew 18:3). Later, when His disciples were trying to prevent people pestering Him with their children, Jesus told them, "I tell you the truth, anyone who will not receive the kingdom of God like a little child will never enter it" (Mark 10:15). The terms "kingdom of heaven" and "kingdom of God" amount to the same thing and include the eternal destiny of the righteous. The teaching here covers the same kind of ground as that which spoke of the need to be "poor in spirit." Jesus used little children as an illustration of the humility and unquestioning faith needed before anyone can get right with God, and the word "receive" emphasizes that salvation must be accepted as a gift. It is not something that can be achieved by our own merits, efforts, or ability; the person who tries to earn his way to heaven is certain to go to hell.

UNANIMOUS

The teaching of Jesus is endorsed by several New Testament writers, who sometimes go into considerable detail about the behavior that will bar people from heaven. Paul's first letter to the Corinthians provides a good example of this: "Do you now know that the wicked will not inherit the kingdom of God? Do not be deceived: Neither the sexually immoral nor idolaters nor adulterers nor male prostitutes nor homosexual offenders nor thieves nor the greedy nor drunkards nor slanderers nor swindlers will inherit the kingdom of God" (1 Corinthians 6:9-10). Paul's warning was aimed at the permissive society of his day, and speaks just as powerfully to ours. He demolishes the idea that people can live as they please because God has guaranteed to see them safe in the end. It is no surprise to find idolatry and immorality (heterosexual and homosexual) singled out, but the list is both longer and deeper. "Swindlers" would have included financial bloodsuckers who ruthlessly extorted money from others, but "thieves" were "petty pilferers, sneak-thieves rather than brigands".[23] The remainder of the list includes sins of word ("slanderers"), thought ("the greedy"), and deed ("drunkards") and is a serious warning that God takes all our behavior into account.

Paul covers similar ground in two other letters. Writing to the Ephesians he says, "For of this you can be sure: No immoral, impure or greedy person—such a man is an idolater—has any inheritance in the kingdom of Christ and of God. Let no one deceive you with empty words, for because of such things God's wrath comes on those who are disobedient" (Ephesians 5:5-6), while he tells the Colossians, "Put to death, therefore, whatever belongs to your earthly nature: sexual immorality, impurity, lust, evil desires and greed, which is idolatry. Because of these, the wrath of God is coming" (Colossians 3:5-6).

It is important to notice that greed is described as idolatry, not a connection we would normally think of making. In both cases, the specific link seems to be with sexual immorality, but the principle extends far beyond that. Idolatry is putting anything before God. Sex, sport, money, business, home, travel, leisure—even religion—can become gods, consuming time, energy, and interest in such a way that the person concerned can be said to worship them. Thinking that one can put these things before God and then avoid His devastating wrath on the Day of Judgment is nothing short of lunacy.

In writing to the Galatians, Paul lists fifteen sins which will keep a person out of heaven: "The acts of the sinful nature are obvious: sexual immorality, impurity and debauchery; idolatry and witchcraft; hatred, discord, jealousy, fits of rage, selfish ambition, dissensions, factions and envy; drunkenness, orgies, and the like. I warn you, as I did before, that those who live like this will not inherit the kingdom of God" (Galatians 5:19-21). These sins are variations on the shameful themes of immorality, occultism, self-promotion, and pleasure-seeking—and they all result in being banned from heaven and bound for hell.

The last two statements in this section come from Revelation, where John says of heaven, "Nothing impure will ever enter it, nor will anyone who does what is shameful or deceitful, but only those whose names are written in the Lamb's book of life" (Revelation 21:27). The important thing to notice here is the way in which John stresses what he is saying by using a double negative. His first phrase could be translated: "By no means may enter into it a single impure thing." Dave Hunt says that for an unrepentant sinner to get to heaven "would be as impossible a contradiction as it would be for a worm to teach calculus or a lion to appreciate great works of art."[24] There will not be so much as a breath of sin in heaven; the nineteenth-century preacher Rowland Hill used to say, "If an unholy man were to get to heaven he would feel like a hog in a flower garden."[25] John's uncompromising words destroy the hopes of those who think in terms of universalism or of a "second chance" after death.

THE FATAL FLAWS

We can now look at a third group of New Testament statements, those which link specific sins with the sinner's condemnation. Beginning again with Jesus, we find Him giving the following warning against a false profession of faith: "Not everyone who says to me, 'Lord, Lord,' will enter the kingdom of heaven, but only he who does the will of my Father who is in heaven. Many will say to me on that day, 'Lord, Lord, did we not prophesy in your name, and in your name drive out demons and perform many miracles?' Then I will tell them plainly, 'I never knew you. Away from me, you evildoers!'" (Matthew 7:21-22). Martyn Lloyd-Jones said that in many ways these are "the most solemn and solemnizing words ever uttered in this world, not only by any man, but even by the Son of God himself."[26] It is difficult to disagree. If many people who, while here on earth, had been doctrinally correct, emotionally fervent, and apparently successful, will be shut out of the kingdom of heaven and condemned to spend eternity in hell, who can afford to be careless or complacent? These people will be condemned because in spite of all their outward show of spirituality and power they were self-deceived. Someone has said, "A man may . . . fondly imagine that he is walking along the right road when he is not. He may use the believer's vocabulary, repeat the believer's formulas, recite the believer's creed, and take part in the believer's activities without being a real believer himself."[27] The moment of truth comes when Jesus dismisses such people as "evildoers," shuts them out of heaven and condemns them to spend eternity in hell. Nothing sends a person to hell faster than hypocrisy.

Jesus also gave uncompromising warnings in connection with the parables of the weeds and the fishing net. He said that His angels would take "everything that causes sin and all who do evil" and "thrown them into the fiery furnace, where there will be weeping and gnashing of teeth" (Matthew 13:41-42); and that the angels "will come and separate the wicked from the righteous and throw them into the fiery furnace, where there will be weeping and gnashing of teeth" (Matthew 13:49-50). Here, the impact comes not from the piling up of specific sins, as in some of Paul's statements, but from the brevity and simplicity of what Jesus says: "sin," "evil," "the wicked." Just as weeds grow alongside wheat and inedible fish swim alongside those which are delicious to eat, so the wicked spend their lives alongside the righteous. They may live in the same house, work in the same office, play in the same team, or attend the same church, but the day is coming when God will draw the final, fatal dividing line, and the sham will be over.

Another fatal flaw was highlighted by Jesus in His final description of the Day of Judgment. After setting the scene, and telling how the "sheep" will be welcomed into heaven, He said that as the judge of all men He would turn His attention to the "goats": "Depart from me, you who are cursed, into the eternal fire prepared for the devil and his angels. For I was hungry and you gave me nothing to eat, I was thirsty and you gave me nothing to drink, I was a stranger and you did not invite me in, I needed clothes and you did not clothe me, I was sick and in prison and you did not look after me." When the wicked express surprise, Jesus tells them, "I tell you the truth, whatever you did not do for one of the least of these, you did not do for me" (Matthew 25:41-43, 45).

What was their fatal sin? In a word, self-interest. They had been so preoccupied with their own little world that they had ignored the needs of others. There is no suggestion that they had been guilty of immorality, extortion, or other sins mentioned elsewhere. They may have been socially acceptable, well-mannered, perfectly respectable; but their lives were thoroughly self-centered. They devoted their time, energy, and money to promoting their own comfort, convenience, and enjoyment while the tears and cries of hurting humanity, whether coming from their television screens or across their garden fences, were callously ignored. By doing nothing to ease the pains of humanity, they had prepared for themselves the pains of hell.

Paul also underlines the dangers of self-serving: "Do not be deceived: God cannot be mocked. A man reaps what he sows. The one who sows to please his sinful nature, from that nature will reap destruction" (Galatians 6:7-8). Nobody can turn his nose up at God. The person who imagines that he can "do his own thing" and escape the consequences is a fool as well as a felon. The person who sows to please himself will reap the endless ruination of hell.

Finally, John records two statements which drive home the relationship between man's behavior and his destiny. In the first, God says, "But the cowardly, the unbelieving, the vile, the murderers, the sexually immoral, those who practice magic arts, the idolaters and all liars—their place will be in the fiery lake of burning sulfur. This is the second death" (Revelation 21:8). In the second, Jesus speaks of the righteous as those who "go through the gates of the city" and adds, "Outside are the dogs, those who practice magic arts, the sexually immoral, the murderers, the idolaters and everyone who loves and practices falsehood" (Revelation 22:15). Most of these characteristics have been mentioned before and require no other comment. Dogs were regarded by the Jews as being unclean, and the term "dogs" was used of people who were "shameless, impudent, malignant, snarling, dissatisfied and contentious."[28] What is clear is that sinners of every kind—even the cowardly—will find themselves doomed.

We have covered a lot of ground in this section—but the New Testament covers much more. Even allowing for overlap, there are well over 100 sins mentioned, every one of them carrying the spiritual death penalty. There is no shortage of roads leading to hell.

THE FINAL PLEAS

Some people try to make out a good case for themselves by claiming that at least they are not guilty of some of the sins traditionally thought of as being the worst. "I have never committed murder or adultery," "I am not perfect, but neither am I a sinner," "I am better than many people I know," and "There are lots worse than me," are phrases I have heard countless times, but there are at least five ways in which reactions like these prove to be pointless.

Firstly, no sin is insignificant. The cowardly are condemned along with the idolaters, the petty thief with the big-time swindler. Hell is the mandatory sentence for every sin, not merely for some.

Secondly, the claim not to have committed murder or adultery collapses when exposed to the Sermon on the Mount, where Jesus emphasized the spiritual nature of God's law. In particular, He taught that to have a resentful attitude about someone was a form of murder, and that "Anyone who looks at a woman lustfully has already committed adultery with her in his heart" (Matthew 5:28). Many who can truthfully plead "Not Guilty" to physical murder or adultery must change their pleas when faced with the full meaning of God's law.

Thirdly, God's law tells us that there are sins of omission as well as sins of commission. James summarizes this by saying, "Anyone, then, who knows the good he ought to do and doesn't do it, sins" (James 4:17). This gives sin a much deeper dimension. Who can truthfully say that he has always done everything he knew to be his duty—to his employer, employees, marriage partner, parents, children, the needy, and everyone else? To avoid God's wrath on the Day of Judgment, it would be necessary not only to have avoided doing everything that was sinful, but also to have done everything that was right. The General Confession in the Church of England's Book of Common Prayer includes the words, "We have left undone those things which we ought to have done. And we have done those things which we ought not to have done. And there is no health in us." Who can honestly say that those words do not apply to them?

Fourthly, God does not just set high standards for us—He demands perfection! James wrote that "Whoever keeps the whole law and yet stumbles at just one point is guilty of breaking all of it" (James 2:10). It is no good claiming to be innocent of one offense if one is guilty of another. God's law is not like an examination paper which says, "Only six questions out of ten need be attempted." It is a unity, and even one sin means that the law as a whole is broken. It would be pointless for a motorist charged with a speeding offense to ask for leniency because the car's lights were in working order, or for a bank robber to do so because he had not broken any windows.

Paul drives this point home by relating it directly to the punishment involved. "All who rely on observing the law are under a curse, for it is written: 'Cursed is everyone who does not continue to do everything written in the Book of the Law.'"(Galatians 3:10). That single sentence is a death-blow to anyone who feels that a decent life can satisfy God, gain a place in heaven and avoid the pains of hell. Nothing could be further from the truth. God's law is not a test we have to pass to get to heaven. Even if it were, we would have to continue to do everything it demands. Not even the best things we do can deliver us from the curse which God pronounces on the lawbreaker.

Fifthly, trying to avoid God's wrath by doing our best ignores the fact that we are condemned not merely or mainly by what we do or fail to do, but by what we are. One of the Bible's clearest statements about this comes when Paul says that "Sin entered the world through one man, and death through sin . . . because all sinned" (Romans 5:12). When Adam sinned, he did so as the representative and head of humanity and dragged everyone of his successors into guilt and condemnation. When Adam sinned, all of humanity sinned—because the whole of humanity is united. When Adam sinned, we sinned; when Adam was pronounced guilty, we were pronounced guilty; when Adam was sentenced to spiritual and physical death, so were we. The clearest evidence of this is the fact that we are all sinning and dying. Adam's sin explains all the other sins that have been committed throughout history.

Many people who read that kind of statement for the first time will immediately protest that it is unfair, and add that they would never do what Adam did. But what is the point of protesting against something God says is true? And in any event, those who protest are copying Adam to the letter by rebelling against God's authority, breaking his law and "doing their own thing."

Paul refers to the origin of human sin when he says, "Like the rest, we were by nature objects of wrath" (Ephesians 2:3). People do not become sinners when they sin; they sin because they are sinners. They are born that way. King David, one of the greatest men in Old Testament history, was even more specific: "Surely I was sinful at birth, sinful from the time my mother conceived me" (Psalm 51:5). It is vitally important not to miss what the Bible is saying here. A person does not become a sinner when he commits his first sin or on the day of his birth. Assuming it has been carried to term, a baby has already been a sinner for nine months the day it is born. Before its umbilical cord is cut and it begins to live independently of its mother, it is already prepared to live independently of its Maker, Strictly speaking, there are no "innocent children"; Jonathan Edwards used to say that they were "little vipers."[29] Babies are guilty before they are born, and as such are under the righteous condemnation of a holy God. Nobody is suggesting that they are guilty of committing any sins but the sinful tendencies and desires are there, waiting to express themselves in the sinful thoughts, words, and actions that will follow as surely as night follows day.

This is in no way to diminish the value of human life. There is no warrant here for embryonic experimentation or abortion. A front-page story in the *Sunday Times* on March 19, 1992 told how vast numbers of abortions in Russia were fueling the French cosmetics industry with tons of human placentas. Rich in nutrients, these produce face creams which give the skin "a softer, smoother look" and, according to one producer, enable the user to age "serenely and in total beauty." Ironically, the report appeared on "Mothering Sunday" and was a stark reminder of the depths to which Western civilization has sunk. As one Christian writer commented, "It means we are killing people by the ton with as much indifference as white settlers hunted bushmen in South Africa in the nineteenth century."[30] Nothing the Bible says about the spiritual nature of unborn children excuses mass murder.

Nor does the Bible's teaching mean that children are not to be loved and cared for. When people brought their little ones to Jesus, "He took the children in his arms, put his hands on them and blessed them" (Mark 10:16), longing, no doubt, that they would one day be saved. Nevertheless, they too were "little vipers," needing the grace of God before they could break out of their sinful syndrome. The root of man's problem lies not in his habitat but in his heart, which is "deceitful above all things and beyond cure" (Jeremiah 17:9). This is why Jesus said that "Out of the heart come evil thoughts, murder, adultery, sexual immorality, theft, false testimony, slander" (Matthew 15:19).

Every sin is significant because it carries a mandatory death sentence. God's law is spiritual and relates to thoughts, desires and motives as well as to words and actions; God requires "truth in the inner parts" (Psalm 51:6). He demands perfection, absolute obedience to every part of His law. Yet we were sinners before birth, guilty, lost and helpless, and unable to do anything that could make us acceptable in God's sight or contribute anything to our salvation. The last point alone is sufficient to damn us all. Any appeal we might one day make to our respectability, our relative goodness, our religion, or our ignorance of biblical truth had already been ruled out before we could even think of making it.

Who then can possibly escape the devastating destiny of spending eternity in hell? The question is not original. Somebody once asked Jesus, "Lord, are only a few people going to be saved?" (Luke 13:23). As we come toward the end of this book, it is very important to notice how Jesus replied. He refused to satisfy His questioner's curiosity about numbers. He said nothing to throw light on any of the "gray areas." He said nothing about children dying in infancy or people who had never heard the gospel. Instead, his reply came in the form of a command: "Make every effort to enter through the narrow door. . . ." (Luke 13:24).

SIXTEEN

The Way to Heaven

A s I explained in the preface, I originally intended this book to be a straightforward (and much briefer) evangelistic presentation, but it gradually grew into one which will, I hope, serve a dual purpose. To bring this double-barreled aim to focus, I want to address these two final chapters to the two separate groups of readers I have in mind, and to apply the messages even more directly by writing them in the second person singular. I appreciate that the purists may protest at this sudden switch, but there are times when style is secondary, and this is one of them. The remainder of this chapter will therefore be written directly to unbelievers.

"YOU ARE THE MAN"

About a year after David, King of Israel, had committed adultery with Bathsheba and then had her husband Uriah killed, God sent the prophet Nathan to bring him to his senses. He began by telling David about a wealthy man who stole a poor neighbor's lamb to provide food for a visitor. David had no problem in pronouncing his verdict on the case: "As surely as the Lord lives, the man who did this deserves to die! He must pay for that lamb four times over, because he did such a thing and had no pit." Nathan immediately replied, "You are the man! . . . You struck down Uriah the Hittite with the sword and took his wife to be your own" (2 Samuel 12:5-6, 9). The direct, personal approach hit home as nothing else could and moments later he confessed his guilt and admitted, "I have sinned against the Lord" (2 Samuel 12:13). As a result, he was forgiven, restored to God's favor, and greatly used in His service.

In reading this book, you may agree with a good deal of it: you may accept that the Bible is the Word of God, that God is holy and just as well as loving and kind, that there must eventually be a day of universal judgment; you may even accept that unrepentant sinners will be condemned to spend eternity in hell. Yet you may have believed all of these truths without realizing that you have endorsed your own terrifying destiny.

One of the most emphatic statements in Scripture about the eternal punishment of the wicked is where Paul writes of the Second Coming of Christ and says, "He will punish those who do not know God and do not obey the gospel of our Lord Jesus. They will be punished with everlasting destruction and shut out from the presence of the Lord and from the majesty of his power" (2 Thessalonians 1:8-9). We have come across this statement several times already in the course of this book, but I now want to focus on Paul's definition of the people who will be sent to hell: "those who do not know God and do not obey the gospel of our Lord Jesus." These two phrases describe the same group of people; knowing God and obeying the gospel go hand in glove. Jesus made this clear when in the course of one of His prayers He said, "Now this is eternal life: that they may know you, the only true God, and Jesus Christ, whom you have sent" (John 17:3). Knowing God and obeying the gospel will take you to heaven; not knowing God and disobeying the gospel will send you to hell. The issue could not be more crucial.

Do you know God? I am not asking whether you know about God, because even if this is the only Christian book you have ever read, it is certain that you now do. So far so good, because knowing about God is an essential foundation for coming to know Him. The Bible says that "Without faith it is impossible to please God, because anyone who comes to him must believe that he exists and that he rewards those who earnestly seek him" (Hebrews 11:6). Yet believing that God exists comes a long way short of saving faith. Millions of people acknowledge the existence of God without knowing Him. Some have denied that anyone can. Albert Einstein once said, "Certainly there is a God. Any man who doesn't believe in a cosmic force is a fool, but we could never know him."[1] Einstein was a brilliant scientist, but on this issue he was catastrophically wrong, because the Bible teaches that we can come to know God. Paul introduced one particular statement to the

Christians at Galatia by saying, "But now that you know God . . ." (Galatians 4:9). In another letter, he assured the believers at Ephesus of his prayers that God "may give you the Spirit of wisdom and revelation, so that you may know him better" (Ephesians 1:17)—which must have meant that they already knew Him.

KNOWING GOD

What does it mean to "know God"? It is not just a matter of intellectual knowledge but of a personal relationship, of which the Bible gives us a number of analogies.[2]

One of these is the picture of a son knowing his father. Paul wrote of the believer, "So you are no longer a slave, but a son; and since you are a son, God has made you also an heir" (Galatians 4:7), while John told his fellow Christians, "How great is the love the Father has lavished on us, that we should be called children of God! And that is what we are!" (1 John 3:1). The image is one of a warm, personal, family relationship. Those concerned love to be in each other's company. The father is actively concerned for his son's welfare, and the son is confidently assured of his father's loving concern for his welfare.

Another picture is that of a wife knowing her husband. Even in the dimmer light of the Old Testament the people of God were told that "Your Maker is your husband" (Isaiah 54:5), while in the New Testament Paul urged husbands to love their wives "just as Christ loved the church and gave himself up for her" (Ephesians 5:25). The picture here is of an even warmer and closer relationship; sometimes in Scripture the verb used about "knowing God" is the one used about the physical union of husband and wife.

A third picture is that of a subject knowing a king. David prayed, "Listen to my cry for help, my King and my God, for to you I pray" (Psalm 5:2). Later, he said,

> "I will exalt you, my God the King;
> I will praise your name for ever and ever.
> Every day I will praise you
> and extol your name for ever and ever"
> (Psalm 145:1-2).

Here, the subject gladly acknowledges the king's right to reign over his life, constantly looks to him for help, and praises him for his goodness.

The fourth picture is that of a sheep knowing its shepherd. Speaking for those who knew God, one of the psalmists said that "We are his people, the sheep of his pasture" (Psalm 100:3), while Jesus added, "I am the good shepherd; I know my sheep and my sheep know me" (John 10:14). His meaning would have been perfectly clear in that rural community. At night, shepherds used to gather their sheep (often given individual names) into a common fold for safety. In the morning, each shepherd would collect his own sheep by calling out their names. Those who belonged to him would ignore every other voice but recognize his and obediently follow him as he led them out to pasture.

The Bible uses other analogies to make the same point, but these four are sufficient for me to repeat the question: do you know God? That one question leads to others. Do you sense that you are a treasured member of God's family? Do you love to come into His presence? Are you confident of His loving concern for you? Do you have an intimate relationship with God, so that you can say, as one Old Testament believer did, "My lover is mine and I am his"? (Song of Songs 2:16). Do you acknowledge Him as your Lord and Master? Do you love to read His Word to find out the kind of person He wants you to be and the kind of life He wants you to live? Do you constantly praise Him for who He is and for what He has done for you? Are you listening for His voice and seeking to obey it? These are some of the signs that a person knows God; to be without them is to be "without hope and without God in the world" (Ephesians 2:12).

Do you realize what this means? Every phrase in that last quotation has a desolating ring to it.

Firstly, you are "*without hope.*" If you remain as you are, you have no hope of forgiveness, peace of mind, or spiritual joy. You have no hope of heaven in the next life and no hope of improvement in this one.

Secondly, you are "*without God.*" Even though you enjoy all the benefits of God's common grace, you have no personal experience of God Himself. You have Him as your Creator and Provider, without knowing Him as your Father and Friend. You are truly God-less; there is no link, no personal relationship between you and God. You know nothing of His love, His friendship, or His fellowship. In times of difficulty or sorrow you are unable to turn to Him in prayer or cry to Him for help. In times of crisis you are unable to ask Him for guidance or direction and, when death finally closes in, you have no Savior to protect you from its power. What a contrast there is between you and someone who knows God, and who can endorse David's words in Psalm 23:

"The Lord is my shepherd, I shall not be in want.
He makes me lie down in green pastures,
he leads me beside quiet waters,
he restores my soul.
He guides me in paths of righteousness
for his name's sake.
Even thought I walk
through the valley of the shadow of death,
I will fear no evil,
for you are with me;
your rod and your staff,
they comfort me"
(Psalm 23:1-4).

Thirdly, you are "*in the world*," a phrase that emphasizes how fragile and futile human life is if cut off from God. Nobody in Scripture expresses this better than the writer of Ecclesiastes (most probably King Solomon and clearly a man of great intelligence, massive wealth, and impressive achievements). Here are some of his reflections on life as seen through the eyes of someone who does not know God:

"I denied myself nothing my eyes desired;
I refused my heart no pleasure.
My heart took delight in all my work,
and this was the reward for all my labor.
Yet when I surveyed all that my hands had done
and what I had toiled to achieve,
everything was meaningless, a chasing after the wind;
nothing was gained under the sun . . .

"For a man may do his work with wisdom, knowledge and skill, and then he must leave all he owns to someone who has not worked for it. This too is meaningless and a great misfortune. What does a man get for all the toil and anxious striving with which he labors under the sun? All his days his work is pain and grief; even at night his mind does not rest. This too is meaningless . . . .

"As a man comes, so he departs,
and what does he gain,
since he toils for the wind?'
(Ecclesiastes 2:10-11, 12-22, 5:16).

These words are as relevant today as when they were first written some 3,000 years ago. What is the value of wealth or popularity, possessions or position when they are all part of "this world," which will soon be a thing of the past? What is the point of all your ambitions and achievements, ideas and engagements, when you know that in a few years' time at most they will be worth nothing to you? One writer hits the nail on the head when he says, "Whatever he may call the path which he walks, no unconverted person has yet succeeded in taking himself off the path of futility."[3]

To be "without hope and without God" is to be in a desperate position. To be without both "in this world" is to be in a highly dangerous one because, if you stay as you are, death will immediately expose you to the wrath of God to a degree that you have never known, and on the Day of Judgment you will be sentenced to be "punished with everlasting destruction."

THE GOOD NEWS

Paul's second way of describing those who will be condemned in this way is to say that they "do not obey the gospel of our Lord Jesus." This invites two obvious questions. What is the gospel? And if disobeying it leads to hell, how does one obey it and find the way to heaven? The word "gospel" simply means "good news," and one of its most basic truths is that "The Father has sent his Son to be the Savior of the world" (1 John 4:14). God has taken the initiative in the salvation of sinners. Paul calls the good news "the gospel of God" (Romans 1:1). It is not something man invented. It is not a piece of metaphysical machinery which religious thinkers have put together over the centuries. Nor is the gospel the Bible's way of telling us that we can get right with God by our own efforts. The Bible says exactly the opposite and warns us that "All our righteous acts are like filthy rags" (Isaiah 64:6). Do you realize what it means? If you are trying to get right with God by going to church, or reading the Bible, or praying, or by some kind of religious observance, or by seeking to do your best to live a decent, respectable life, you are simply adding to your sins while trying to get them removed.

In 1741, Jonathan Edwards preached what some people have called the most famous sermon delivered in the United States. It was entitled "Sinners in the Hands of an Angry God" and was full of graphic and moving images of the endless punishment of the wicked in hell. In the course of his sermon, he warned his hearers of the folly of trusting in their own righteousness to save them: "You cannot save yourselves . . . all your righteousness would have no more influence to uphold you and keep you out of hell than a spider's web would have to stop a fallen rock."[4] God will not be palmed off with filthy rags, and the gospel is the good news that although we are helpless and hopeless God has done something to rescue us from our sin and bring about our salvation.

What did He do? He "sent his Son to be the Savior of the world." Paul underlines this by writing of "the gospel of God . . . regarding his Son" (Romans 1:1-2). God did not send an angel to rescue sinners, nor did He create some other being to carry out His plan. Instead, He came in the person of His Son. The amazing truth that Jesus is God blazes across the pages of Scripture: "He is the image of the invisible God" (Colossians 1:15). "God was pleased to have all his fullness dwell in him" (Colossians 1:19). "For in Christ all the fullness of the Deity lives in bodily form" (Colossians 2:9). "The Son is the radiance of God's glory and the exact representation of his being" (Hebrews 1:3). When Jesus came into the world He added our human nature to His divine nature. From that moment onward He has been both God and man; not a mixture of both, but fully God and fully man. The gospel is not the news that God sent a third party to save sinners but that He Himself came.

How was the rescue mission carried out? What did Jesus do that saves people from going to hell and enables them to go to heaven? The astounding answer to that question is that in His life and death He fulfilled all the demands of God's law, and did so on behalf of others.

Firstly, *He fulfilled the demands of God's law in His life*. The New Testament makes it crystal clear that Jesus was genuinely human. As a baby, a child, an adolescent, and a fully grown man He went through all the normal stages of physical, psychological, and emotional development. He had to be taught to stand, to walk, to wash, to speak, to write, and to feed and dress himself. His hair and nails grew; His muscles expanded; His voice broke: He passed naturally and normally through puberty into manhood. Like everyone else, He needed food, drink, sleep, fresh air, and exercise. Like everyone else,

He expressed a whole range of emotions from joy to sorrow; when He realized that the city of Jerusalem was heading for disaster, "he wept over it" (Luke 19:41); when His disciples brought back reports of success in their ministry He was "full of joy" (Luke 10:21). And, like everyone else, He was tempted. We are told of one particular onslaught when He was alone in the desert and "For forty days he was tempted by the devil" (Luke 4:2), but this was not His only experience of temptation, because when the devil withdrew it was only "until an opportune time" (Luke 4:13). Later in the New Testament we get an even fuller picture and are told that He "was tempted in every way, just as we are—yet was without sin" (Hebrews 4:15).

Here is the first way in which Jesus met the requirements of God's law; He obeyed every detail of its demands. After living in His company for about three years, Peter could say, "He committed no sin, and no deceit was found in his mouth" (1 Peter 2:22). Jesus never had an unclean thought, never said anything untrue, unkind, unjust or unfair, never did anything selfish or dishonest. Yet the quality of His character was not merely negative, in the sense that He did no wrong, but positive, in the sense that He always did that which was right. On one occasion, speaking of His relationship with God, He quite openly said, "I always do what pleases him" (John 8:29). Do you know of anyone else who could seriously make that claim and then produce the evidence to back it up? Every virtue known to man was present in His life, and every vice known to man was absent from His life. He was perfect. Later, God spoke to Jesus' inner circle of friends, Peter, James, and John, and said, "This is my Son, whom I love; with him I am well pleased. Listen to him!" (Matthew 17:5). The phrase "I am well pleased" means much more than a verbal pat on the back; it shows that Jesus was everything His Father wanted Him to be and fulfilled to perfection the plan He had for Him.

If at this point you are thinking, "But the life that Jesus lived is irrelevant. A perfect example set 2,000 years ago is of no help to me today and will be of no help to me on the Day of Judgment," you are absolutely right. If all the gospel told us was that Jesus lived a perfect life and taught us to do the same, what good would that do? C. S. Lewis has a typically shrewd comment on this: "If Christianity only means one more bit of good advice, then Christianity is of no importance. There has been no lack of good advice for the last four thousand years. A bit more makes no difference."[5]

I would even dare to take that one step further and say that if the gospel consists only of Christ's perfect example and instructions, it only makes matters worse. We often try to excuse our own sins by noticing that other people are behaving in the same way, or we shelter behind the fact that "Nobody is perfect"; so when we discover that someone was perfect it is not good news but exactly the opposite, because it exposes us as guilty failures. If the gospel says merely that the Son of God became a human being and lived a perfect life, it is a contradiction in terms; it is not good news. Yet this is not all it says; there is a second way in which Jesus fulfilled the demands of God's law.

THE SUBSTITUTE

Much earlier in this book we saw that the result of sin is physical and spiritual death. When Adam sinned, he dragged all of humanity with him, so that "There is not a righteous man on earth who does what is right and never sins" (Ecclesiastes 7:20). The "first installment" of sin's death penalty is being paid here and now, as sinners are "separated from the life of God" (Ephesians 4:18) and the "second installment," physical death, is certain to follow. The Bible calls this "the law of sin and death" (Romans 8:2). It is inevitable and inescapable: "The wages of sin is death" (Romans 6:23). If we turn that last statement around (which will not alter its meaning in any way but help to clarify the point I want to make here) we could say that "Death is the wages of sin." Yet this immediately raises a huge question mark when we place it alongside what Jesus did, because although He had no sin of any kind He died. As "the law of sin and death" is a law of cause and effect, how can someone experience the consequences of sin when there was no sin in his life to bring about those consequences? The Bible's astonishing answer is that *when Jesus died He did so on behalf of others and in their place.*

This is confirmed by one New Testament writer after another. Paul says, "You see, at just the right time, when we were still powerless, Christ died for the ungodly" (Romans 5:6). "But God demonstrates his own love for us in this: While we were sinners, Christ died for us" (Romans 5:8). "God made him who had no sin to be sin for us" (2 Corinthians 5:21). "He died for us" (1 Thessalonians 5:10). Peter says the same thing: "He himself bore our sins in his body on the tree" (1 Peter 2:24). "For Christ died for sins once for all, the righteous for the unrighteous, to bring you to God" (1 Peter 3:18). The same truth is endorsed by John: "This is how we know what love is: Jesus Christ laid down his life for us" (1 John 3:16). "This is love; not that we loved God, but that he loved us and sent his Son as an atoning sacrifice for our sins" (1 John 4:10).

PAID IN FULL

So many tremendous truths came pouring out of these statements that it will be impossible to do more than touch on them here. One is *God's amazing love*. When Paul says that the death of Jesus on behalf of sinners "demonstrates" God's love he employs a word we would use about putting up a huge billboard to catch everyone's eye. The Scottish theologian James Denney used to say that he would like to go into every church in the land and walk down the aisle holding a cross in the air and shouting, "God loved like this!' There has never been a greater demonstration of love than the death of Jesus, who gave His life on behalf of those who were "powerless," "ungodly," and "sinners." One writer says that it is "without parallel and without analogy,"[6] and another agrees that "A love which sacrifices itself not for its friends but for its enemies has no parallel in our world."[7]

Another truth we see here is that *God's plan of salvation was not an emergency operation*. Jesus died "at just the right time," not "in the nick of time." There is a difference! Paul says elsewhere that Jesus was born "when the time had fully come" (Galatians 4:4), in other words, at exactly the moment when God determined He would be born. The Bible also says that Jesus was "slain from the creation of the world" (Revelation 13:8). His death was not an afterthought or "Plan B." Before the world was made, before man was created, before time came into existence, God's plan to save sinners was complete in every detail, and ready to be brought into operation at the moment He chose.

A third great truth underlined here is that of *God's perfect justice*. When Jesus took the place of sinners, He became as accountable for their sins as if He had been responsible for them. God is inflexibly holy and so determined to punish sin that when Jesus took the sins of others upon Himself He had to bear *in full* the penalty their sins deserved. The words I have emphasized are all-important because they are at the very heart of the gospel. When people think about the death of Jesus, they tend to think of His physical death, the separation of His soul from His body. Yet to stop there is to come short of the gospel's message, which is that Jesus paid the full penalty for sin.

As He was dying on the cross, He cried out, "My God, my God, why have you forsaken me?" (Matthew 27:46). What did He mean? At this point, we are on holy ground. As one commentator has put it, "Here is the heart of the cross; here is the mystery which no painting or sculpture, with distorted face, can ever show."[8] He is right, of course, but we dare not flinch from the fact that for the first time Jesus sensed that His Father had rejected Him, leaving Him without any awareness of His presence.

As we consider the crucifixion of Jesus, we can see that His physical death was genuine. It had all the elements we expect to find; His soul left His body, His temperature dropped, rigor mortis set in, there was a corpse to be buried. Yet His spiritual death was infinitely worse. As the representative of sinners, Jesus was exposed to the wrath of God against the sinners He represented and the sins they had committed—and God held nothing back. The full fury of His holy anger was unleashed against His own beloved Son, so that when He cried out, "Why have you forsaken me?" His cry met with nothing but holy, angry silence. In His spiritual and physical death Jesus suffered everything the Bible means when it describes hell as a pit, a prison, darkness, and a lake of fire, and He felt in His own body and soul all of hell's shame, contempt, punishment, banishment, separation, deprivation, torment, and agony.

The Apostles Creed (so called not because the apostles wrote it, but because it is based on their teaching) says that Jesus "suffered under Pontius Pilate, was crucified, dead and buried," and that "he descended into hell." Those who framed those words around the end of the fourth century may have meant no more than that Jesus' soul went to Sheol, or Hades, the place of all the departed, and obviously had in mind Peter's statement that after His death Jesus "went and preached to the spirits in prison" (1 Peter 3:19), but they could not have put more concisely the awesome truth of what happened at Calvary. As my friend Geoff Thomas has written, "Hell is the place where the fellowship of God is absent and the wrath of a sin-hating God remains."[9] That is what Jesus experienced—and He did so on behalf of others.

THE RECEIPTED BILL

Let me anticipate your next question: "How do we know that God accepted what Jesus did?" The Bible's answer is both simple and stupendous: He raised Him from the dead. Beginning three days after His death, Jesus met with His friends and followers (several hundred of them altogether) over a period of about seven weeks, giving them what Luke called "many convincing proofs that he was alive" (Acts 1:3) before being "taken up into heaven" (Mark 16:19). There is more proof for the resurrection of Jesus than for the Roman invasion of Britain by Julius Caesar, but this is not the place to examine the details.[10] Lord Darling, a former Chief Justice of England, once did so very carefully and came to the following conclusion: "There exists such overwhelming evidence, positive and negative, factual and circumstantial, that no intelligent jury in the world could fail to bring in a verdict that the resurrection story is true."[11]

The resurrection of Jesus did several things. It confirmed *His identity*: Paul says that Jesus was "declared with power to be the Son of God by his resurrection from the dead" (Romans 1:4). It proved *the truth of His teaching*: He staked everything He said on His prophecy that He would rise from the dead. Above all, it declared that *God had accepted His sacrifice on behalf of others*, and that Jesus had accomplished what He came to do. Many years ago, Britain used to have debtors' prisons. If someone contracted a debt and then ran away without paying it, anyone who had stood surety for him could be arrested and imprisoned in his place until the debt had been settled and justice satisfied. If a debtor who had done this returned to his hometown sometime later and saw his surety walking along the street, he would know that the debt had been paid in full. That helps to illustrate the tremendous truth that the resurrection of Jesus is proof that God's justice was satisfied by the death of His Son on behalf of sinners. The one who paid the debt was released from the prison of death. That is why Paul can say that in the death of Jesus, God "canceled the written code, with its regulations, that was against us and that stood opposed to us; he took it away, nailing it to the cross" (Colossians 2:14). Jesus met the demands of God's law not only by living a perfect life, but by paying in full the penalty it imposes on the disobedient. His resurrection is the receipted bill.

OBEYING THE GOSPEL

Surely this is the best news you have ever heard? Jesus Christ, the eternal Son of God, came into the world as a human being, lived a perfect life, then died in the place of sinners, bearing their sins, satisfying every demand of God's holy justice, and throwing the gates of heaven wide open. I can already hear the next questions! "Then how can the Bible say that sinners will be condemned if they fail to 'obey the gospel'? And if the gospel is the good news of something God did and not something God demands, how can I possibly obey it?" The answer is both definite and demanding.

It is certainly true that if you are to be saved, it can only be on the basis of what Jesus did. As Peter said, "Salvation is found in no one else, for there is no other name under heaven given to men by which we must be saved" (Acts 4:12). Yet you must still obey the gospel. The root of the word "obey" means "to hear beneath," and the picture is of submissively listening to what is being said, accepting it as true, and applying its implications to one's life. As far as obeying the gospel is concerned, it means that you are called to "turn to God in repentance and have faith in our Lord Jesus" (Acts 20:21).

Repentance means *a wholehearted turning from sin*. Are you willing for this? Are you prepared to acknowledge not only that you have committed sins, but that you are a sinner?

Think firstly of the number of sins you have committed. Assuming that you broke God's law once in every waking hour, this would amount to about 16 sins in a day, over 100 in a week, well over 3,000 a month and nearly 6,000 a year. If you died at the age of 70 you would stand before a holy God with over 400,000 sins to be accounted for, any one of which would be sufficient to bar the way to heaven and open the door to hell.

This is serious enough, but your situation is even worse because "All have sinned and fall short of the glory of God" (Romans 3:23). This means that you are continuously falling short of the perfection God requires, constantly adding to the mountain of your sins and to the punishment they deserve. Think of the past month, the past week, even the last twenty-four hours. What does your conscience tell you? Would you not be ashamed to share every detail of you thoughts, words, and actions with your friends, your neighbors, or members of your family? How then can you face the prospect of having every one of them count against you on the Day of Judgment?

When asked which was the greatest of the commandments in God's law, Jesus replied, "Love the Lord your God with all your heart and with all you soul and with all your mind and with all your strength" (Mark 12:30). Are you doing this? Have you constantly done so? If not, then remember that breaking the greatest commandment is committing the greatest sin.

If you are still clinging to the thought that you are better than some people you know, and not guilty of any really serious sin, you are clinging to tinsel in a tornado. For many people, this "tinsel" is their religion. In his amusing little autobiography, the renowned British actor Sir Alec Guinness wrote about his spiritual search, which took in Anglicanism, Presbyterianism, Communism, Buddhism, and Roman Catholicism. Yet, at the end of the chapter, he confessed, "The fear I mostly entertain is that my personal religion is notional rather than real."[12] Far from saving anyone, formal religion is a sin which needs to be abandoned.

Repentance involves *confession* not only of *sins* but of *sin*. It means acknowledging that you are a sinner by nature, a sinner at heart, that (to quote Jonathan Edwards again) you were born a "little viper" and have remained corrupt and depraved ever since. If you are not prepared to admit this, there is no hope for you, because Jesus said, "I have not come to call the righteous, but sinners" (Matthew 9:13). If you proudly insist on claiming to have sufficient natural goodness to save yourself, or at least to make some contribution to your salvation, you are not obeying the gospel and are heading for disaster.

Repentance also involves *sorrow for sin*, the recognition that all sin, every sin, is vile and loathsome in God's sight. Do you understand this? It is not enough to sense what sin has done to you: do you sense what it has done to God? It is not enough to feel miserable about your own failure, stupidity, weakness, or inadequacy. That could be nothing more than self-pity, which will add to your sins, rather than do anything to remove them. There is a big difference between God-centered sorrow, which grieves over the wickedness of sin and what it has done to God, and self-centered sorrow which is concerned only about what it has done to you. The Bible is clear about this: "Godly sorrow brings repentance that leads to salvation and leaves no regret, but worldly sorrow brings death" (2 Corinthians 7:10). Brownlow North once described himself as "a man whose sins crucified the Son of God." Do you sense that about your sins, your pride, your selfishness, your greed, your dishonesty, even your reliance on your religion, and respectability? If not, you have never truly repented; you are still not obeying the gospel.

True repentance has yet another dimension; there must be *a gen-*

uine desire to turn from sin and to live a life that is honoring to God
and obedient to His Word. When David came to repentance he cried,
"Create in me a pure heart, O God, and renew a steadfast spirit within
me" (Psalm 51:10). He longed to turn his back on sin, to have nothing more to do with it, and to live a changed life. You must turn to
God in the same spirit. God is not willing to forgive any sin that you
are not willing to forsake. Repentance is not a request for God to
sweep your sins under the carpet; it involves an honest longing to live
a life that is pleasing to God. Isaiah says,

> "Let the wicked forsake his way
> and the evil man his thoughts.
> Let him turn to the Lord, and he will have mercy on him,
> and to our God, for he will freely pardon"
> (Isaiah 55:7).

Repentance without turning from sin is a contradiction in terms.
Have you truly repented? Are you willing to do so now? Do you
acknowledge that you are a sinner by nature, by desire, by habit, and
by choice? Are you broken-hearted and disgusted as you realize the
true nature of sin, and what it did to the Son of God? And are you
willing to lead a new life, one that is God-centered and not self-centered? This is part of what it means to obey the gospel, and it is
absolutely essential.

SAVING FAITH

The second element in obeying the gospel is to have "faith in our Lord
Jesus." When the Bible speaks about having faith in God, or in the
Lord Jesus Christ, it means much more than believing certain biblical
facts. Obviously it includes that. Jesus once said, "If you do not
believe that I am the one I claim to be, you will indeed die in your
sins" (John 8:24). Where do you stand on this issue? Do you believe
with Peter that Jesus is "the Christ, the Son of the living God"?
(Matthew 16:16). If so, that is good; but it is not good enough. As we
saw in chapter 12, there were occasions when evil spirits acknowledged Jesus to be "the Holy One of God" (Mark 1:24) and "the Son
of God" (Luke 4:41), but their confessions neither kept them from
hell nor took them to heaven. Saving faith in Christ means turning to
Him, committing your life to Him, trusting Him and Him alone to
save you from the guilt and consequences of your sin.

Are you willing to do this and to do it now? Much of what I have been trying to get across in the latter part of this book—the love of God, the sending of His Son, the fact that sinners will perish and the gospel promise of eternal life—is crammed into one statement which many Christians call "the gospel in a nutshell": "For God so loved the world that he gave his one and only Son, that whoever believes in him shall not perish but have eternal life" (John 3:16). Here is the marvelous promise of the gospel in all its wonder and glory, but notice that eternal life is conditional upon believing in Christ, taking and trusting Him as your own personal Savior.

Are you prepared to do this? If not, why not? When God sent His servant Ezekiel to preach to a stubborn and rebellious nation, He told him, "Say to them, 'As surely as I live, declares the Sovereign Lord, I take no pleasure in the death of the wicked, but rather that they turn from their ways and live. Turn! Turn from your evil ways! Why will you die, O house of Israel?'" (Ezekiel 33:11). God's message to you is exactly the same. If you come to the end of this book, decide this message is not for you, and turn away from the Savior it offers, then even the time you have spent reading these pages will add to you guilt and, unless you change your mind, will add to your punishment. How can you bear such a thought? Why would you choose such a thing? Why would you refuse the forgiveness of sins and eternal life? Why are you prepared to despise God's goodness to you, ignore His voice and trample the blood of His Son under your feet? Do you think God will take kindly to that? My questions only echo what the Bible asks: "Do you show contempt for the riches of his kindness, tolerance and patience, not realizing that God's kindness leads you toward repentance? But because of your stubbornness and your unrepentant heart, you are storing up wrath against yourself for the day of God's wrath, when his righteous judgment will be revealed" (Romans 2:4-6).

If you are still resisting what God is saying, or are hesitant about what to do, I urge you to change your mind and to obey the gospel while you have the opportunity. The Bible says, "Today, if you hear his voice, do not harden your hearts" (Hebrews 3:7). Delayed obedience is disobedience, whatever excuse you choose to make for it. Saying that you will turn to Christ tomorrow means refusing to turn to Him today. That is an insult to God, flinging His invitation back in His face and telling Him that you will accept it if and when it suits you. Why should God tolerate such a thing? As Jonathan Edwards put it, "Why should you not have wrath as great as that love and mercy which you despise and reject?"[13]

THE DANGERS OF DELAY

Putting off turning to Christ is also a highly dangerous thing to do, because every rejection of the gospel leads to a hardening of the heart. There is evidence to suggest that nobody who deliberately rejects Christ is ever quite the same again. What the Bible calls "sin's deceitfulness" (Hebrews 3:13) sees to that. The realities of death and judgment, heaven and hell will fade; day to day business and busyness will crowd in; excuses will be easier to come by. Delay is also dangerous because you can come to God only when the Holy Spirit calls you. God's warning in the early days of humanity's history, "My Spirit will not contend with man for ever" (Genesis 6:3) applies to every individual who hears the gospel. If you sense that God has spoken to you through the pages of this book, but you refuse to respond to His invitation, what guarantee do you have that He will ever speak to you in such a way again? As a friend of mine has put it, "Even if you live as long as you hope, the day of opportunity may be shorter than your life."[14] Trading on God's patience is a fearful folly. The time for repentance and faith is always now and never tomorrow. In the Bible's words, "Seek the Lord while he may be found; call on him while he is near" (Isaiah 55:6).

Finally, the most obvious danger in delay is that you dare not presume that you will live to see another day. The Bible's warnings could not be clearer: "Death is the destiny of every man; the living should take this to heart" (Ecclesiastes 7:2). "Do not boast about tomorrow, for you do not know what a day may bring forth" (Proverbs 27:1). "What is your life? You are a mist that appears for a little while and then vanishes" (James 4:14). God has appointed the day of your death as surely as He appointed the day of your birth, and the clock is relentlessly ticking away. However young, or fit, or strong you may be, death is closer to you now than it was last year, last month, last week; closer than when you began reading this book or reached the top of this page. An eleventh-century theologian once said, "Death is oftentimes as near to the young man's back as it is to the old man's face."[15] It is only by God's grace that you are continuing to hold the tenancy of life; He is under no obligation to give you even a moment's notice to quit.

In the sermon we mentioned earlier in this chapter, Jonathan Edwards warns his hearers of the danger of delaying repentance: "You have offended [God] infinitely more than ever a stubborn rebel did his prince; and yet it is nothing but his hand that holds you from falling into the fire every moment. It is to be ascribed to nothing else that you did not go to hell the last night; that you were suffered to awake again in this world after you closed your eyes to sleep. And there is no other reason to be given why you have not dropped into hell since you arose in the morning, but that God's hand has held you up . . . There is nothing else that is to be given as a reason why you do not this very moment drop down into hell."[16] If you are still unconverted, every single one of those words is true of you at this very moment, even as you read this sentence. Surely it is lunacy to ignore them?

Death is the great uncertain certainty. Are you ready to meet your Maker? Are you sure that your sins are forgiven and that you are right with God? Or are you still obstinately refusing to obey the gospel, determined to take your chances when you come to the Day of Judgment? If so, your chances are nil. Jesus said, "Whoever does not believe stands condemned already because he has not believed in the name of God's one and only Son" (John 3:18). The only escape from the "condemned cell" is to turn from sin and trust in Christ—and God promises to give you the grace to do so if you will truly call upon Him: "You will seek me and find me when you seek me with all your heart" (Jeremiah 19:13). Jesus makes a promise that is equally emphatic: "I tell you the truth, whoever hears my word and believes him who sent me has eternal life and will not be condemned; he has crossed over from death to life" (John 5:24). Eternal life does not begin after death, but the moment a person obeys the gospel by turning from sin and trusting in Christ.

What reason can you possibly give for not accepting God's invitation and taking Him at His word? You are already on the road to hell, but in His amazing love God has set before you the way to heaven. May He graciously enable you to find it and follow it!

P. S.

If this was the book I had originally intended to write, this chapter might not have been relevant, but as things have worked out I must add a brief postscript specifically geared to the reader who is already a Christian.

There is a sense in which so far you have been on the outside looking in (although in one sense on the inside looking out). Before reading this book you had no doubt that the Bible was "the living and enduring Word of God" (1 Peter 1:23). You knew that God was holy and just and that all humanity will stand before Him on the Day of Judgment. You were already aware that the Bible had some very serious things to say about hell, yet you rejoiced in the good news that "Christ Jesus came into the world to save sinners" (1 Timothy 1:15). You also knew from experience that because Jesus Christ rose again from the dead and is alive today, "He is able to save completely those who come to God through him" (Hebrews 7:25).

Then is this book of no more than academic or theoretic interest to you and of no practical value? I sincerely hope not. The American preacher A. W. Tozer once wrote, "There is scarcely anything so dull and meaningless as Bible doctrine taught for its own sake. Truth divorced from life is not truth in its biblical sense, but something else and something less . . . Theological truth is useless until it is obeyed. The purpose behind all doctrine is to secure moral action."[1] For all its limitations, I have sought to base this book solidly on biblical doctrine, and I pray that God will use it to produce the moral action the doctrine of hell demands. The previous chapter makes it clear what the unbeliever should do, which is to "turn to God in repentance and have faith in our Lord Jesus" (Acts 20:21). What about the Christian? What kind of responses should you make to the teaching of Scripture about the eternal punishment of the lost? We shall look at some of the most obvious ones.

"SNATCHED FROM THE FIRE"

When John Wesley was five years old, the house in which he was living (the Rectory at Epworth, now in Humberside) was burned to the ground. Thanks to prompt action by two of the villagers, the boy was hauled out seconds before the roof crashed in. Much later in life, as a powerful preacher of the gospel, he wrote these words in his Journal: "At about eleven o'clock it came into my mind that this was the very day and hour in which forty years ago I was taken out of the flames. I stopped and gave a short account of that wonderful providence. The voice of praise and thanksgiving went up on high and great was our rejoicing before the Lord."[2] John Wesley was converted to Christ in a meeting at Aldersgate Street in London on May 24, 1738, and he always looked on his conversion as the second time that he had been snatched from the flames, this time in a spiritual sense. There is a point in the Old Testament at which God refers to His redeemed people as "a burning stick snatched from the fire" (Zechariah 3:2) and it seems that Wesley had this in mind as he praised God for His saving goodness to him. As he lay on his deathbed in February 1791, he repeated the words of a great hymn by Isaac Watts, the last one Wesley had announced in the course of his ministry:

> *I'll praise my Maker while I've breath*
> *And when my voice is lost in death,*
> *Praise shall employ my nobler powers;*
> *My days of praise shall ne'er be past,*
> *While life, and thought, and being last*
> *Or immortality endures.*

In the fifty and more years that had passed since he was brought to faith in Christ, he never stopped praising and thanking God for having "taken him out of the flames."

You should be no less thankful! Even if you were born into a Christian family, or had lived a reasonably respectable life, you still came into this world as what Jonathan Edwards called a "little viper," guilty, lost, and helpless. Before you became a Christian you were "dead in your transgressions and sins" (Ephesians 2:1), yet God in His mercy ensured that you were exposed to the gospel, brought you to spiritual birth, enabled you to turn from sin and trust in Christ, granted you the forgiveness of sins and eternal life, and joined you to all those able to say with Paul that "Since we have been justified through faith, we have peace with God through our Lord Jesus Christ" (Romans 5:1), and to rejoice that you have "an inheritance that can never perish, spoil or fade—kept in heaven for you" (1 Peter 1:4).

What is more, the Bible assures you that you were chosen in Christ "before the creation of the world" (Ephesians 1:4). Your salvation had nothing to do with your own merits or efforts. As Paul admits, "Like the rest, we were by nature objects of wrath. But because of his great love for us, God, who is rich in mercy, made us alive with Christ even when we were dead in transgressions . . . For it is by grace you have been saved, through faith—and this not from yourselves, it is the gift of God—not by works, so that no one can boast" (Ephesians 2:3-5, 8-9). Were it not for God's indescribably love you would be as surely on your way to hell as the vilest human being who has ever lived. Then never let a day go by without praising God for having had mercy upon you and bringing you to himself.

In one of his Psalms, David says,

"I will extol the Lord at all times;
his praise will always be on my lips . . .
Glorify the Lord with me;
let us exalt his name together"
(Psalm 34:1, 3).

This is an invitation you should always be delighted to accept! In another psalm, David talks to himself, as it were, and says,

"Praise the Lord, O my soul;
all my inmost being, praise his holy name.
Praise the Lord, O my soul,
and forget not all his benefits"
(Psalm 103:1-2).

It will be impossible for you to remember all God's benefits (the word means something like "bounties") because, like His compassions, they are "new every morning."(Lamentations 3:23), but, surely, it will be equally impossible ever to forget the greatest of all, that He has rescued you from hell, assured you of a place in heaven, and promised you His presence and power all the way there!

THE GREAT AND FUNDAMENTAL LAW

If praising God is an obvious response that the doctrine of hell should produce in the Christian, then godliness of life is another. Matthew Henry used to say that God's command to His people, "Be holy because I, the Lord your God, am holy" (Leviticus 19:2) is "the great and fundamental law of our religion." This one command summarizes the Christian's moral responsibility in the light of the Bible's teaching, and it is often given in the context of God's saving goodness to His people. Having said that God had chosen us in Christ before the creation of the world, Paul immediately adds the purpose of our being chosen: "to be holy and blameless in his sight" (Ephesians 1:4). Elsewhere he says, "For God did not call us to be impure, but to live a holy life" (1 Thessalonians 4:7), and on another occasion tells Timothy that God has "saved us and called us to a holy life" (2 Timothy 1:9). Notice that in all of these cases there is a close and direct link between salvation and holiness.

Peter makes the same point: "But you are chosen people, a royal priesthood, a holy nation, a people belonging to God, that you may declare the praises of him who called you out of darkness into his wonderful light" (1 Peter 2:9). The word "declare" which Peter uses here virtually means "advertise." A Christian is to be a living advertisement for God, a human visual aid to show a sinful and skeptical world that God is real, Jesus is alive, and the Holy Spirit can change a person's life.

In his second letter, Peter refers to holiness in the context of the end of the world and the Second Coming of Christ (and therefore of the Day of Judgment): "But the day of the Lord will come like a thief. The heavens will disappear with a roar; the elements will be destroyed by fire, and the earth and everything in it will be laid bare. Since everything will be destroyed in this way, what kind of people ought you to be? You ought to live holy and godly lives as you look forward to the day of God and speed its coming" (2 Peter 3:10-12). Notice how Peter makes the connection. The fact that the world as we know it is coming to an end has moral implications. As the present state of affairs is going to give way to what Peter goes on to call "a new heaven and a new earth, the home of righteousness" (2 Peter 3:13), you should be striving to be ready for that great change, not allowing your day-to-day behavior to be molded by this world's passing standards and values.

Vance Havner once wrote, "If you are a Christian, you are not a citizen of this world trying to get to heaven; you are a citizen of heaven making your way through this world."[3] This is exactly the point Paul makes when he says that "Our citizenship is in heaven" and that "We eagerly await a Savior from there, the Lord Jesus Christ"(Philippians 3:20). This message would have come across loud and clear to his original readers who, as residents of the Roman colony of Philippi, had all the rights and privileges of Roman citizens. Building on this background, Paul reminds them of their "dual citizenship" and makes it clear that their greater allegiance is to the heavenly kingdom of which God had graciously made them members.

As a Christian, you share in their great responsibility, and you should have a heightened sense of this whenever you think of the fact that Christ is coming back. The Seventh Earl of Shaftesbury, a prominent nineteenth-century social reformer, said near the end of his life, "I do not think that in the last forty years I have lived one conscious hour that was not influenced by the thought of our Lord's return."[4] The same impending event should have a powerful influence on the way you live. Unless God had intervened, you would be a citizen not of heaven but of hell, and the Second Coming of Christ would spell not deliverance but disaster. The thought that when God calls humanity to judgment you will be saved from the holocaust of hell and welcomed into the everlasting bliss of heaven ought to be a constant incentive to you to live "in a manner worthy of the gospel of Christ" (Philippians 1:27).

If it is possible to be an effective Christian without being wealthy, or trendy, but not without being holy. God has given you a great responsibility, but also great resources; Peter says, "His divine power has given us everything we need for life and godliness through our knowledge of him who called us by his own glory and goodness" (2 Peter 1:3). C. H. Spurgeon once told his hearers, "I should like to coin my heart to pass it round to you in living medallions, bearing each one this inscription—for Jesus' sake be holy."[5] God's love means that you should—and His power means that you can.

GUILTY SILENCE

A third response to the doctrine of hell is to do all you can to reach others with the gospel. At one point in the Old Testament, Israel was in a deep economic recession, made worse by a bitter and costly war against Syria. When the nation's capital, Samaria, was under siege, and the situation seemed hopeless, some lepers decided to make their way to an enemy camp and surrender, in the hope that they would be given enough food to stay alive. When they reached the camp they found it deserted but, to their amazement, fully stocked. Hardly daring to believe what was happening, they piled into the food and drink and helped themselves to as much gold, silver, and clothing as they could carry. Suddenly, they came to their senses—and to a sense of their responsibility: "We're not doing right. This is a day of good news and we are keeping it to ourselves . . . Let's go at once and report this to the royal palace" (2 Kings 7:9).

Sadly, many Christians are behaving as those lepers did in the first part of the story. They are loading themselves up with all the blessing they can get from preaching, Bible teaching, and Christian fellowship—but are keeping it to themselves. They have discovered "good news," but are doing little or nothing to share it with those who need to hear it if they are to be rescued from the pains of hell.

There are millions of people in the world today who have never heard the gospel—more than made up the whole world population in 1955—and without the gospel they are lost. Every day adds hundreds of thousands to their number. As a Christian you have a responsibility to take your share in obeying the last command Jesus gave the church before He returned to heaven: "Go into all the world and preach the good news to all creation" (Mark 16:15). C. H. Spurgeon told his Bible College students, "Shun all views of future punishment which would make it appear less terrible, and so take the edge off your anxiety to save immortals from the quenchless flame. If men are indeed only a nobler kind of ape, and expire as the beasts, you may well enough let them die unpitied; but if their creation in the image of God involves immortality, and there is any fear that through their unbelief they will bring upon themselves endless woe, arouse yourselves to the agonies of the occasion, and be ashamed at the bare suspicion of unconcern."[6]

The perilous state of unbelievers is not the only biblical incentive for evangelism, nor is it the greatest, but it is the one that most clearly relates to the subject of this book. This comes across in a statement Paul made to the Corinthians, part of which we noted in an earlier chapter: "For we must all appear before the judgment seat of Christ, that each one may receive what is due to him for the things done while in the body, whether good or bad. Since, then, we know what it is to fear the Lord, we try to persuade men" (2 Corinthians 5:10-11).

There are two obvious incentives here. The first is that "We must all appear before the judgment seat of Christ." Christians need have no fear that they will be condemned on that day—as Paul says elsewhere, "There is now no condemnation for those who are in Christ Jesus" (Romans 8:1)—but the Bible makes it clear that the quality of their lives and the faithfulness of their service as Christians will be taken into account in determining the measure of their reward. Jesus told a number of parables which emphasized this particular truth, and Paul laid down a principle that runs through them all: "Now it is required that those who have been given a trust must prove faithful" (1 Corinthians 4:2). Are you a faithful steward of all that God has given you? Are you using your talents, energies, finances, and opportunities as you should in order to reach a lost world with the gospel? It is surely sobering to realize that you will one day be judged for the way you have responded to the spiritual needs of others?

The second motive for evangelism in Paul's words is equally obvious: on the Day of Judgment unbelievers will hear the dreadful sentence, "Depart from me, you who are cursed, into the eternal fire prepared for the devil and his angels" (Matthew 25:41). How can you possibly accept that multitudes of people—including many you know personally—are on a collision course with an announcement of God's righteous and terrifying condemnation and yet do nothing to warn them of their danger? To change the metaphor, how can you go on gorging yourself on spiritual food and not share it with those who are starving to death? John Stott has rightly said that "The neglect of my neighbor's spiritual needs, on whatever pretext, is incompatible with the claim to love him. Such neglect is criminal irresponsibility. To suppress the good news in silence is to incur guilty."[7]

BY ALL POSSIBLE MEANS

In underlining his passionate concern for the lost, Paul told the Corinthians, "I have become all things to all men so that by all possible means I might save some" (1 Corinthians 9:22). He did not mean that he was prepared to compromise on matters of principle, but rather that he was prepared to "sacrifice his own legitimate interests and preferences completely, if thereby he might save some."[8] He was willing to forego any non-essentials in his life if by so doing he would help to ensure that men and women on their way to hell would hear the life-giving gospel. All Christians should have the same driving concern and be prepared to make the same determined effort. You may not be called, as he was, to be a public preacher—that is a privilege granted to comparatively few—but there are many other ways in which you can and should be involved in reaching others with the gospel.

Firstly, you can *pray*. When Jesus saw crowds of people "harassed and helpless, like sheep without a shepherd," He told His disciples, "The harvest is plentiful but the workers are few. Ask the Lord of the harvest, therefore, to send out workers into his harvest field" (Matthew 9:36-38). There is an urgent need for preachers, those committed to a lifelong work of reaching people with the gospel. Many churches are struggling along with inadequately equipped leaders, missionary societies are crying out for recruits, evangelistic agencies are short-staffed. The lack of earnest prayer for God to raise up faithful, capable gospel preachers is one of the greatest weaknesses in the church today. You can play an important part in changing this situation.

Secondly, you can *give*. As someone has rightly said, "The kingdom of God is not built on finances, but it cannot be extended without them."[9] The Old Testament records an occasion when there was an urgent need to replace the temple at Jerusalem, destroyed by invaders many years earlier. A rebuilding program was initiated by the country's spiritual leaders, but it got a very sluggish response from the rank and file, who suggested that the project be delayed until their financial situation improved. God's reaction swept this flimsy excuse aside and showed that the real problem had to do with their selfish priorities: "Is it a time for you yourselves to be living in your paneled houses, while this house remains a ruin?" (Haggai 1:4). It is not difficult to apply these words to today's situation, when one Christian cause after another is struggling to make ends meet and many Christians are giving them no more than nominal support while moving selfishly up the social scale, constantly improving their own material standard of living. One writer has said, "The gulf between what affluent Christians give and what they could give is a terrifying tragedy."[10] Not all Christians are affluent, but when Christians fail to support God's work as they should it is nothing short of sinful.

When people complained at a woman's extravagance in honoring Jesus by anointing Him with expensive perfume, He silenced them by saying, "She did what she could" (Mark 14:8). Can the same be said of you? Leaving aside the many other ways in which you can support evangelistic work, are you doing all you can in this area? What are your financial priorities? How much are you giving directly to the work of the gospel? There is no shortage of opportunity, including your local church, evangelistic agencies, foreign missions, the work of Bible translation and evangelical Bible colleges and training centers. All of these have great needs which can be met only as Christians obediently fulfill their financial responsibilities.

Are you giving God what is right—or what is left? Few things test a Christian's spirituality more than the use of money, and nothing should focus your thinking more on this subject than the fact that funds at your disposal could be used to help in rescuing people from everlasting destruction. The seventeenth-century preacher Richard Baxter once wrote, "Stretch your purse to the utmost, and do all the good you can."[11] Anything less is not good enough.

PERSON TO PERSON

Thirdly, you can *take the gospel directly to others*. To think in terms of billions of lost people numbs the mind. Even the thought of millions in one's own country is overwhelming—but there is another way to approach the issue. Every day you meet people who are lost, "without hope and without God in the world" (Ephesians 2:12): colleagues at work, fellow students, neighbors, social contacts, and others. Members of your own family may well be in the same terrible position. None of these is excluded from the promise that "Everyone who calls on the name of the Lord will be saved" (Romans 10:13), but notice how Paul continues: "How, then, can they call on the one they have not believed in? And how can they believe in the one of whom they have not heard? And how can they hear without someone preaching to them?" (Romans 10:14-15). "Preaching" is not limited to standing in a pulpit and delivering a sermon. It includes all direct communication of the gospel.

Personal evangelism has always been one of the most effective means that God has used to bring people to Himself. In Acts 8, we are told that when a great persecution hit the church in Jerusalem "All except the apostles were scattered throughout Judea and Samaria," and that "Those who had been scattered preached the word wherever they went" (Acts 8:1, 4). Notice that all the professional preachers remained in Jerusalem; those who "preached the word" all over Judea and Samaria were the rank and file Christians, men, women, and young people whose lives had been transformed by the power of the gospel and who were delighted to share the good news with others. Nor are we told that they built churches or held formal services in order to do so. As the contemporary British writer Michael Green puts it, "Evangelism was the spontaneous chattering of the good news. It was engaged in naturally, continuously, easily and joyfully by Christians wherever they went."[12] This was the pattern in the early church, and it was powerfully effective.

In *A History of the Expansion of Christianity*, Kenneth Scott Latourette wrote, "The chief agents in the expansion of Christianity appear not to have been those who made it a profession or a major part of their occupation, but men and women who earned their livelihood in some purely secular manner and spoke of their faith to those whom they met in this natural fashion."[13] It would be very easy to show that the same is true today. I have been in meetings where up to ninety percent of those present said that the major influence in their conversion was personal contact with someone who was a Christian. What an exhilarating prospect that raises for you! There is no need to call in an evangelist in order to evangelize; God has given you the command and your day-to-day contacts provide the opportunity.

None of this means that anyone's salvation ultimately depends on your obedience, the amount of your evangelistic activity, or your ability to communicate the gospel. You can no more save another person than you could have saved yourself. As the Bible makes crystal clear, "Salvation belongs to our God" (Revelation 7:10). If anyone is to be saved, it is entirely by the sovereign grace of God, so that neither the sinner nor the person who shared the gospel with him or her can take any of the credit.

When Robert Murray M'Cheyne first heard of someone coming to Christ through his ministry, his response struck exactly the right note: "How blessed an answer to prayer, if it be really so . . . It has refreshed me more than a thousand sermons. I know not how to thank and admire God sufficiently . . . Lord, I thank thee that thou hast shown me this marvelous working, though I was but an adoring spectator, rather than an instrument."[14] Even though he poured himself into his ministry with tremendous energy (he died when he was just twenty-nine years of age) he knew that the salvation of others was

due not to his work but to the work of the Holy Spirit in bringing sinners to repentance and faith.

You should always bear this in mind and get involved in the work
of evangelization, not in a spirit of guilt and fear, but grateful for the
privilege of being one of "God's fellow-workers" (2 Corinthians 6:1).
This will not lessen your sense of responsibility, but it should deliver
you from the crushing sense that you are personally accountable for
preventing sinners going to hell. As one contemporary writer puts it,
"Trying to be even the unconscious savior of a nation is an unbear-
ably heavy burden to carry."[15]

Yet those important principles have to be balanced with the
inescapable fact that the brevity of life, the certainty of death and
judgment and the everlastingness of hell mean that reaching others
with the gospel is a matter of urgency. People are hurtling toward a
terrible disaster without any hope of being saved unless they hear the
gospel and respond to it in repentance and faith. No wonder the Bible
urges Christians to "snatch others from the fire and save them" (Jude
23). Commenting on Jude's striking metaphor, John Calvin wrote,
"When there is a danger of fire, we hesitate not to snatch away vio-
lently whom we desire to save; for it would not be enough to beckon
with the finger, or kindly to stretch forth the hand."[16] Do you have
that sense of urgency? Do you have a genuine concern for the eternal
destinies of those with whom you are in contact, or are you content
to escort them gently on their way to hell without ever warning them
of their danger? J.C. Ryle adds another dimension to the challenge:
"The highest form of selfishness is that of the man who is content to
go to heaven alone. The truest charity is to endeavor to share with
others every spark of religious light we possess ourselves, and so to
hold our own candle that it may give light to every one around us . . .
No candle which God lights was ever meant to burn alone."[17]

Sharing the gospel with others will not always be easy, especially
if you are faithful in warning people of its "dark side." The subject of
hell is so traumatic that there will often be the temptation to blur the
issue for fear of raising people's hackles or embarrassing them in some
way. When Dr. Knightley Chetwood, Dean of Gloucester, was preaching at a court on one occasion he said rather diffidently that unrepentant sinners would be punished after death "in a place it is not
decent to mention in so polite a company"![18] Along the same lines,
C.S. Lewis tells of hearing a young man end a sermon on judgment
by warning his hearers that those who did not turn to Christ would

suffer "grave eschatological ramifications." After the service, Lewis asked him whether he meant that these people would go to hell. "Precisely," the preacher replied. "Then say so," Lewis told him.[19] Always remember that people's response to the gospel is literally a matter of life or death—eternal life or eternal death. Evangelism is vital, serious and urgent.

On December 12, 1984 dense fog shrouded the M25, a highway near Godstone, in Surrey, a few miles south of London. The hazard warning lights were on, but were ignored by most drivers. At 6:15 A.M. a truck carrying huge rolls of paper was involved in an accident, and within minutes the carriageway was engulfed in carnage. Dozens of cars were wrecked. Ten people were killed. A police patrol car was soon on the scene, and two policemen ran back up the motorway to stop oncoming traffic. They waved their arms and shouted as loud as they could, but most drivers took no notice and raced on toward the disaster that awaited them. The policemen then picked up traffic cones and flung them at the cars windscreens in a desperate attempt to warn drivers of their danger; one told how tears streamed down his face as car after car went by, and he waited for the sickening sound of impact as they hit the growing mass of wreckage farther down the road. The plight of the lost is so terrible, the power of sin so great and the horror of hell so fearful—how can you possibly do nothing to warn people of their danger and to point them to the Savior?

In the course of his ministry John Wesley's brother Charles wrote over 7,000 hymns, one of which has a verse which crystallizes his own response to the challenge of his day:

> *My talents, gifts and graces, Lord*
> *Into thy blessed hands receive;*
> *And let me live to preach thy word,*
> *And let me to thy glory live;*
> *My every sacred moment spend*
> *In publishing the sinner's Friend.*

Nearly 300 years have passed since Wesley wrote those words. The need for Christians who can pray those words—and mean them—has never been greater. May God make you one of them!

References

PREFACE

1. Published by the Banner of Truth Trust.

CHAPTER ONE: *Fact or Fantasy?*

1. "Only 4% of Minnesotans Feel They're Hellbound," *EP News Service*, March 25, 1978.
2. *Newsweek*, March 27, 1989.
3. *The Bulletin*, May 24, 1988.
4. *Sunday Telegraph*, December 24, 1989.
5. David Lodge, *How Far Can You Go?*
6. Cited in *Newsweek*, March 27, 1989.
7. As above.
8. *The Bulletin*, May 24, 1988.
9. *A Brief History of Hell*, BBC2, January 6, 1991.
10. *The Bible Almanack*, ed. J. I. Packer, M. C. Tenney, W. White.
11. *Handbook of Contemporary Theology*, ed. Bernard Ramm, Wm. B. Eerdmans Publ. Co.
12. See H. Buis, *The Doctrine of Eternal Punishment,* Presbyterian & Reformed Publ. Co., p.x.
13. *Daily Telegraph*, December 23, 1989.
14. *Daily Telegraph*, December 13, 1990.
15. *Cable News Network*, January 17, 1991.
16. *Daily Telegraph*, August 21, 1991.
17. *Daily Telegraph*, January 10, 1990.
18. *Daily Express*, August 29, 1990.
19. *Prime Time,* ABC Television, October 11, 1990.
20. *Daily Mail*, July 5, 1990.
21. *Sunday Express,* June 24, 1990.
22. *Daily Mail*, December 12, 1990.
23. Tommy Armour, *How To Play Your Best Golf All The Time*, Coronet Books, p.105.
24. *International Daily Express*, March 23, 1990.

25. *Sydney Morning Herald*, March 17, 1990.
26. *Daily Telegraph*, December 7, 1990.
27. As above.
28. *Daily Telegraph*, January 4, 1992.
29. *Observer*, April 12, 1992.
30. *Golf World*, February 1990.
32. *Daily Telegraph*, December 13, 1990.
33. Song "Imagine" on album *Imagine*, produced by John Lennon, Yoko Ono, and Phil Spector, EMI Records.
34. Cited by Buis, *Doctrine of Eternal Punishment*, p.147.

CHAPTER TWO: *Database*

1. *The Concise Oxford Dictionary of Current English*, 7th Edition, Clarendon Press, p.1240.
2. Clark H. Pinnock, *Biblical Revelation*, Moody Press, p.48.
3. Robert Dick Wilson, *A Scientific Investigation of the Old Testament*, Moody Press, p.70.
4. As above.
5. Nelson Glueck, *Rivers in the Desert; History of Neteg*, Jewish Publications Society of America, p.31.
6. William Ramsay, *The Bearing of Recent Discoveries on the Trustworthiness of the New Testament*, Hodder & Stoughton, p.222.
7. C. S. Lewis, *They Stand Together: The Letters of C. S. Lewis to Arthur Greeves*, ed. Walter Hooper, Macmillan, p.503.
8. Some of the New Testament writers were apostles in a more general sense than others, and Paul received his apostolic authority after Jesus' death and resurrection. For a simply written explanation of the apostolic authority of all the New Testament books, see the chapter 'Why there are only twenty-seven books in the New Testament' in Brian H. Edwards, *Nothing But the Truth*, Evangelical Press.
9. Pinnock, *Biblical Revelation*, p.149.
10. Karl Barth, *Kirchliche Dogmatik*, I.2., cited by R. C. Sproul in "The Case for Inerrancy: A Methodological Analysis," in *God's Inerrant Word*, ed. John Warwick Montgomery, Bethany Fellowship Inc., p.256.
11. Sproul, as above.
12. D. Martyn Lloyd-Jones, *Studies in the Sermon on the Mount*, Inter-Varsity Press, vol. 1, p.118.
13. Martin Kahler, *The So-Called Historical Jesus and the Historic Biblical Christ*, trans. Carl E. Braaten, Fortress, p.75.
14. K. S. Kantzer, "The Christ-Revelation as Act and Interpretation" in *Jesus of Nazareth: Savior and Lord*, ed. Carl F. H. Henry, Wm. B. Eerdmans Publ. Co., p.252.
15. Cited by Harold Lindsell, *God's Incomparable Word*, Victor Books, p.39.
16. Lloyd-Jones, *Studies in Sermon on the Mount*, p.187.

17. John Wesley, *Journal*, vol. VI.

CHAPTER THREE: *Windows on the Words*

1. The only other place in the New Testament where "hell" is used to translate the original language is in 2 Peter 2:4, where we are told that "God
   did not spare angels when they sinned, but sent them to hell, putting them
   into gloomy dungeons to be held for judgment." The phrase "sent them
   to hell" translates a verb based on the Greek word *tartarus*, which in
   Greek literature always meant a place of conscious torment.
2. Peter Cotterell, *I Want to Know What the Bible Says About Death*,
   Kingsway Publication, p.81.
3. George Eldon Ladd, *A Theology of the New Testament*, Wm. B.
   Eerdmans Publ. Co., p.194.
4. S. F. D. Salmond, *Christian Doctrine of Immortality*, 2nd edition, T. &
   T. Clark, p.204.
5. Buis, *Doctrine of Eternal Punishment*, p.4.
6. C. S. Lewis, *The Great Divorce*, Collins, p.18.
7. J. A. Motyer, *After Death*, Hodder & Stoughton, p.23.
8. Buis, *Doctrine of Eternal Punishment*, p.12.
9. *Septuaginta* is the Latin word for seventy; it is thought that about this
   number of Jewish translators were involved in making the translation.
10. *Dictionary of New Testament Theology*, ed. Colin Brown, Paternoster
    Press, vol. 2, p.206.
11. W. E. Vine, *Expository Dictionary of New Testament Words*, Oliphants,
    p.187.
12. James B. Ramsey, *The Book of Revelation*, Banner of Truth Trust, p.67.
13. Robert A. Morey, *Death and the Afterlife*, Bethany House Publishers,
    p.87.
14. Cited in the *Daily Telegraph*, May 31, 1991.

CHAPTER FOUR: *The Forbidden Subject*

1. *Daily Telegraph*, April 22, 1992.
2. Fred Carl Kuehner, "Heaven and Hell," in *Fundamentals of the Faith*, ed.
   Carl F. H. Henry, *Christianity Today*, p.24c.
3. Laurence Sterne, *The Life and Opinions of Tristram Shandy, Gentleman,
   and Sentimental Journey through France and Germany*, Macmillan, vol.
   1, p.119.
4. *Daily Express*, February 11, 1984.
5. Thomas Brooks, *The Complete Works*, Banner of Truth Trust, vol. V,
   p.452.
6. Joseph Hall, *Epistles*, 3.2.
7. See Sheldon Vanauken, *A Severe Mercy*, Hodder & Stoughton, p.227.
8. Samuel E. Waldron, *A Modern Exposition of the 1689 Baptist
   Confession of Faith*, Evangelical Press, p.84.

9. *USA Today*, August 4, 1992.
10. *Daily Telegraph*, October 11, 1991.
11. Sigmund Freud, *The Complete Psychological Works,* vol. 14, cited by Eryl Davies, *Condemned for Ever!*, Evangelical Press, p.13.
12. *Daily Telegraph*, February 7, 1992.
13. Alex MacDonald, *Love Minus Zero,* Christian Focus Publications, p.136.
14. Woody Allen, "Death" (a play) in *Without Feathers.*
15. Dave Hunt, *Whatever Happened to Heaven?*, Harvest House Publishers, p.11.
16. John Calvin, *Commentaries,* trans. William Pringle, Baker Book House, vol. XVII, p.442.
17. Waldron, *Exposition of 1689 Confession*, p.380.
18. C. Stephen Evans, *The Quest for Faith,* Inter-Varsity Press, pp.122-123.
19. Cited by Spiros Zodhiates, *Life After Death*, Wm. B. Eerdmans Publ. Co., p.34.
20. This verse is widely used by those who say that man's nature has three parts, body, soul and spirit, but the theory does not stand up to biblical examination. For an excellent discussion of the issue, see William Hendriksen, *New Testament Commentary: I and II Thessalonians,* Banner of Truth Trust, pp.146-50.
21. J. M. Pendleton, *Christian Doctrines,* cited by Emery H. Bancroft, *Elemental Theology,* Zondervan, p.179.
22. J. Gresham Machen, *The Christian View of Man,* Banner of Truth Trust, p.147.
23. Ernest F. Kevan, *Salvation,* Baker Book House, p.13.
24. Emery H. Bancroft, *Elemental Theology,* Zondervan, p.179.
25. James Montgomery Boice, *Foundations of the Christian Faith,* vol. II: God the Redeemer, Inter-Varsity Press, p.18.
26. Motyer, *After Death*, p.40.
27. Blaise Pascal, *Selections from Thoughts,* trans. Arthur H. Beattie, Appleton-Century-Crofts, p.68.
28. Hunt, *Whatever Happened to Heaven?*, p.12.
29. A. A. Hoekema, *The Bible and the Future,* Paternoster Press, p.82.
30. Bruce Milne, *Know the Truth,* Inter-Varsity Press, p.109.

CHAPTER FIVE: *Is Anyone There?*

1. A. A. Hodge, *Evangelical Theology,* Banner of Truth Trust, p.388.
2. An archaic word meaning "boundary."
3. William Shakespeare, *Hamlet,* Act III, Scene 1.
4. Cited by Hunt, *Whatever Happened to Heaven?*, p.14.
5. John Dryden, *Aurengzebe,* 4.1.
6. Cited by Billy Graham, *Peace With God, The World's Work* (1913) Ltd, p.67.
7. John Betjeman, "Before the Anaesthetic, or A Real Fright."
8. Robert Morley, *Around the World in 81 Days,* Coronet Books, p.176.

9. Aristotle, *Nicomachean Ethics*, 3:9.

10. Epicurus, "Letter to Menoeceus," in *Letters, Principal Doctrines and Vatican Sayings*, trans. Russel M. Geer.

11. Seneca, *The Trojan Women*, trans. Frank Justus Miller, p. 97.

12. Bertrand Russell, cited by J. W. N. Sullivan, *The Limitations of Science*, p.175.

13. Bertrand Russell, *Why I am Not a Christian*, p.111.

14. Tom Stoppard, *Rosencrantz & Guildenstern Are Dead*, Faber.

15. John Benton, *Looking for the Answer*, Evangelical Press, p.38.

16. Cited by Michael Green, *Man Alive!*, Inter-Varsity Press, p.9.

17. As above, p.12.

18. American Humanist Association, "Humanist Manifesto II," *The Humanist*, vol. 33, September-October 1973.

19. M. J. Savage, *Life After Death*, cited by Augustus H. Strong, Systematic Theology, Pickering & Inglis, p.989.

20. Hunt, *Whatever Happened to Heaven?*, p. 13.

21. Arthur C. Custance, *The Sovereignty of Grace*, Baker Book House, p.328.

22. Hunt, *Whatever Happened to Heaven?*, p.12.

23. Daniel Webster, on Mr. Justice Story, September 12, 1845.

24. Peter Singer, as cited in "Death Act Dies in California," by Martin Mawyer, *Fundamentalist Journal*, vol. 7, June 1988, p.61.

25. Joseph Fletcher, as cited by Mawyer, as above.

26. Marvin Harris, "Our Pound of Flesh," in *Natural History*, vol. 88, August-September 1979, p.36.

27. Robert Burns, "Man was Made to Mourn."

28. Paul Oestreicher, *Thirty Years of Human Rights* (The British Churches' Advisory Forum on Human Rights, 1980).

29. Francis A. Schaeffer, *Death in the City*, Inter-Varsity Press, pp.86-7.

30. David Watson, *Is Anyone There?*, Hodder & Stoughton, p.66.

31. E. F. Kevan, "Genesis," *The New Bible Commentary*, ed. F. Davidson, A. M. Stibbs, E. F. Kevan, Inter-Varsity Press, p.77.

32. Francis A. Schaeffer, *Genesis in Space and Time*, Hodder & Stoughton, p.47.

33. Kevan, "Genesis," p.78.

34. Bancroft, *Elemental Theology*, p.178.

35. Louis Berkhof, *Systematic Theology*, Banner of Truth Trust, p.691.

36. *Wisdom of Solomon*, 2:23.

37. Vanauken, *A Severe Mercy*, p.203.

38. Hunt, *Whatever Happened to Heaven?*, p.17.

39. Cited by Professor William Hendricks in "Death: A Theological Perspective," a lecture given at Southwestern Baptist Theological Seminary, Fort Worth, Texas, October 26, 1976.

40. Morey, *Death and the Afterlife*, p.40.

41. Spiros Zodhiates, *Life After Death*, p.65.

42. As above, p.100.
43. Calvin, *Commentaries*, vol. XVIII, p.222. I have modernized the language of this quotation.
44. Motyer, *After Death*, p.19.

CHAPTER SIX: *Where Do We Go from Here?*

1. *The Independent*, May 31, 1990.
2. Schaeffer, *Genesis in Space and Time*, p.101.
3. See Waldron, *Exposition of the 1689 Confession*, p.81.
4. *BBC Television News*, December 29, 1990.
5. C. G. Berkouwer, *De Wederkmost van Christus*, Kok, vol.1, p.79.
6. Hoekema, *Bible and the Future*, p.103.
7. J. C. Ryle, *Expository Thoughts on the Gospels*, Baker Book House, vol. 2., p.473.
8. The word used here is *tartarus*; see chapter 3, note 1.
9. W. G. T. Shedd, *The Doctrine of Endless Punishment*, Klock and Klock, p. 59.
10. Cited by Loraine Boettner, *Roman Catholicism*, Banner of Truth Trust, p.286.
11. Cited by Roland Bainton, *Here I Stand*, Lion Publishing, p.78.
12. Cited by Boettner, *Roman Catholicism*, p.370.
13. See Ernest G. Schwiebert, *Luther and His Times*, p.312.
14. Boettner, *Roman Catholicism*, p.288.
15. Bruce M. Metzger, *An Introduction to the Apocrypha*, p.146.
16. Cited by Peter Toon, *Heaven and Hell*, Thomas Nelson, p.119.
17. Boettner, *Roman Catholicism*, p.288.
18. Alexander Hislop, *The Two Babylons*, p.167.
19. See *Book of Homilies*, p.390, cited by Motyer, *After Death*, p.59.
20. See Davies, *Condemned for Ever!*, p.106.
21. Irenaeus, *Against Heresies*, Book II, chapter xxxiii.
22. J. Stafford Wright, *What is Man?*, Paternoster Press, p.140.
23. Morey, *Death and the Afterlife*, p.183.

CHAPTER SEVEN: *The Moment of Truth*

1. J. I. Packer, Hodder & Stoughton, p.155.
2. Hoekema, *Bible and the Future*, p.109.
3. Milne, *Know the Truth*, p.255.
4. See *Let God Be True*, Watchtower Bible and Tract Society, pp.198-199.
5. Cited by David Watson, *Is Anyone There?*, p.68.
6. Ryle, *Expository Thoughts*, vol. 3, p.292.
7. John Benton, *How Can a God of Love Send People to Hell?*, Evangelical Press, p.41.
8. John Calvin, *Institutes of the Christian Religion*, trans. Henry Beveridge, James Clarke & Co. Ltd., vol. 2, p.271.

CHAPTER EIGHT: *The Great Day*

1. Rousas John Rushdoony, *Salvation and Godly Rule*, ed. Carl F. Henry, p.380.
2. David Watson, *My God is Real*, Falcon Books, p.36.
3. John W. Wenham, *The Goodness of God*, Inter-Varsity Press, p.174. This book was republished in 1985 under the title *The Enigma of Evil.*
4. Earl Kelly, *James: A Practical Primer for Christian Living*, Craig Press, p.218.
5. Leon Morris, *The Biblical Doctrine of Judgment*, p.72.
6. Thomas Watson, *A Body of Divinity*, Banner of Truth Trust, p.90.
7. Packer, *Knowing God*, p.156.
8. Kuehner, "Heaven and Hell." p.24f.
9. Motyer, *After Death*, p.36.
10. Davies, *Condemned for Ever!*, p.77.
11. A. W. Pink, *The Attributes of god*, Reiner Publications, p.75.
12. William Eisenhower, "Sleepers in the Hands of an Angry God," *Christianity Today*, March 20, 1987.
13. R. C. Sproul, *The Holiness of God*, Tyndale House Publishers, pp.224, 228.
14. David Watson, *In Search of God*, Falcon Books, p.45.
15. J. L. Dagg, *Manual of Theology and Church Order*, Gano Books, p.356.
16. Peter Cotterell, *Mission and Meaninglessness*, SPCK.
17. Clark H. Pinnock, "The Destruction of the Finally Impenitent," *Criswell Theological Review*, 4.2 (1990), p.252.
18. Stuart Olyott, *The Gospel as it Really Is*, Evangelical Press, p.77.
19. Bob Sheehan, "A Self-Revealing God," *Reformation Today*, no.127, May-June 1992, p.6.
20. Cornelius Van Til, *Apologetics*, Presbyterian & Reformed Publ. Co., p.38.
21. Cornelius Van Til, *Common Grace and the Gospel*, Presbyterian and Reformed Publ. Co., p.162.
22. Ronald Blue, "Untold Billions: Are they Really Lost?" *Bibliotheca Sacra*, October-December 1991, p.340.
23. Cited by David Watson, *In Search of God*, p.65.
24. G. I. Williamson, *The Westminster Confession of Faith*, Presbyterian & Reformed Publ. Co., p.91.
25. Toon, *Heaven and Hell*, p.112.
26. Christopher E. Luthardt, "The Final Judgment of Jesus Christ and its Eternal Consequences for All Mankind" in *That Unknown Country*, C. A. Nichols Co., p.621.
27. William James, *Reader's Digest*, October 1959.
28. Vine, *Expository Dictionary*, p.36.
29. Ryle, *Expository Thoughts*, vol. 1, p.344.
30. John Murray, *Collected Writings*, vol. 2, Banner of Truth Trust, p.416.

CHAPTER NINE: *The Ultimate Horror*

1. See William Rounseville Alger, *The Destiny of the Soul: A Critical History of the Doctrine of a Future Life,* Greenwood Press, vol.1, p.204.
2. As above, p.109.
3. Wendy Donigher O'Flaherty, cited *Newsweek*, March 27, 1989.
4. Cited in *Everyman, "A Brief History of Hell,"* BBC TV, January 6, 1991.
5. Cited by Buis, *Doctrine of Eternal Punishment,* p.67.
6. Dante, *The Inferno,* trans. John Ciardi, Mentor, p.128.
7. As above.
8. John Milton, *Paradise Lost,* Book 1, Scott Foresman & Co., p.79.
9. *Call Nick Ross,* BBC Radio 4, April 21, 1992.
10. Cited by P. B. Coombs, *Life After Death,* Church Pastoral-Aid Society, p.9.
11. *Easter Enigma,* BBC Radio 4, April 19, 1992.
12. Wenham, *Goodness of God,* p.27.
13. Isaac Watts, "The Day of Judgment," Stanza VII, in *Works,* vol. 4, 1st edition, A. M. S. Press.
14. Cited by Edward Fudge, "Putting Hell in Its Place," *Christianity Today,* August 6, 1976.
15. Jesus did not of course speak in "verses," but this figure gives a fairly accurate indication of the emphasis he placed on the topics concerned.
16. Nels F. S. Ferre, *The Christian Understanding of God,* SCM Press, p.245.
17. C. S. Lewis, *The Problem of Pain,* Macmillan, p.125.
18. Cited by G Campbell Morgan, *The Acts of the Apostles,* Pickering & Inglis, p.305.
19. Calvin, *Commentaries,* vol. VII, p.182.
20. See Morey, *Death and the Afterlife,* p.127.
21. Basil F. C. Atkinson, "The Gospel According to Matthew," *New Bible Commentary,* p.779.
22. Milne, *Know the Truth,* p.274.
23. Luther Poellot, *Revelation,* Concordia Publishing House, p.285.

CHAPTER TEN: *The Pains of Hell*

1. Brooks, *Works,* p.127.
2. Thomas Vincent, *Christ's Certain and Sudden Appearance to Judgment,* cited by Eryl Davies, *The Wrath of God,* Evangelical Press of Wales, p.50.
3. William Shakespeare, *Richard III,* Act V, Scene 3.
4. John Flavel, *Works,* Banner of Truth Trust, vol. 3, pp.137-8.
5. As above, p.136.
6. Hoekema, *Bible and the Future,* p.268.
7. *Daily Telegraph,* July 14, 1981.
8. *Daily Telegraph,* May 8, 1992.
9. Shedd, *Doctrine of Endless Punishment,* p.145.
10. Packer, *Knowing God,* p.170.

11. Kenneth L. Woodward, "Heaven," *Newsweek*, March 27, 1989.
12. *Crimes and Misdemeanors*, Orion Pictures Corporation.
13. Lewis, *Great Divorce*, pp.66-67.
14. MacDonald, *Love Minus Zero*, pp.139-140.
15. Lewis, *Problem of Pain*, p.127.
16. Matthew Henry, *Commentary on the Holy Bible*, Marshall Morgan & Scott, vol. 2, p.137.
17. Shedd, *Doctrine of Endless Punishment*, p.163.
18. Ralph Venning, *The Plague of Plagues*, Banner of Truth Trust, p.73.
19. *US News and World Report*, March 25, 1991.
20. John Donne, cited by John Blanchard, *Gathered Gold*, Evangelical Press, p.66.
21. See Bauer, Arndt, Gingrich and Danker, *Greek-English Lexicon*, 2nd edition, The University of Chicago Press, p.134.
22. John Chrysostom, cited by Brooks, *Works*, vol. 5, p.137.
23. Vine, *Expository Dictionary*, p.58.
24. Kenneth Wuest, *Wuest's Word Studies: Romans in the Greek New Testament*, Wm. B. Eerdmans Publ. Co., p.42.
25. Ethelbert W. Bullinger, *A Critical Lexicon and Concordance to the English and Greek New Testament*, Zondervan, p.862.
26. William Hendriksen, *New Testament Commentary: The Gospel of Matthew*, Banner of Truth Trust, p.398.
27. T. Hood, "Ode To Melancholy," *A Dictionary of Quotations*, ed. Philip Hugh Dalbiac, Thomas Nelson & Sons Ltd, p.278.
28. Venning, *Plague of Plagues*, p.79.
29. Cited in *Evangelical Times*, January 1991.
30. Cited by Davies, *Condemned for Ever!*, p.59.
31. Brooks, *Works*, vol.6, p.208.
32. Flavel, *Works*, vol. 3, p.142.
33. Jonathan Edwards in sermon entitled, "There is such a thing as eternity," p.5.
34. Haynes Bayly, "Odes to Rosa," *Dictionary of Quotations*, p.61.
35. Henry Blocher, Fourth Edinburgh Conference on Christian Dogmatics, August 1991.
36. Cited by Larry Dixon, *The Other Side of the Good News*, Victor Books, p.162.
37. See D. Martyn Lloyd-Jones, *Romans: An Exposition of Chapters 3:20-4:25; Atonement and Justification*, Banner of Truth Trust, p.79.
38. Packer, *Knowing God*, p.172.
39. As above, p.166.
40. "The Campaign for Real God," *Punch*, April 7, 1989.
41. R. V. G. Tasker, "Wrath," *The Illustrated Bible Dictionary*, Inter-Varsity Press, p.1657.
42. Davies, *Wrath of God*, p.11.

CHAPTER ELEVEN: *Too Bad to be True?*

1. Arthur Conan Doyle, cited by Buis, *Doctrine of Eternal Punishment*, p.146.
2. *Reconciliation*, cited by J. Oswald Sanders, *Heresies: Ancient and Modern*, Marshall Morgan & Scott, p.81.
3. *Textbook of Theosophy*, cited by Buis, *Doctrine of Eternal Punishment*, p.147.
4. M. J. Savage, *Life After Death*, cited by Strong, *Systematic Theology*, p.1035.
5. Ferré, *Christian Understanding of God*, p.228.
6. David L. Edwards and John Stott, *Essentials*, Hodder & Stoughton, p.295.
7. John A. T. Robinson, *But That I Can't Believe*, New American Library, p.69.
8. John A. T. Robinson, "Universalism: Is it Heretical?" *Scottish Journal of Theology*, June 1949, p.155.
9. Lewis, *Problem of Pain*, Macmillan, p.106.
10. Edwards and Stott, *Essentials*, p.312.
11. Paul Helm, *The Last Things: Death, Judgment, Heaven and Hell*, Banner of Truth Trust, p.108.
12. Wenham, *Goodness of God*, p.20.
13. John Hick, *Death and Eternal Life*, Fount Paperbacks, Collins, p.200.
14. Pinnock, "The Destruction of the Finally Impenitent," p.253.
15. Motyer, *After Death*, p.12.
16. As above, p.35.
17. Robert Mounce, *The Book of Revelation*, Wm. B. Eerdmans Publ. Co., p.295.
18. Motyer, *After Death*, p.13.
19. Dixon, *Other Side of the Good News*, p.65.
20. *Theological Wordbook of the Old Testament*, ed. R. Laird Harris, Moody Press, p.795.
21. As above, p.976.
22. John Hercus, *David*, Inter-Varsity Press, p.115.
23. Helm, *The Last Things*, p.113.
24. Benton, *How Can a God of Love . . . ?*, p.19.
25. William V. Crockett, "Wrath that Endures For Ever," *Journal of the Evangelical Theological Society*, June 1991, p.197.
26. John Sanders, "Is Belief in Christ Necessary for Salvation?", *Evangelical Quarterly*, vol. 60, p.241.
27. Dixon, *Other Side of the Good News*, p.177.
28. Donald G. Bloesch, *Essentials of Evangelical Theology*, vol.2: *Life, Ministry and Hope*, Harper and Row, p.226.
29. Dixon, *Other Side of the Good News*, p.107.
30. *The Complete Poetical Works of Tennyson*, Cambridge Edition, Houghton-Mifflin, p.163.

31. Cited by R. D. Dickinson, *The Future Life*, p.89.
32. As above. I have tidied up the distracting punctuation in this quotation.
33. As above, p.93.
34. As above, p.97.
35. George B. Cheevers, "Well Daubed Badly Built," as above, p.99.
36. Nels F. S. Ferre, *Christ and the Christian*, Harper & Bros., p.245.
37. Ferré, *Christian Understanding of God*, p.240.
38. See David Pawson, *The Road to Hell*, Hodder & Stoughton, p.140.
39. Cited by Sanders, "Is Belief in Christ Necessary . . . ?" pp.249-250.
40. As above, p.250.
41. Cited by Pawson, *Road to Hell*, p.142.
42. Robert Young, *Literal Translation of the New Testament*, Guardian Press, p.160.
43. Alan M. Stibbs, *The First Epistle General of Peter*, Tyndale New Testament Commentaries, p.142.
44. Bullinger, *Critical Lexicon & Concordance*, p.596.
45. Ludovic Kennedy, *Pursuit*, Book Club Associates, p.154.
46. J. I. Packer, *The Apostles' Creed*, Tyndale House Publishers, pp.54-5.
47. Ferré, *Christian Understanding of God*, p.237.
48. Maurice Roberts, in *The Banner of Truth* Trust, March 1990, p.4.
49. *Monthly Record of the Free Church of Scotland*, January 1987, p.3.
50. Robert Murray M'Cheyne, *A Basket of Fragments*, The Banner of Truth Trust, p.166. M'Cheyne believed that the redeemed in heaven would see the lost in hell and rejoice in the vindication of God's righteousness and justice. The work quoted has several moving passages on this.
51. Dixon, *Other Side of the Good News*, p.126.
52. Richard Brooks, *The Lamb is all the Glory*, Evangelical Press, p.153.
53. *Monthly Record of the Free Church of Scotland*, November 1986, p.240.
54. Cited by John H. Gerstner, *Jonathan Edwards on Heaven and Hell*, Baker Book House, p.65.
55. Jonathan Edwards, *Works*, The Banner of Truth Trust, vol. II, p.122.
56. John Lawson, *Introduction to Christian Doctrine*, Zondervan, p.262.
57. *The Sunday Telegraph*, August 30, 1992.
58. As above.

CHAPTER TWELVE: ". . . Happily Ever After?"

1. *Concise Oxford Dictionary*, p.1147.
2. R. C. Sproul, *Reason to Believe*, Lamplighter Books, (Zondervan), pp.99-100.
3. *Sunday Telegraph*, November 18, 1990.
4. See Peter Alliss, *An Autobiography*, Collins, p.128.
5. J. I. Packer, "'Good Pagans' and God's Kingdom," *Christianity Today*, January 1986.
6. Cited in *Christianity Today*, March 20, 1987.

7. J. G. G. Norman, "Origenism," *The New International Dictionary of the Christian Church*, ed. J. D. Douglas, Paternoster Press, p.374.

8. Darrel Bigham, "Universalism," *New International Dictionary of the Christian Church*, p.1003.

9. Barth, *Kirchliche Dogmatik*, vol. I, part 2, p.507.

10. As above, vol. I, part 2, p.59.

11. As above, vol. IV, part 1, p.99.

12. Emil Brunner, *Religionsphilosophie*, cited by Paul King Jewett, *Inspiration and Interpretation*, ed. John F. Walvoord, Wm. B. Eerdmans Publ. Co., p.211.

13. Emil Brunner, *Eternal Hope*, cited by Kuehner, "Heaven and Hell," p.24p.

14. Nels F. S. Ferré, *Evil and the Christian Faith*, Harper & Brothers, p.120.

15. Ferré, *Christ and the Christian*, pp.63-64.

16. See Millard J. Erickson, *Christian Theology*, Baker Book House, p.1017.

17. C. H. Dodd, *New Testament Studies*, University Press, p.119.

18. Cited by Vernon C. Grounds, "The Final State of the Wicked," *Journal of the Evangelical Theological Society*, September 1981, p.213.

19. *Redemptor Hominus*, (1979), cited by John Stott in Edwards & Stott, *Essentials*, p.325.

20. William Hendriksen, *A Commentary on 1 and 2 Timothy and Titus*, Banner of Truth Trust, p.93.

21. Calvin, *Commentaries*, vol. XXI, p.112.

22. Kuehner, "Heaven and Hell," p.24t.

23. M. R. Vincent, *The Epistles to the Philippians and to Philemon, in The International Critical Commentary*, cited by Hendriksen, *A Commentary on the Epistle to the Philippians*, Banner of Truth Trust, p.115.

24. Robert L. Dabney, *Discussions: Evangelical and Theological*, Banner of Truth Trust, vol. 1, p.132.

25. Shedd, *Doctrine of Endless Punishment*, pp.129-131.

26. Kenneth Kantzer, "Troublesome Questions," *Christianity Today*, March 20, 1987.

27. Fitzjames Stephen, cited by Grounds, "Final State of the Wicked," p.211.

28. C. E. Graham Swift, "The Gospel According to Mark," *New Bible Commentary*, p.814.

29. A. A. Hodge, *The Confession of Faith*, The Banner of Truth Trust, p.394.

CHAPTER THIRTEEN: *The Last Loophole*

1. *TIME Magazine*, February 19, 1990.

2. Morey, *Death and the Afterlife*, p.250.

3. Helm, *The Last Things*, p.117.

4. See Edward Fudge, *The Fire that Consumes*, Providential Press, p.365.

5. See P. Schaff, *History of the Christian Church*, Wm. B. Eerdmans Publ. Co., pp.858ff.

6. As above.

7. As above.
8. Robert G. Clouse, "Socinianism," *New International Dictionary of the Christian Church*, p.912.
9. *Evangelicals Now*, June 1991.
10. Wenham, *Goodness of God*, p.41.
11. Edwards and Stott, *Essentials*, p.320.
12. Stephen Travis, *I Believe in the Second Coming of Jesus*, Hodder & Stoughton, p.198.
13. *Evangelicals Now*, June 1991.
14. Calvin, *Institutes*, vol.1., p.162.
15. Shedd, *Doctrine of Endless Punishment*, p.151.
16. As above.
17. As above.
18. E. M. Golbourn, *Everlasting Punishment*, p.68.
19. C. S. Lewis, *Spirits in Bondage*, Macmillan, p.41.
20. Kevan, *Salvation*, p.98.
21. Dixon, *Other Side of the Good News*, p.76.
22. Berkhof, *Systematic Theology*, p.691.
23. As above, p.672.
24. Clark H. Pinnock & Delwin Brown, *Theological Crossfire: An Evangelical/Liberal Dialogue*, Zondervan, p.226.
25. Motyer, *After Death*, p.36.
26. LeRoy Edwin Froom, *The Conditionalist Faith of Our Fathers*, Review and Herald Publishing Assn, vol. 1, p.107.
27. John H. Gerstner, *Repent or Perish*, Soli Deo Gloria Publications, pp.36-37.
28. Fudge, *The Fire that Consumes*, p.88.
29. Fourth Edinburgh Conference on Christian Dogmatics, August 1991.
30. As above.
31. Edwards and Stott, *Essentials*, p.319.
32. P. E. Hughes, *The True Image—the Origin and Destiny of Man in Christ*, Inter-Varsity Press, p.viii..
33. Edwards and Stott, *Essentials*, p.319.
34. Helm, *The Last Things*, pp.116-17.
35. Dixon, *Other Side of the Good News*, p.159.
36. *Celebration*, June 1990.
37. Robinson, "Universalism: Is it Heretical?", pp.143-4.
38. Packer, *Knowing God*, p.132.
39. Maurice Roberts, in *The Banner of Truth*, February 1990, p.5.
40. William Hendriksen, *The Bible on the Life Hereafter*, Baker Book House, p.80.
41. Fourth Edinburgh Conference on Christian Dogmatics, August 1991.
42. Harold O. J. Brown, "Will the Lost Suffer For Ever?", *Criswell Theological Review*, 4.2 (1990), p.272.
43. This point is persuasively argued by Jonathan Edwards in his "Sermon

on the Eternity of Hell Torments," cited in *The Writings of James Henly Thornwell,* Banner of Truth Trust, vol. 2, pp.251-2.

44. Helm, *The Last Things,* p.62.
45. Gerstner, *Repent or Perish,* pp.61-2.
46. Cited by Thomas Brooks, *Works,* vol. 4, p.75.
47. Basil F. C. Atkinson, *Life and Immortality: An Examination of the Nature and Meaning of Life and Death as they are revealed in the Scriptures,* published privately, cited by Toon, *Heaven and Hell,* p.178.
48. Shedd, *Doctrine of Endless Punishment,* p.92.
49. Alan W. Gomes, "Evangelicals and the Annihilation of Hell," Part 1, *Christian Research Journal,* Spring 1991, p.11.
50. Poellot, *Revelation,* p.268.
51. Clark H. Pinnock, "Fire then Nothing," *Christianity Today,* March 20, 1987.
52. Wenham, *Goodness of God,* p.78.
53. Roger Nicole, "The Punishment of the Wicked," *Christianity Today,* June 9, 1958.
54. *Celebration,* June 1990.
55. Pinnock, "Destruction of the Finally Impenitent," p.256.
56. Hoekema, *Bible and the Future,* p.272.
57. Edwards and Stott, *Essentials,* p.316.
58. As above, p.314.
59. As above. p.315.
60. Hoekema, *Bible and the Future,* p.273.

CHAPTER FOURTEEN: *The Decisive Words*

1. *The Second London Confession,* later known as the *1689 Baptist Confession of Faith.*
2. Edwards, *Nothing But the Truth,* p.38.
3. See Galatians 3:15-16.
4. Vine, *Expository Dictionary,* p.302.
5. J. I. Packer, *The Problem of Eternal Punishment,* Fellowship of Word and Spirit, p.4.
6. J. Thayer, *Greek-English Lexicon of the New Testament,* Zondervan, p.36.
7. Davies, *Condemned for ever!,* p.100.
8. F. W. Conrad in *That Unknown Country,* p.195.
9. René Pache, *The Future Life,* trans. Helen I. Needham, Moody Press, p.293.
10. Dabney, *Discussions,* vol. 1, p.656.
11. M. Horbery, *An Enquiry into The Scripture Doctrine Concerning the Duration of Future Punishment,* cited by Wenham, *The Goodness of God,* pp.29-30.
12. Hendriksen, *Bible on the Life Hereafter,* p.197.
13. Edwards and Stott, *Essentials,* p.318.

14. Fudge, *Fire that Consumes*, p.300.
15. Kendall S. Harmon, Fourth Edinburgh Conference on Christian Dogmatics, August 1991.
16. Pawson, *Road to Hell*, p.164.
17. Harold E. Guillebaud, *The Righteous Judge*, Phoenix Press, p.26.
18. J. I. Packer, *God's Words,* Inter-Varsity Press, p.205.
19. Augustine, *City of God*, 21.23.
20. Roberts, *Banner of Truth*, February 1990, p.3.
21. Ryle, *Expository Thoughts*, vol. 1, p.344.
22. Strong, *Systematic Theology*, Pickering & Inglis, p.1045.
23. Hodge, *Evangelical Theology*, p.391.
24. A. A. Hodge, *Outlines of Theology*, Banner of Truth Trust, p.582.
25. Loraine Boettner, *Immortality*, The Presbyterian & Reformed Publ. Co., p.120.
26. Motyer, *After Death*, p.45.
27. Packer, *God's Words*, p.205.
28. See E. B. Pusey, *What is of Faith as to Eternal Punishment?* James Parker, p.44.
29. Morey, *Death and the Afterlife*, p.31.
30. Cited by Buis, *Doctrine of Eternal Punishment*, p.54.
31. McClintock & Strong, cited by Morey, *Death and the Afterlife*, p.236.
32. Edwards, *Works*, vol. 2, Banner of Truth Trust, p.88.
33. Stoppard, *Rosencrantz and Guildenstern are Dead.*

CHAPTER FIFTEEN: *The Roads to Hell*

1. Cited by Sproul, *The Holiness of God*, Tyndale House Publishers, p.222.
2. *Des Moines Register*, December 25, 1977.
3. "Only 4% of Minnesotans feel they're Hellbound," *EP News Service*, March 25, 1978.
4. *Newsweek*, March 27, 1989.
5. *US News and World Report*, March 25, 1991.
6. *Daily Mail*, April 15, 1992.
7. *BBC Television News*, December 22, 1989.
8. *Daily Telegraph*, January 17, 1991.
9. *The Bulletin*, May 24, 1988.
10. John Bunyan, *Sighs from Hell or Groans of a Damned Soul*, cited by Buis, *Doctrine of Eternal Punishment*, p.84.
11. *US News and World Report*, March 25, 1991.
12. As above.
13. Toon, *Heaven and Hell*, p.201.
14. *USA Today*, April 5, 1991.
15. As above.
16. I. Howard Marshall, *Christian Beliefs*, Inter-Varsity Fellowship, p.90.
17. See Loraine Boettner, *The Reformed Doctrine of Predestination*, Presbyterian & Reformed Publ. Co., pp.145-6.

18. Custance, *Sovereignty of Grace*, p.323.
19. J. Caird, cited by Blanchard, *Gathered Gold*, Evangelical Press, p.270.
20. See Flavel, *Works*, vol. 3, pp.183-225.
21. A. J. Macleod, "The Gospel According to John," *New Bible Commentary*, p.871.
22. Lloyd-Jones, *Studies in the Sermon on the Mount*, vol. 1, p.207.
23. Leon Morris, *The First Epistle of Paul to the Corinthians*, Tyndale New Testament Commentaries, Tyndale Press, p.97.
24. See Hunt, *Whatever Happened to Heaven?*, p.28.
25. Cited by Blanchard, *Gathered Gold*, p.140.
26. Lloyd-Jones, *Studies in the Sermon on the Mount*, vol. 2, p.261.
27. R. V. G. Tasker, *The Gospel According to Matthew*, in Tyndale New Testament Commentaries, Tyndale Press, pp.83-84.
28. Albert Barnes, *Notes on the New Testament*, Kregel Publications, p.1038.
29. Cited by Gerstner, *Repent or Perish*, p.193.
30. "The Friend of the Unborn," *Evangelical Times*, September 1992.

CHAPTER SIXTEEN: *The Way to Heaven*

1. Cited by John MacArthur, *The MacArthur New Testament Commentary: Hebrews*, Moody Press, p.309.
2. Packer, *Knowing God*, pp.35-36.
3. Stuart Olyott, *A Life Worth Living and a Lord Worth Loving*, Evangelical Press, p.40.
4. Cited by Dixon, *Other Side of the Good News*, p.18.
5. C. S. Lewis, *Mere Christianity*, Macmillan p.133.
6. Olyott, *Gospel as it Really Is*, p.43.
7. Michael Green, *Why Bother with Jesus?*, Hodder & Stoughton, p.42.
8. R. A. Cole, *The Gospel According to St. Mark*, Tyndale New Testament Commentaries, Tyndale Press, p.243.
9. Geoff Thomas, "He Descended into Hell," *Evangelical Times*, April 1987.
10. For a discussion of the evidence see John Blanchard, *Will the Real Jesus Please Stand Up?*, Evangelical Press.
11. Cited by Green, *Man Alive!*, p.54.
12. Alec Guinness, *Blessings in Disguise*, Fontana/Collins, p.82.
13. Edwards, *Works*, vol.2, p.82. I have modernized the language of this quotation.
14. Malcolm Watts, *The Messenger*, vol.15, no.18., December-January, 1986-1987, p.3.
15. Bernard of Clairvaux, cited by Brooks, *Works*, vol.1, p.225.
16. Cited by Sproul, *Holiness of God*, p.225.

CHAPTER SEVENTEEN: *P.S.*

1. A. W. Tozer, *The Best of A. W. Tozer*, ed. Warren Wiersbe, Christian Publications Inc., p.141.
2. Wesley, *Journal*, vol. 3, pp.453-4. Cited by Arthur Skevington Wood, *The Burning Heart*, Paternoster Press, p.29.
3. Cited by Blanchard, *Gathered Gold*, p.29.
4. Cited by James Montgomery Boice, *Philippians*, Zondervan, p.248.
5. C. H. Spurgeon, *The Metropolitan Tabernacle Pulpit*, vol. 30, Banner of Truth Trust, p.368.
6. C. H. Spurgeon, *Letters to My Students*, Marshall, Morgan & Scott, pp.314-315.
7. John Stott, *Our Guilty Silence*, Hodder &Stoughton, p.19.
8. Normal Hillyer, *The New Bible Commentary Revised,* cited by Geoffrey B. Wilson, *1 Corinthians*, Banner of Truth Trust, p.138.
9. Cited by Billy Graham, *A Biblical Standard for Evangelists*, World Wide Publications, p.89.
10. Ronald J. Sider, *Rich Christians in an Age of Hunger*, Hodder & Stoughton, p.161.
11. Richard Baxter, *The Reformed Pastor*, The Banner of Truth Trust, p.66.
12. Michael Green, *Evangelism—Now and Then*, Inter-Varsity Press, p.118.
13. K. S. Latourette, *A History of the Expansion of Christianity*, vol. 1, Paternoster Press, p.116.
14. Cited by Andrew A. Bonar, *The Life of Robert Murray M'Cheyne*, Banner of Truth Trust, p.31.
15. David Sitton in *Evangelical Times*, September 1992.
16. Calvin, *Commentaries*, vol. XXII, p.448.
17. Ryle, *Expository Thoughts*, vol. 2, p.257.
18. Cited by A. Skevington Wood, *The Burning Heart*, p.285.
19. See Frank E. Gabelein, "The Bible: Both the Source and Setting for Learning," *Christianity Today*, February 6, 1981.

INDEX OF NAMES

Note: Some entries refer to the sources of quotations who may not actually be named in the text.

INDEX OF SUBJECTS

SCRIPTURE INDEX